HOME/BODIES

HOME/BODIES:
Geographies of Self, Place, and Space

Wendy Schissel, Editor

On behalf of the Women's Studies Research Unit
University of Saskatchewan

UNIVERSITY OF
CALGARY
PRESS

Published by the
University of Calgary Press
2500 University Drive NW
Calgary, Alberta
Canada T2N 1N4
www.uofcpress.com

We acknowledge the financial
support of the Government
of Canada through the
Book Publishing Industry
Development Program (BPIDP),
and the Alberta Foundation
for the Arts for our publishing
activities. We acknowledge the
support of the Canada Council
for the Arts for our publishing
program.

Canada Council   Conseil des Arts
for the Arts   du Canada

Canadä

LIBRARY AND ARCHIVES OF
CANADA CATALOGUING IN
PUBLICATION:

Home/bodies : geographies of self,
place, and space / edited by Wendy
Schissel.

Includes bibliographical references
and index.

ISBN 10: 1-55238-184-6
ISBN 13: 978-1-55238-184-7

1   Women – Social conditions –
    Textbooks.
2   Women's rights – Textbooks.
3   Feminism – Textbooks.
I   Schissel, Wendy, 1950–

HQ1155.H64 2006   305.42
C2006-903441-9

Cover design, Mieka West.
Internal design & typesetting,
    Jason Dewinetz.

To the dancers of the Kids in Motion Dance Program
whom you will meet in the last paper in this volume
who just happen to use their wheelchairs as part of
their artistic expression,

and

to Dr. Lillian Dyck, Canadian Senator, neurochemist,
National Aboriginal Achievement Award in Science
and Technology winner, and former Co-Chair and
Executive member of the Women's Studies Research
Unit, University of Saskatchewan,

with profound and humble admiration.

ACKNOWLEDGEMENTS

This collection of papers would not have existed were it not for the seed planted at the "Lived Environments of Girls and Women" conference in Saskatoon, Saskatchewan, in July 2001, sponsored by the Women's Studies Research Unit (WSRU) at the University of Saskatchewan. And the conference would not have existed were it not for the hard work and dedication of co-chairs Dr. Meg Smart and Dr. Linda Wason-Ellam, all the conference committee WSRU Executive members at the time, and most importantly, the Executive Director of the WSRU, Marie Green, who has for so long been the heart and soul of that Unit. When I undertook this project I was serving a second time as Co-Chair of the WSRU Executive, so this work was undertaken a few years and a country ago on behalf of that Unit.

My thanks go to all the contributors to this volume. They include seasoned veterans of the academy and budding academics, two of whom I had the pleasure of teaching some years ago in Women's and Gender Studies classes. It is such a privilege to see one's students go on to other institutions to fulfill their destinies.

I wish to thank as well the Office of Research Services at the University of Saskatchewan for a Publication Fund grant awarded to the Women's Studies Research Unit for this volume.

And finally, my thanks go to the University of Calgary Press for its commitment to this project, with special appreciation to John King, Senior Editor of the Press, and Joyce Hildebrand, copy editor for *Home Bodies: Geographies of Self, Place, and Space*. An accomplished copy editor is surely a thing of beauty!

Wendy Schissel, PhD
Dean, Humanities Division
Mt. Hood Community College
Gresham, Oregon
December 2005

INTRODUCTION

Wendy Schissel

Despite its title, this is not a book on human or physical geography per se, although two chapters are written by geographers. The geographies that the writers in this collection explore are more often metaphorical than physical. The essays that follow are about how we live in and through identities, bodies, places, and spaces in non-linear, incoherent, and fragmented ways.

Our lived environments, physical and conceptual, our desire to feel "at home" for the myriad of reasons and with the many connotations that concept implies, is a theme that runs explicitly or implicitly through these papers. Home is a fluid concept that needs to be constantly "negotiated." Home is also, variously but not exclusively, a homeland – indigenous or adopted – a sexuality, a body prescribed by moral or ableist codes, cyberspace, a community, or a place where caring occurs, sometimes at substantial cost to the caregiver. On the other hand, it may also be what we are prevented from achieving. The writers in this book talk about the "insider" view and about "embeddedness." Perhaps it is not surprising, then, that the prevailing methods of research reflected here are qualitative: the authors have employed interviews, focus groups, case studies, and narrative research.

The titles of the subsections of this book also work in metaphorical fashion. They imply, by section, first, that fractures inhere in the very foundations of our social system even though it is the individual who feels the break and its compounding; second, that the materials from which we build a feeling of being at home are tentative at best; and third, that there are some models by which we can build home habitats that are conducive to social and personal health.

In the first section, "Compound Fractures," three papers speak to the breaks in the socio-political foundations that determine homeland or define sexuality. The fractures are compounded because systemic racism, sexism, and heterosexism intensify each other. Such *isms* fail to account for the effects of the past on the present, as seen in chapter 1, nor do they understand the fluidity involved in home and identity making, which chapters 2 and 3 reveal, respectively, as part of the immigrant woman's or the transgendered individual's experience.

The title of section 2, "Ruptured Sutures," continues the home/bodies metaphor, its purpose being to reveal how tenuous are the "gut" threads that tie us to the need to feel "at home" in place, space, or body. Nothing is without rupture in the four chapters of this section: neither the adoption practices of the 1960s and 70s; nor the facility with which girls may be using the Internet today; nor the best intentions of a daughter trying to care for her dying mother at home; nor the discourse of marginalization originating in both ecofeminism and labour studies, a discourse which has not sufficiently accounted for the reasons, forms, and sites of women's activism in industrial forestry.

The third section, as its title suggests, discusses some successful attempts to create "Habitats for/of Humanity," attempts that include intercultural friendships, professional mentorship, sexual health services responsive to the young generation who uses them, and a form of physical activity that challenges our notions of disability.

Several of the papers in this collection had their genesis in a conference held July 4–7, 2001, in Saskatoon, Saskatchewan. "The Lived Environments of Girls and Women" conference, organized by the Women's Studies Research Unit at the University of Saskatchewan, brought together activists and scholars, non-governmental agencies, and government-sponsored agents. Keynote speakers included Winona LaDuke – a Native American environmentalist, social critic, and vice-presidential running mate to Ralph Nader in 1996 – and Jean Kilbourne, a writer, speaker, and documentary-maker well known for her critiques of advertising. But the conference also showcased the work of young feminists, scholars, and activists, some of whom are represented here. This book is intended for all readers with an interest in the topics it includes.

Part 1: Compound fractures

This section opens with J. Maria Pedersen's "Oppression and Indigenous Women: Past, Present and Future. An Australian Kimberley Aboriginal Perspective." Pedersen focusses particularly on the "fractured social context" of Aboriginal families and the places that the Kimberley Aborigines have historically called home. Pedersen and others in this book remind us that history hurts. According to Pedersen, a history of simultaneous colonization, assimilation, and neglect reverberates in the lives of Australian Aboriginal women and their children today. Her discursive analysis is supplemented by her own story, an autoethnography tightly interwoven with the vast number of stories of her people and other Aboriginal peoples of Australia who continue to live in a "limbo of nothingness."

Pedersen's story also has a familiar ring for the First Nations of Canada: the Australian *Aborigines Act* of 1905 was very similar in its sweeping powers to the Canadian *Indian Act* of 1874, which set a despicable standard for the treatment of Aboriginal peoples throughout the British Empire. Common inheritances for Australia and Canada of such acts have included assimilationist practices of "scooping up" Aboriginal children from their homes and families so they could be sent to residential schools; the sexualizing of Aboriginal women for white men's purposes and the denial of the resulting half-caste offspring; cycles of poverty, alcoholism, and welfare dependency, telltale statistics of violence against Aboriginal women; and Aboriginal self-injury and suicide.

What Pedersen adds to this picture is the paradoxical reality of lived experiences for Australian Aboriginal women. They are sometimes reluctant "to instigate and embrace change," she says, because of the internalized and fragmenting self-censure that is a result of colonial oppression.

Simultaneously, "articulate, educated, and empowered" Australian Aboriginal women are reaching beyond "soul-destroying dependency." Both realities are affecting the Reconciliation process in which Australia is engaged. Pederson sees a more promising future in Aboriginal self-determination and in flatly refusing to "accept identities imposed by other cultures."

Pedersen's paper about Australia exemplifies the difficulties that Canadian critic Sherene Razack identifies in her concept of the "culturalization of racism" (1998, 60). Pluralizing ideologies such as multiculturalism in Canada or Reconciliation in Australia use a "cultural differences" approach, which too often "descends, in a multicultural spiral, to a superficial reading of differences that makes power relations invisible and keeps dominant cultural norms in place" (Razack 1998, 9). Pedersen illuminates Razack's idea by making us aware of the "damned if you do, damned if you don't" scenario for Australian Aboriginal people. In Australian society, she says, Aboriginal people are typically condemned by a rhetoric that dismisses them for not being "real": according to this logic they have no culture – they "cannot sing the songs, do not know the dances, have lost their language and do not display the genetics of their heritage." Pluralizing national policies, the preferred way to handle "cultural difference," are thus made more problematic: it is impossible to celebrate cultural diversity when, apparently, the natives have lost their culture somewhere! Victims of a century of systemic racism are thus blamed for not living up to the view of them held by the dominant society.

Another "compound fracture" to the foundations of Western hegemony comes in the form of Islam, particularly after 9/11. Tabassum Ruby's paper, "Who Am I and Where Do I Belong? Sites of Struggle in Crafting and Negotiating Female Muslim Identities in Canada," gives voice to women who recognize themselves as disruptive to a predominantly Christian or even post-religious Western ethos. Ruby says that the singular identity projected upon all Muslim women denies their multiple ethnic identities as emigrants from a dozen countries where practices of Islam differ dramatically. However, Ruby's paper also makes us aware that the Islamic terrorist threat is but another blind for a systemic racism that keeps visible minority women "othered," even if they were born in Canada or have acquired Canadian citizenship.

Many women describe their lived experience of being collectively identified with terrorism as something quite different from the general meaning of the word *terrorism* in the West: it is they who "*feel* the terror of discrimination because of their religious and ethnic backgrounds." The terror the women describe is about more than one moment in history in 2001 that radically affirmed for Western popular culture their difference. While the immediate effects of the destruction of the Twin Towers and the indiscriminate American retaliations on Islamic fundamentalism in the Middle East have added yet another aspect of "otherness" to their sense of selves in North American culture, what preoccupies these women is their difficulty in being "at home" in Canada.

Paradoxically, however, it is difficult for them to keep alive the memories of "back home" that came with them from their various nations of birth as the world and they themselves change. For the women in Ruby's focus groups, "home" is what problematizes identity: these women are insiders and outsiders in both their country of residence and their countries of birth. Home becomes a hybrid place composed of emotional, spatial, and psychological fragments, complicated by gender and constructed by and contributing to fluid, discontinuous identities.

The third paper in part 1, "'Transgendered' Perspectives as a Challenge to Sex, Gender, and Sexuality" by Coralee Drechsler, fractures yet another foundation of Western hegemony: heterosexism. In effect, what Drechsler set out to do with her interview research was to test the theories of Judith Butler (1990; 1993). What Drechsler discovered in interviewing the participants in her study – all of whom responded to her call for "transgendered" subjects, but all except one of whom refused the designation "transgendered" – was that the lived experiences of people who inhabit a space outside of the heterosexual imaginary (Ingraham 1994) are even more incoherent and individually performed than Drechsler (reading Bulter) anticipated. While Drechsler's participants claimed definitive identities, all indicated destabilized understandings of sexuality. These "transgendered" participants' language "often contained contradictions ... because of their simultaneous rejection of and subscription to the expectations and understandings prescribed by the sex/gender system." Drechsler discovered, in writing about her participants' experiences, how difficult it is to use the universalizing terms of the ideologically laden dominant sex/gender/sexuality imaginary (as witnessed by her self-conscious way of using single and double quotation marks).

Part 2: Ruptured sutures

This section begins with another paper that shows how much history hurts; it does so by illuminating how important maintaining the status quo of heterosexual, white families was from the 1960s through the 1970s and beyond in Canadian society. Sandra Jarvie's "Silenced, Denigrated, and Rendered Invisible: Mothers Who Have Lost Their Babies to Adoption in the 1960s and 1970s" is as disturbing a paper as any in this collection because of a history in Canada of deliberate and calculated silencing and victimizing of "unwed" mothers.

Over the course of less than twenty years during the 1960s and 1970s, one quarter of a million Canadian babies and children were "surrendered" to adoption. While Jarvie does not comment on the term "surrendered" directly for its connection to the language of criminal apprehension and prospective punishment, her paper does make clear the Catch 22 conundrum of "unwed" adolescent mothers who were coerced into signing adoption forms without knowing their legal or human rights. On the one hand, these girls and young women were stigmatized and punished for sexual precocity and moral non-conformity, which their society saw as the reasons for their unsanctioned pregnancies. Family, society, and the very "experts" who purportedly had these girls' and their babies' best interests in mind worked in concert to promote adoption of babies born "out of wedlock." On the other hand, these same girls were victimized for being "uncaring" mothers who did not deserve their babies because they were willing to give them up. The implicit assumption was that they were neither desirable nor capable homemakers for babies because they were unwed.

Jarvie sees a connection between authenticity issues for social workers and their care for "unwed mothers": "the rise and claim to professional status through social workers' control and expertise in the area of 'illegitimacy' and 'unmarried' mothers." Furthermore, the need for professional recognition coincided with the need for babies by childless couples; indeed, social workers colluded – perhaps for the most part unknowingly and with other, more personal and professional goals in mind – in the commodification of infants. Indeed, newborn, healthy, and white babies were the products of choice.

Ideologies of punishment, professional validation, and supply-and-demand drove social service responses to the "problem" of "illegitimate" births during the 1960s and the 1970s. The resulting poor support structures prevented the creation of a solid social contract that should have provided supportive and educative means for and efforts on behalf of pregnant girls and women. The "homes" and hospitals for "unwed mothers" should have sutured the abrasions caused by social stigma, but instead what efforts to heal the girls' psychological and emotional wounds were made – and according to Jarvie these were few – dissolved the moment they gave their babies up and left the home or hospital. No follow-up services were offered, and the experiences of the unwed mothers were ignored.

The next chapter in this section, Ellen Whiteman's "tell-me-what-I-want.com: Adolescent Girls, Consumer Society, and Information Technologies," allows us a glimpse at how unregulated marketing on the Internet targets young people. If you are a teenager, for example, and want a pet but your parents will not let you have one or you are allergic to everything with fur, you can get one "free" at a virtual pet site! Of course, you will want to take good care of your virtual pet, feed it and buy things for it. In order to do this, you can earn credits at the virtual pet store by playing advertisement-laden games or agreeing to have advertisements sent to your Web site. Advertisers count on several things with this ploy: first, the buying power of adolescents; second, their power to convince those with buying power in their households to buy certain products; third, and most disturbing of all, as Jean Kilbourne

(1999) has told us for three decades, the cultivating of brand loyalty for life among young people.

A virtual pet is a disturbing enough idea, especially because, as Whiteman reminds us, children who have virtual pets can, in fact, virtually ignore them anytime without consequences. But more disturbing yet, and more fitting for our discussion of the geographies of self, even the self of virtual space, is the fact that the girls in Whiteman's study were accessing a site where they could create a virtual guy, a "cybersweetie," a fantasy boy (*www.gurl.com*). And this site is a link on the most popular adolescent magazine site online, *www.seventeen.com*. Like the paper version, the online version of the magazine is really about selling girls to advertisers (Kilbourne 1999): hence the "tell-me-what-I-want" of Whiteman's title. The articles in *Seventeen* remain what they always have been: "blueprints to which adolescent girls must measure up in order to perform their femininity correctly." They are a means by which girls can internalize gendered scripts that tell them they are never good enough as they are, a means of setting them up to buy products – makeup, clothes, diet books, and so on – that will give them access to the good life depicted in advertising.

Whiteman opens a Pandora's box of concerns about self-image, relationships, fantasy identities, competition among girls, compulsory heterosexuality, virtual relationships taking the place of real ones, and most importantly, security. All but one of the girls in Whiteman's study freely gave out personal information in order to access sites, get free sample products, or use various kinds of "free" e-mail and chat sites (such as ICQ or MSN). Whiteman sees hope in the forms of resistance that her interviewees exhibit and in the increasing abilities that girls seem to be gaining in using information sources online. But I cannot help but wonder if these are false hopes in the face of the stronger messages of gendered identities and roles that adolescent girls are getting from the newest and perhaps the most pervasive media of all, the Internet.

Home may be where the computer portal to the world is for girls, but at the other end of the age spectrum, geographer Allison Williams examines home as a "therapeutic landscape" for those who care for elderly palliative family members. In "The Impact of Palliation on Familial Space: Home Space from the Perspective of Families Living (and Caring) for Dying Loved Ones at Home," Williams uses the case study of one mother/daughter palliative patient/caregiver relationship to explore and begin to challenge a body of research and thought that suggests that "home" may be the best place for a dying patient to experience quality of life up to the end. The problematic that Williams introduces is the fragmentation of self and health that may be the cost to the loving caregiver.

In her Sorokin Lecture of 2001, Meg Luxton talked about neo-liberal policies of deinstitutionalization that make sweeping assumptions about the composition of family and ignore what feminist scholars have been trying to say about it for some time. The postmodern family more often than not has no reserve army of caregivers – unemployed, stay-at-home women who have the youth, physical ability, "natural" nurturing qualities, and economic stability to bring a dying or even aging parent into their homes. In Williams' case study, both mother and daughter had to give up their respective homes, while the daughter attempted to create "home" in a city apartment. Moreover, the daughter herself suffered from a disabling condition. It is interesting to chart, with Williams, the difference between what the daughter intended to do when first interviewed and her level of burnout, fatigue, and guilt when interviewed after a period of a few months.

What this particular case study makes clear is that the "changing geographies of care," which look to home care for palliation – among other things – serves state purposes of health restructuring, with all of its rhetoric of wellness, at the expense of other individuals in the "home." In the discursive first section of her paper, Williams reviews the changes in thinking that have recently been a part of health/medical geographers' research. Though she talks of the multiplicity of meanings that attach themselves to the concept of being "at home," Williams seems particularly drawn to incorporating "existential insidedness" or "place identity," with all of the attendant humanist assumptions and psychological imperatives those terms might imply, into her analysis. Clearly, the daughter caregiver did not find the social service network, supposedly put in place to provide home support and caregiver respite, to give her much relief at all. If a caregiver's health and well-being suffer, surely the health of the (supposedly) advantaged palliative patient must as well.

Maureen Reed's "Spinning Yarns of Women's Activism in Support of Industrial Forestry on Canada's West Coast" is at the end of this section because it takes issue with the very research tools and language used by feminists and labour studies theorists to construct a healthier habitat for humanity. "Ironically," she says in a footnote, "the act of labelling has marginalized these women [in her study] ... making them ripe subjects for a new generation of feminist research agendas such as my own." Reed is aware of herself both as a feminist researcher imposing concepts such as marginalization on groups that might not categorize themselves that way, and unhappy with the either/or choices presented through the feminist activism and theorizing she finds in ecofeminism and labour studies. Moreover, with her notion of "embeddedness," Reed gives us a term for the concept of "home" with all its multitude of meanings: "embeddedness refers to a sense of rootedness of place and social life, in one sense, a growing up together of space and place." Reed says that "women's activism [particularly rural women's activism] is embedded within local social and spatial contexts." Reed does not imply that only women's activism is thus embedded – men lobby at local levels, too – but women are the focus of her research because women in rural communities or one-industry locales remain the main caregivers, as well as the primary recipients and deliverers of social services.

Part 3: Habitats for/of humanity

Part 3 of this collection differs from the previous two sections in that it discusses environments in which the multi-layered complexity, fragmentation, and fluidity of being at home in place or body are at least momentarily accommodated by habitats, again more metaphorical than physical, and more fitting for and of humanity. In "Crafting Selves: Impact of Identity on Intercultural Friendships Among Women," Kim Morrison analyses the identity-defining descriptors that a group of intercultural grandmothers use (related to age, race, culture, parenthood, gender, etc.) through their inclusive and simultaneously definition- and category-defying attempts to expand the effect of the attributes commonly associated with grandmothering. To be a grandmother in our society is, typically, to be essentialized with innate female characteristics of maternalism that reach mythic proportions in the concept of grandmothering. The grandmothers of Intercultural Grandmothers United (whose region ranges over Treaty 4 territory in present-day Saskatchewan) recognize, however, that grandmothering is a diverse, not a common experience, especially when viewed through an intercultural lens: First Nations and Metis women tend far more often than white women to be primary caregivers of grandchildren; "spoiling" of grandchildren attends much more often to the experiences of non-Aboriginal women; the elderliness associated with grandmothering in dominant society is a different thing from being an elder as Aboriginal peoples have traditionally conceived that position of privilege; and "grandmothers can be caring individuals who may never have had biological children or grandchildren."

Like Reed in the previous essay, Morrison notes that contemporary feminists could learn something about the lived experiences of the women who make up IGU. The grandmothers, who are uncomfortable with their own intentional reversing of typical race categories in the naming their organization (note the order of "First Nations, Metis, and other Canadian women"), know they have some distance to go in welcoming and retaining "other" grandmothers, particularly visible minority women. The master's tool of language cannot dismantle the master's house of societal oppression, but the grandmothers' abilities to "construct humanity and grandmothering as overarching commonalities" work as changing performative acts of friendship rather than definitions of identity for Morrison.

The habitat fit for inhabiting that Denise Larsen and Jennifer Boisvert *et al.* describe was created when six women at various stages of training in or practicing of psychology came together to form a mentor relationship. They came away from the experience as friends, having found career support and in the process, created a "women's" work of art, a quilt. "Women's Professional Mentorship in Psychology and the Academy: One Group's Stories of Quilting and Life" is a celebration and example of how mentorship can work, but it is also a critique of the "chilly" and competitive academic climate, chartering process, and clinical practice that the authors experienced in common. All of these women overcame the isolation to meet with one another and in the process discovered that "the distinction between mentor and mentoree blurs when we begin to realize that in the teaching/helping relationship, the mentor or teacher not only provides direction but also benefits from the encounter." To one of the group members, the experience of being part of the mentoring group was one of "coming home."

The authors of this paper talk about having to take risks to share their pasts and dreams; they speak of their awareness of quilt making as traditional women's work and an activity "unusual for our profession." Theirs is a collective response to collective disappointment at not having found feminist mentorship and pedagogy in the academy or the profession. A primary reason for establishing the group, and one of the commitments they bespeak as a result of their mentorship experience, is the desire to make a difference in their field, both in the academy and in clinical practice –to make other women psychologists feel "at home" in the profession.

The writers of the last two chapters in this book have done something that is crucial to creating a healthier habitat for children: they have listened to and privileged what children and young people have to say about *their* worlds. "Sexual Health of Young Women: Context of Care Make a Difference," by Mary Hampton, Barb McWatters, Bonnie Jeffery, and Pamela Smith, connects with several of the previous papers. It exposes, so as to replace, heterosexual assumptions of the right kinds of families, the right kinds of and times for sexual intercourse, the right kinds of responses to non-hegemonic sexual practices, and the right kinds of assumptions about the universality and policing of adolescence. If indeed adolescents are to find, in their own words, a "comfortable" place, a "home" space in which to learn more about the process of identity making and healthy sexual choices, then the geographies they choose must be those that are not commonly offered to them at home, in school, in society. In studying the successes of Planned Parenthood, Regina's Sexual Health Centre, Hampton *et al.* begin with the astute observation that the "sexual health of adolescents receives attention *only* when it is constructed as a problem within individuals" (emphasis added). As a society, as the young people in this study make clear with their comments, we have failed to provide what our young people need in the area of sexual health – a social contract that is honest and forthright in developmentally appropriate ways. We choose not to recognize the sexual activity of Canadian adolescents: in the Regina sample of 2,393 grade 10 and grade 12 students, 44 per cent of adolescent respondents to a city-wide survey reported having had sexual intercourse. I doubt that the children in Regina are any more sexually active than those in any other Canadian city, yet we continue to pretend kids are not sexually active and to punish them when they are.

The other extremely important aspect of Hampton *et al.*'s research was the training of gender-balanced teams of young research assistants to distribute and collect the surveys and to facilitate focus groups. This is an empowering model for young people at both ends of the research.

The participants in the survey were very clear about their preference for the Sexual Health Centre over the services provided by walk-in clinics or family doctors. More young women than young men have used the Centre, and this paper charts the priorities of young women. They want to feel "comfortable," and for them that means friendly, non-judgmental, well-informed staff in a comfortable, non-clinical space with couches and a TV they can adjust. They want communication that is confidential and that validates their individuation. And finally, they have learned that the medical procedures at the Sexual Health Centre are non-compulsory and non-threatening, and they have passed the message on to other teens.

The last paper in this section and collection, "Voices of Dancers with Mobility Impairments," by Donna Goodwin, Joan Krohn, and Arvid Kuhnle, makes for a fine conclusion to the essays collected in this book. When I read it, I see again the grace and joy and commitment of the two young wheelchair dancers whose performance I witnessed as part of the presentation of the authors' research. The study involved interviews with six wheelchair dancers aged six to fourteen, five female and one male, who were also encouraged to journal or draw pictures of their dance experiences. In addition, the mothers of the dancers did interviews and took twenty-four photographs of each of their children in dance or practice situations; one mother also kept a journal. The resulting research findings were analysed for common themes, of which four predominated: the children and parents feel that these dancers are "breaking the mould" imposed upon them by society because of their impairments; in their dance, they find a space "beyond the wheelchair" that enables them to be expressive and creative; the dancing is "more than an extracurricular activity" in that it makes the usually invisible impaired child visible; and finally, and most impressive of all, the children want to "share the dance," to educate the general public about what disabled people are capable of doing and to act as models for other children with impairments.

What Goodwin *et al.* facilitate with their research is the "insider" self so often left out of disability research. And in this case, we hear the insider voice of children who are seldom given voice in any research about them. We learn from them what we should have heard a long time ago: people who must negotiate functional changes in their bodies amidst social expectations and physical barriers are disabled by the environments we create, environments that too often prevent them from feeling at home with their bodies and from finding a strong sense of identity. "Disablement" is a process of becoming disabled in large part because that is the social and historical expectation.

It is fitting, I think, to end this collection with a paper that speaks of empowerment to the next generation.

Part 1

COMPOUND FRACTURES

Chapter 1

OPPRESSION AND INDIGENOUS WOMEN: PAST, PRESENT, AND FUTURE – AN AUSTRALIAN KIMBERLEY ABORIGINAL PERSPECTIVE

J. Maria Pedersen

> "If they have not been caught and deported as children, because their mothers have been victimised by white men, one day they will be caught and deported with their children because *they* have been victimised by white men.... What Australia's Aboriginal and half-caste daughters need is their own mothers who love them, and their own homes among their own people, and teaching, until such time as they shall have attained legal and economic and political freedom."
>
> — *Excerpt from the witness statement by Mary Montgomery Bennet to the Royal Commission Appointed to Investigate, Report and Advise on the Condition and Treatment of Aborigines in Western Australia, 19 March 1934 (Moseley 1935)*

Introduction: A personal perspective

The history of Western Australia is a tangled tapestry of tragedy and experiences, so preparing this paper has been a challenge. I can only provide a brief encounter with my people from the Kimberley Region because there are so many stories from the different points of contact between first and later peoples of the area.

The Kimberley region of Western Australia covers some 422,000 square kilometres, and has a stable population of around 28,000 people. This region is in the northwestern corner of Australia, in the top section of the state of Western Australia. The area contains six main urban centres and an increasing number of Aboriginal communities. Summer is characterized by a tropical monsoonal "wet" season, with winter a mild, "dry" time of year. The region has a diverse and complex geology resulting in spectacular, harsh, and seasonally inaccessible landscapes. Prior to white settlement, a large number of language groups were spread over the Kimberley region.

I would like to share some of my history so that this paper will have significance and so that my world view can be considered in the context of both Australia's official history and the world's indigenous cultures. Three of my grandparents were taken from their black mothers and placed in Beagle Bay Mission because they were not full-blood Aboriginal children. My mother's mother was a very young girl when she was sent from the Roebourne area, which is about seven hundred kilometres south of Broome. She never returned to her country or saw her family again. My father's parents were taken from the Fitzroy Crossing area, which is about six hundred kilometres north of Broome. I have eight sisters and one brother. I was born and raised in Broome, Western Australia, where I live now with my four sons, aged eighteen, seventeen, eight, and six. I have been a full-time parent for the last nine years and a single parent for the last five. When my youngest child commenced school, I began my studies toward a Bachelor of Indigenous Australian Studies (BIAS) at Notre Dame University Australia, Broome Campus. I recently completed my degree.

I was not born a legal citizen of Australia; in fact, my children represent the first generation of my family who were actually born citizens of this country. My father had to apply for his family to become citizens so that we could access a better education and those rights demanded as a matter of course in today's society. He was, however, still expected to show his "papers" on demand. I was born at a time when Aboriginal Australians were not allowed automatic citizenship, despite their histories on this continent that spanned thousands of years and many generations. We came under the protection of the government and this meant that the police had jurisdiction over our every movement at all times.

I discovered from Native Welfare records, which I obtained under the Freedom of Information laws, that the police, as agents for the Protector, in fact searched for my mother because she was not a full-blood Aboriginal child and my grandmother did not have permission from the Protector to have custody of her daughter. My family was fortunate that the nuns at the local convent took in and cared for our mother from approximately five years of age, when my grandmother, who was going blind, became very ill.

My mother was a very forward-thinking woman, deciding to educate her nine daughters at a time when education for women was very restricted. Even rarer than comprehensive education for Aboriginal people who were not "legal citizens" was comprehensive education for Aboriginal girls. To access this education, my family had to travel to Perth, some 2,500 kilometres south of Broome. Because we were non-citizens of our country, we were not legally allowed this geographical movement. So in 1964 my father applied for and was granted citizenship rights for my sisters and me. We could then legally access sound and appropriate mainstream education beyond remote primary institutions. My mother has been a formidable role model for us; she still works full-time, cooking at our local hospital. As a result, my sisters and I have been able to develop a balanced sense of social interaction that enables us to operate successfully in both the Aboriginal and non-Aboriginal spheres.

I am a member of the Broome Local Drug Action Group, a regional member of the Women's Legal Service, Inc., Western Australia, and a long-serving member of the Aboriginal Student Support and Parental Awareness Committee, which is designed to improve educational outcomes for Aboriginal students and to develop parental participation in their children's education. I have also completed the Gatekeeper Certificate, which is a youth suicide-prevention initiative. My paper provides some insights into the oppression of Australian Aboriginal women who, despite significant disadvantages, are forging a new power in the embers of our continued resistance to oppression.

An Australian Kimberley Aboriginal perspective

In a history characterized by dispossession and oppression since colonization, Australia's Kimberley Aboriginal people have resisted European attempts to render their culture and race extinct. Dispossession typically meant the denial of access to land for survival, economic, and ceremonial purposes. The oppression of Aboriginal people was largely determined by the prevailing dominant ideologies attendant upon British imperialism that denied equality and self-determination to Aboriginal people at a number of levels within colonial society. For Kimberley Aboriginal people, this oppression was characterized by the process of dehumanization (Freire 1972), the effects of which continue to resonate throughout the Aboriginal community today. Aboriginal people were considered to be little more than animals who could be bred out of the general population. In addition, assimilationist policies based in notions of quantum-blood classified Aboriginal people as full-bloods, half-castes, and quadroons. All Aboriginal people were denied equality of access to the social resources that gave power and wealth to the dominant European society (Sidanius and Pratto 1999). As a consequence of the generations of systemic dehumanizing and assimilationist practices, Aboriginal people continue to experience oppression in contemporary society. These experiences are characterized by disproportionate amounts of poverty, crime, and imprisonment (Sidanius and Pratto 1999).

Aboriginal people inhabited the harsh and largely inaccessible Kimberley region for hundreds of generations (Pedersen and Woorunmurra 1995, 14; Lambert 1993, 3). Sophisticated social and kinship systems determined an ordered society: a structure of responsibilities within and between the various family units maintained strong familial and social ties (Bell 1998; Berndt and Berndt 1988, 143). Traditional Aboriginal society was a highly spiritual, egalitarian, and sharing co-operative. That is not to say that conflict did not occur between family or clan groups.

Being connected to and caring for the land are premises fundamental to the very existence of Aboriginal people. This custodianship is inherent in kinship systems and is part of kinship obligations because ancestors rest on the land, thus sanctifying particular areas. The presence of ancestors figures largely in Aboriginal Dreaming, which is characterized by a spiritual reality that exists in cyclical rather than linear space and time. A shared or collective oral history founded on the past creates a continuous connection to and sharing of information and knowledge among all participants of life. It is through the Dreaming that Aboriginal Law is transmitted throughout the generations. Aboriginal Law could be described as the guidelines for all actions necessary for survival within society. Dreaming for Aboriginal people was so essential to the Aboriginal psyche that it was never completely suppressed.

In the early 1800s, European explorers discovered that the Kimberley region was rich in grazing land suitable for the pastoral industry, and by the 1860s, white settlement in the region had begun (Pedersen and Woorunmurra 1995, 16). Aboriginal people were forced from their traditional hunting grounds, and pastoralists abused sites sacred to Aboriginal ways of life. The Aboriginal people inhabiting the Kimberley region were a threat to the European pioneers, never ceding their land but fighting to retain custodianship (Pedersen and Woorunmurra 1995, 33, 68, 87). While Aboriginal people on foot with spears and boomerangs were ill-matched to a superior force of armed men on horseback (Elder 1998; Pedersen and Woorunmurra 1995, 67; Austen 1998), they used their superior knowledge of the land and their survival skills to resist the appropriation of their country and the destruction of their culture.

Any resistance or retaliation by the Aboriginal people was swiftly answered by punitive expeditions that in some instances wiped out whole families, simply because they were there. Aborigines lived in a limbo of nothingness that has endured since colonization. They were generally included in pastoral leases as part of the property ceded to Europeans. The fate of any resident Aborigines was left to the will of the lessee. In the initial stages of the colonization process, indigenous Australians were romanticized as noble savages; however, competition for land and resources, and Aboriginal resistance to colonization led to changes to this perception.

Settlement in the Kimberley region occurred some seventy to eighty years later than on the east coast, and by this time stereotypical views of Aboriginal peoples had become entrenched in the ideologies of the fledgling Australian state. Aborigines, already dehumanized, became demonized, generally portrayed as "short, ugly and heavy featured" savages (Elder 1998, 5). They were considered subjects of the British Empire and therefore answerable to British law; however, because they were not citizens of Australia, they had no legal, social, political, or economic rights in this country (Chesterman and Galligan 1997; Haebich 1992, 129). Australia engaged in exclusionary policies and oppressive practices in its dealings with the indigenous population.

But it was the *Aborigines Act* (1905) that gave the government complete control over the lives of Aboriginal people, including whom they were allowed to marry, whether they were allowed to raise their children, and where they were allowed to live (Haebich 1992, 67, 85). The European proponents of social Darwinism who created and controlled the Act believed that the Aborigines were a race so low on the scale of humankind that they were doomed to extinction; therefore, the increasing emergence of half-caste children was of great concern. Such children were seen as better than their kin because of their European blood, so they were taken from their families and sent to the missions and institutions to be "domesticated." Because of their Aboriginal heritage, these children of mixed blood were considered suitable only for training to be servants for the European population (Haebich 1992, 82; Huggins 1998, 17) or deserving of no better than lower-order manual and labouring positions. Half-castes became little more than slave labourers.

Aboriginal women were typically viewed from ethnocentric perspectives and were therefore overlooked and exploited (Bain 1982, 21-28; Elder 1998; Haebich 1992, 77, 107). They were used as concubines or sexual partners for the settlers and pioneers at a time when white women were scarce in the region (Haebich 1992, 116, 324). It became an accepted practice for pastoralists and/or their workers to kidnap and abuse Aboriginal women and girls. Females working for European employers reported many instances of sexual abuse. Their lack of power (Haebich 1992, 130) resulted in their abuse without redress (Chesterman and Galligan 1997, 47-48).

In the late 1800s, this sexualization of Aboriginal womanhood was reflected in government-assigned Northern Protector Walter Roth's belief that without government intervention, half-caste girls were destined to become prostitutes. The government, he believed, was removing them from their families and homes "for their own protection" (Chesterman and Galligan 1997). In the terms of the parochial attitude that Roth embraced, government intervention was required to protect half-caste girls from an inherent biological deficit. In the early 1900s, in accordance with what can now be recognized as victim-blaming paradigms, the government began removing Aboriginal females following instances of abuse and misuse by non-indigenous men and sending these abused women to institutions and missions. The excerpt below is taken from the Moseley Royal Commission and is part of a petition that was forwarded by half-caste women from Broome (Moseley 1935). It reflects the fate of many Aboriginal women and girls.

> Some of us have fatherless children supported by ourselves that have been brought into this world through no fault of our own, but through fear. And should we disclose who were the fathers truthfully. By being on the Act [Aborigines Act 1905] we might not be believed, because the Officers have not to take the word of the mother alone. And those men who are the fathers of some of those children know this and take good care that the girl they want is alone. And in a place and at a time when no witnesses for the woman is or can be there.

Rather than the Europeans acknowledging that white men were committing offences of rape and sexual assault and that they should accept some responsibility for those criminal activities, the colonizers punished Aboriginal women through oppressive processes that removed them from their families and country. Mary Bennet, in evidence given to the Moseley Royal Commission of 1935, stated that "[t]he native woman never gets justice" (Moseley 1935).

Aboriginal women became accustomed to being invisible. Being noticed meant potential removal from family or exposure to abuse and ridicule. The psychology of oppression has become an intergenerational way of life and has distorted the potential for Aboriginal women to be fully human (Freire 1972, 20). In 1967 the Australian public voted overwhelmingly to give Aborigines full citizenship rights. The legislative changes did not occur for some years after 1967, however. It could even be argued that more equitable access to social resources has only occurred in the last ten to fifteen years.

The effects of this history have never been adequately addressed. In fact, there has been public and political denial of the severity of the atrocities perpetrated against Aboriginal people, and denial that some of these atrocities even occurred. But Aboriginal people believe that the negative social repercussions of these atrocities have resulted in generations of alcohol and substance abuse, which are now the avenues of escape for many of today's Kimberley Aboriginal young people (*Choose Life Report* 1999). Associated risk-taking behaviours continue the cycle of poverty, oppression, and welfare dependency. The *Choose Life Report* (1999) found that hospitalization due to intentional self-injury among Aboriginal peoples was over seventeen times more common than death due to suicide. Increased access to and availability of alcohol has also resulted in increased violence against women (E.M. Hunter 1991). As mothers and grandmothers of a culturally extensive family network, Kimberley Aboriginal women in the twenty-first century are still coping with the manifestations of a psychological immobility resulting from the fear of intercultural and intracultural violence (E.M. Hunter 1991). Thus, "'the weary round goes on'" as one Aboriginal woman, Mary Bennett, reported to Moseley (1935). The result is another generation continuing the cycle of poverty and dysfunction. Myths about Aboriginal people are still apparent in the opinions, perceptions, and behaviours of many Australians, while for many Aboriginal people, their perception of themselves as oppressed is, as it is with indigenous peoples worldwide, "impaired by their submersion in the reality of oppression" (Freire 1972, 22).

Experiencing post-colonial trauma, far too many Aboriginal people "confuse freedom with maintenance of the status quo" (Freire 1972, 16). The reluctance to instigate and embrace change simply perpetuates oppression. There is an unwillingness to reach beyond this shadow of being. Aboriginal women are also confronted by the self-censoring psychology of internalized oppression from within their own communities. Then there are those non-Aboriginal people who do not wish to alter the status quo and who attempt to silence those who would speak out about oppressive practices. Such people would prefer to have token representatives who are well-spoken but never outspoken. Thus, Aboriginal women are confronted by both internal and external constraints.

While the process of Reconciliation in Australia has attempted to highlight Australian Aboriginal history, the expectation has been that Aboriginal people would of their own accord emerge from an abyss of nothingness and take their equal places in society. These expectations are clearly based on liberal assumptions of the existence of a level playing field for all.

The reality of life for Kimberley Aboriginal people is quite different from the dominant liberal view. For example, the Centre for Aboriginal Economic Policy Research identified Aboriginal Australians as the most disadvantaged and the poorest sector of Australian society (B. Hunter 1999). The history of Aboriginal women has left them in little doubt as to their lack of power and credibility in a male-dominated society that was founded on the paradigms of European ideologies. Aboriginal women in the twenty-first century are still coping with the long-term effects of dispossession, forcible removals, dispersal, alienation, and denigration.

Other research reveals the following realities for Kimberley Aboriginals:

- Aboriginal people make up less than 3 per cent of the State of Western Australia's population, but Aboriginal people comprise approximately 40 per cent of the total Kimberley population (Healy and Acacio 1998, 2).
- Forty per cent of the Kimberley Aboriginal population are below fifteen years of age (Kimberley Development Commission 1997).
- Aboriginal juveniles aged ten to fourteen are twenty-five times more likely to be arrested and charged by police (Aboriginal Justice Council 1999, 7).
- Young Kimberley Aboriginal people are eighteen times more likely to be held in detention than other Australian youth, setting a pattern for future contact with police and the courts (Council for Aboriginal Reconciliation 1997).
- The suicide rate for Kimberley Aboriginal youth is more than twelve times the national average (*Choose Life Report* 1999, 11).
- Homicide is the leading cause of death among young Kimberley Aboriginal women aged fifteen to twenty-nine (Kimberley Aboriginal Medical Services Council 2000).
- Aboriginal women are fourteen times more likely to be arrested by police than non-Aboriginal women (Blagg 2000, 9).

- Aboriginal women are twelve times more likely to be victims of assault than non-Aboriginal women (Blagg 2000, 12).

These are just some of the social indicators that impact significantly on the lives of Kimberley Aborigines, invariably leading to consistent negative contact with all facets of the legal system. As the agency historically responsible for enforcing the *Aborigines Act (1905)*, the police retain a stereotypical view that Aboriginal people have criminal tendencies (Haebich 1992, 92–93, 95). The police view is still symptomatic of the history of the colonization of Australia, which was characterized by the imperialist and masculinist ideologies of the British Empire: "the consequent air of penal discipline and official insistence on the maintenance of order had a tragic role in shaping relations with the Indigenous people" (Eddy 1992, 9).

The over-representation of Aboriginal males in custody and the high incidence of family violence result in many women becoming the sole primary caregivers of young people who are regularly confronted with the stereotypical assumptions of their having anti-social behaviour. Non-indigenous perceptions of Aboriginal people continue to be characterized, as they have since colonization, by stereotypical and negative assumptions. For example, young Aboriginal women are still viewed primarily as potential sexual partners, while young Aboriginal males have been stereotyped as potential criminals. Consequently, many Aboriginal young people in the Kimberley Region are still regularly and repeatedly stopped by the police for questioning – simply because these young people can be stopped.

Substance abuse and associated risk-taking behaviours are negative ways of responding to the stereotypes and consequences of oppression and to the poverty that characterizes many Kimberley Aboriginal environments. At another level, however, such behaviours may provide the only means by which some Aboriginal people feel they can continue to exist each day. Aboriginal women in particular are required to cope in oppressive and often tragic circumstances, the consequences of which can operate to disrupt the health and well-being of families and communities. These disruptions to healthy functioning can interfere with opportunities and aspirations to acquire the skills necessary to overcome the oppressive environments within which many Kimberley Aboriginal people exist.

That lack of opportunity perpetuates oppression. Aboriginal lawyer Noel Pearson (1999) has identified education as the single motivating factor that can potentially mobilize Aboriginal people and provide them with the basic tools for dealing with the existing social and legal constructs that often operate to further disadvantage them through abuses of power, misinformation, and the manipulation of processes. Mothers, grandmothers, and aunts are typically the primary caregivers for young Aboriginal people. Because such women are uninformed and uneducated in dominant-culture ways, future generations are susceptible to remaining on the margins of Australian society.

Given the historical and continuing trend of Kimberley Aboriginal women trying to hold families together in a fractured social context, the challenges described above need to be addressed. Kimberley Aboriginal women need to take a leading role in rebuilding and promoting stronger communities in order that we may find more effective ways of dealing with and countering life in an oppressive society. Strategies aimed at achieving such goals must include a multifocal approach in order to accommodate the diversity of circumstances within Kimberley Aboriginal communities. In addition, Kimberley Aboriginal women must be involved at all levels of change.

Emerging from a history of oppression, however, there are today a number of articulate, educated, and empowered Australian Aboriginal women who are reaching beyond a fragmented history of soul-destroying dependency (Williams *et al.* 1992). They are challenging the barriers imposed by society and attempting to expose and address the factors undermining Aboriginal self-determination.

Ironically and sadly, amidst the notable accomplishments of these Aboriginal women, Australians can be dismissive of those who are not seen as "real" Aboriginal people. In the general view, these non-real Aboriginals have no real culture; they have nothing and are nothing (Huggins 1998, 143). They cannot sing the songs, do not know the dances, have lost their language, and do not display the genetics of their heritage. Australians commonly overlook the fact that dispersal of Aboriginal children resulted in a removal from the language and practices of their lineage. Also overlooked is the notion that aboriginality is about a connectedness to the soul, not about genetically inherited features. Aboriginal people are once again being constructed as a race of nobodies, living in a limbo of nothingness. And once again, the social practice of "divide and rule" (Freire 1972, 111) occurs as a reaction to Aboriginal women who are reasserting their identities on their own terms (Oxenham 1999) and have the skills to be strong agents for change.

Institutionalized racism (Sullivan 1996, 44, 61) is another huge obstacle confronting Kimberley Aboriginal women. Officially, however, such racism conflicts with the principles of Reconciliation. Many Aboriginal people are still denied access to resources and assistance because they are confounded by language difficulties, administrative obstructions (Bennett 1999), and geographical isolation. For example, the Western Australian Department of Training found that "Aboriginal women appear to be far removed [more so than Aboriginal men] from decisions that affected them" (1997, 19). Many Aboriginal women return to education after they have raised families, but changes to educational allowances for remote and mature students mean this group of students will again be the most disadvantaged.

It is encouraging, however, to note that despite these challenges, there are now numerous Aboriginal professionals who can undertake research from positions of shared history and experience. For them, education has been a means of empowerment. Their backgrounds should help to assure that a true reflection of the state of the Aboriginal Nation can be achieved. In the sphere of indigenous Australian social interaction, a growing number of articulate, educated, and strong representatives are challenging existing ideologies, practices, and written material.

For example, a study exploring responses to oppression and its implications for identity development in a group of Aboriginal youth residing in Perth, Western Australia found that these young people responded to oppression in a number of ways that challenge the ethnocentric paradigms of black self-hatred and hopelessness (Hovane 2000). In addition, this group of young people demonstrated a well-developed critical consciousness about their status within society and were able to employ this awareness to successfully foster a strong sense of self, cultural identity, and self-esteem (Hovane 2000). On such research and young people rest the hopes for the future of Australian Aboriginal people.

Conclusion

Australian Aboriginal women are discriminated against because of gender, but even more because of race. We are fighting for more than the material. We are fighting for cultural recognition and for historical recognition, and we are reasserting identities based in our lived experiences (Oxenham 1999), thus rejecting identities previously constructed through the paradigms of ethnocentric Europeans. As Aboriginal women, we are now saying that we have a history, we are not invisible, we have a voice, and we are reclaiming our humanity. Our future must embrace change and this change can only happen through education. Without a holistic societal and political approach that includes those factors that impact on every aspect of Aboriginal life, change will be difficult.

We perceive a partnership of mutual reciprocity among all Australians, and rather than espousing the political rhetoric of Reconciliation, we are actively pursuing our path to self-determination. In refusing to accept identities imposed by other cultures, we are stepping outside of the confines of our cultural prisons.

Our young people are the future and the measure of our success as a society. Ours is a collective social responsibility to ensure a safe and nurturing environment for their development. We have experienced the depths of despair at the sheer magnitude of the task ahead of us, but our determination to create a better life for our children and grandchildren far outweighs the fear of failing.

Chapter 2

WHO AM I AND WHERE DO I BELONG? SITES OF STRUGGLE IN CRAFTING AND NEGOTIATING FEMALE MUSLIM IDENTITIES IN CANADA

Tabassum Ruby

> Even though I have been here since I was four years old, the
> first thing people ask wherever I go is, where are you from?
> You know. You have to look a certain way I think in order to be
> accepted as Canadian. (Bilqis)

Introduction

"May I ask you where you are from, if you do not mind?" asks a middle-aged woman with a young daughter while we stand to catch a bus that will take us downtown. "I am from Pakistan," I reply. "Most probably Muslim then," the woman states, and I confirm her assertion. The girl, who is no more than five years old (and I like to call her "Joy"), surprisingly steps back, trying to be as close to her mother as she can, and utters "Bin-Laden." "No, honey, no, it has nothing to do with Bin-Laden." The mother endeavours to comfort her daughter. I am stunned. A few moments before, Joy greeted me with a warm smile, complaining about the cold December afternoon in Saskatoon and telling me that she was going to buy a Christmas present for her father. We also learned each other's names and Joy tried to pronounce my name correctly. I appreciated her effort and felt faith in humanity, despite our cultural differences. The situation, nonetheless, changed upon my response to her mother's assessment of my religious affiliation. Joy's friendly smile turned to fright. What makes her relate me with Bin-Laden? Why is she so upset by hearing that I am Muslim?

While these thoughts fill my mind with great curiosity and distress, I inquire of Joy who Bin-Laden is. "He is mean," Joy answers. But why is he mean? What has he done? "He is a bad guy," she replies. Joy's mother, still comforting and holding her daughter close, tells me that since September 11, 2001, Joy has been afraid of Muslims. This elucidation explains the young girl's anxiety. Joy feels panic because her young mind sees a link between a Pakistani-Muslim and Bin-Laden. Even to this child, I am a potential "terrorist," like the one presented in the media as an enemy of the Western world.[1] She did not know earlier that I am a Muslim because I do not wear a headscarf, a prominent symbol of a Muslim woman. Her mother acknowledges the media influence on her daughter and states that the negative images of Muslims shown repeatedly in the media have led Joy to believe that it is important to stay away from Muslims. The warm feelings of mutual humanity that we exchanged a few moments ago, therefore, turn into chilly fright due to stereotypical depictions of Muslims in the media.[2]

Neither Joy's mother's question regarding my country of origin, nor Joy's perception of me as a potential "terrorist," nor my experience of confronting negative stereotypes of Muslims walking down a Western street is an isolated case. The results of my study show that many immigrant Muslim women living in Canada often face the question of identity and confront clichéd images of Muslims.

In this chapter, I explore the ways in which immigrant Muslim women negotiate the categories of woman, immigrant, and Muslim, and also how these women situate themselves as to who they are and where they belong. The multiple identities of the participants in my study are not necessarily compatible and often generate tensions because the women position themselves as "insider" as well as "outsider" in their resident country. The participants frequently referred to "back home," a place where they think they belong, while realizing that they have been uprooted from their countries of origin. Memories of countries of origin have led many participants to conduct their lives according to their "back home" traditions, a result of their strong commitment to their cultures and religion. Simultaneously, they have also adapted to the lifestyle of mainstream Canadian society, sometimes enthusiastically and sometimes out of compulsion. Thus their identities appear to be very fluid, altering in order to adjust to a non-Muslim environment.

Methodology

Using three focus groups, I conducted one interview session with each group. I divided my participants into groups on the basis of their use of the *hijab*.[3] In one focus group all of the participants wore the *hijab* and in another, the women did not wear it. There were five informants in each of these two groups and each interview session was one and half hours long. My third group consisted of mixed informants: some wore the *hijab* and some did not. The mixed group had four participants and the session lasted for one hour and fifty minutes. The interviews were audiotaped with the participants' permission.

Sampling

In order to protect the anonymity of my participants, details such as their places of birth, ages, and occupations cannot be fully described here, but general characteristics are as follows. The informants' countries of origin include Afghanistan, Bangladesh, Brunei, Burma, Egypt, Guyana, India, Iran, Jordan, Kuwait, Pakistan, and Turkey. The women's ages range from sixteen to sixty. The participants' occupations include physician, accountant, writer, insurance officer, and student. The immigrant experiences of my participants range from those who arrived in Canada a few years ago to those who immigrated more than two decades ago.

Immigrant Muslim women and the question of identity

Harris (1995) writes that identity is a very abstract word that refers simply to "an individual's sense of uniqueness, of knowing who one is, and who one is not" (1). Knowing about oneself very much depends on the culture in which one lives. The language, the food, the dress codes, the values, as well as the beliefs and the social institutions, are all part of a culture and contribute significantly to one's understanding of one's identity. A person's identity, however, is multi-faceted. I, for instance, walking down Saskatoon's street, was not only viewed as a woman by Joy and her mother, but also as a woman of colour, an immigrant, and a member of an ethnic and a religious group. Thus, the use of the word "identities" as a plural is more appropriate in discussing the sites of struggle of immigrant Muslim women living in Canada.

As immigrants

Non-Caucasian immigrants often face racial discrimination in Western societies; part of that discrimination manifests itself under the category of "immigrant." Ng (1981, 1987, 1993) states that women of colour are frequently seen to be "immigrant" by other members of society regardless of their place of birth. Technically, the term refers to those who have a certain legal status in Canada, such as landed immigrants. However, as Ng points out, in everyday life the word "immigrant" encompasses negative stereotypes of non-English-speaking women who have lower paid jobs and belong to certain ethnic groups. The term is less often associated with white English-speaking immigrants, but is readily used to describe "visible minorities."

Similarly, many of my informants indicated that since they do not fit the image of white European immigrants, they often encounter racism in Canada. Their legal documents show that they are citizens of Canada, but in their everyday social life, they are often considered to be "aliens." In response to my question about what it is like to be a Canadian, Haleemah commented that having a Canadian nationality did not confirm her as Canadian in the society, and people often inquired about her place of birth: "And you look different, you know. When people say where are you from, if I say I am Canadian, yeah, I mean where [were] you born? You know. You have to say, from India or Pakistan or whatever, you know."

Even though Haleemah has been here for twenty years and identifies herself as Canadian, she is not accepted as one because her dark skin marks her, in her own words, as "different." She is often asked about her country of origin, a constant reminder that she is an outsider and does not belong here. Her status is associated with her racial background rather than with her legal status, suggesting that only Caucasian immigrants embody the image of Canadian citizens.

For those who came here as children or adolescents, the perception of "outsider" usually played out in their school experiences. As young newcomers, they experienced racial discrimination because children in their schools had the idea that only white students who spoke without accents were Canadian. When Di'ba went to high school in Saskatoon, it was difficult for her schoolmates to accept her as one of them: "People in high school are not very mature. And they are not understanding, you know. So it is hard for them to accept new people who come here so.... But I mean you get used to it, you just got to prove yourself, you know."

Through childhood socialization, children learn what distinguishes them from others and who belongs to their group and who is a "stranger" (Papanek 1994). Di'ba, however, did not situate racist attitudes within the broader social context. She viewed racism as individual rather than systemic. She therefore adopted an individualist approach to the racism that she experienced, as evidenced in her comment that every individual needed to prove him/herself and get used to the behaviour.

As Muslim immigrants

Racial discrimination in the case of my participants occurs partly because they belong to a religious and ethnic group that is associated with negative images, such as "terrorist" and "extremist." The word *terrorism* is frequently used in the media, as well as in daily conversations; nonetheless, researchers such as Farrell (1982), Buckelew (1984), and Wheeler (1991) have pointed out that there is no agreed-upon inclusive definition and that the term "means different things to different people" (Kushner 1998, 8). For instance, the United States may bomb a country and "claim it is defending national interests. Yet, it may condemn another country for doing the same thing" (White 2002, 4). Double standards and contradictions lead to confusion; therefore, the term *terrorism* is difficult to define.

There are, however, some definitions that help to identify some of the features of terrorism. For instance, White (2002) states that terrorism is "the use or threatened use of force designed to bring about a political change" (8). It may also be thought of as "the systematic use of random violence against innocents in order to bring about political change through fear" (Miller 1982, 1). Yet another definition is "the unlawful use of force or violence against person or property to intimidate or coerce a government, the civilian population, or any segment thereof, in furtherance of political or social goals" (Smith 1994, 6, citing the FBI's definition). These vague definitions do not tell us the criteria for defining "threat," "violence," and "unlawful use of force." They do, however, indicate general aspects of the word that people can recognize.

Many of my participants used the term *terrorism* as a way of showing that immigrant Muslim women *feel* the terror of discrimination because of their religious and ethnic backgrounds. Some of them also believe that Muslim identities are wrongly connected to "terrorists." Di'ba, in particular, argued that people have many false impressions about Muslims and that stereotypical images need to be terminated. She stated that if she had a chance to make some changes in Canada, she would clear up some of the misconceptions about Muslims.

> I like to clear some of the misconceptions about us, like in general as being terrorists and all that. We are not and people

should know that. And people need to understand also that we are not here to change them, because being different is one thing, but people think that if you are different then maybe you are going to try to change things around here and people do not usually like change. So, we are not here to change anybody, we are just here to live and, you know, we are just like anybody else.

The constant association of the term *terrorist* with Muslims disturbs Di'ba, for she believes that people have the wrong perception. She recognizes that as a Muslim, she follows a belief system that makes her *different* and confirms her distinct identities. However, demanding her human rights, she argues that she is "like anybody else," and should not be discriminated against on the basis of ethnicity and/or religion.

Terror through terrorism

Hall (1991) argues that "history changes your conception of yourself" (6), and the history of being an immigrant Muslim woman in the West changed after the destruction of the Pentagon and the World Trade Centre towers in the United States. Many of my participants mentioned the aftermath of the event at a personal level, as well as at a worldwide level, and they felt that Muslim identities were at risk because of the United States' response to the events of September 11, 2001. In particular, the informants referred to the bombing of Afghanistan. They believed that massive damage was inflicted on Afghan people without justification. Di'ba remarked that "[the American government] can't tell the difference between the terrorists, the Taliban, and the normal people. So you kill a lot of innocents and you said you are going after terrorists – like, you are being the terrorist by doing that." Smith (1994) states that "some persons are labeled as terrorists, while others who commit similar crimes avoid that label" (7). Similarly, even though Di'ba identified the Taliban as terrorists, she argued that by killing Afghan civilians, the United States became a terrorist, too. In Di'ba's view, the United States, therefore, defeated the purpose of attacking Afghanistan.

In addition to commenting on the casualties, some participants also stated that the attack brought many difficulties to the people of Afghanistan that were not evident before the war. Noreen, for example, remarked on the issue of drugs as well as on the political violence in Afghanistan. Before the attack, "the women were covered, and now see the drugs start again in Afghanistan. People kill each other – they just make the Muslim people attack on each other. You can see the difference they have made in Afghanistan." Zulaika and Douglass (1996) argue that "terrorism news is framed according to a definite worldview that opposes countries and cultures within a hierarchy of values in which 'we' are at the top and the practitioners of terrorism [are] at the bottom" (13). Although media coverage of Afghani women's *burqa* was an important issue in Canada, particularly before and after September 11, 2001, Noreen (who wears the *hijab*) does not consider women's covering as one of the most pressing social issues in Afghanistan. For her, the use of drugs and "Muslim killing Muslim" are greater problems.

From conversations with Noreen and many other participants, it became clear to me that the informants believed that the United States government's attack on Afghanistan revealed the worldwide hostility toward Muslims. Di'ba, for instance, observed – with good reason, as it turns out – that after bombing Afghanistan, the United States was planning to attack Iraq. She said that Muslims across the globe were at risk: "It seems that [the United States is] targeting the small, weak, countries right now and then they just move on to the bigger ones, and it's, like, what are you trying to do, you know, just to wipe out the whole nation." On the basis of a shared bond of Islam, Di'ba and many other participants feel connected with fellow believers, and this promoted a sense of collective victimization among the participants. Thus, many interviewees were concerned about Muslim countries and the collective well-being of Muslims who were at risk because of the American aggression.

The events of September 11, 2001 and their aftermath have had a direct personal impact on some participants. In particular, they informed me that travelling has become difficult for Muslims. They argued that Muslim travellers often face longer inquiries about their identification and their luggage at airports, and that increased airport security, which is targeted especially at Muslims, shows biases. Di'ba went to Florida after September 11th to attend a conference with her two Euro-Canadian friends, and at the Toronto airport she was the only one asked about her luggage: "They just told them, oh yeah, go ahead you know, whatever. For me, they actually checked for everything.... I mean, I can understand, but do it to everybody, not just to me. It is not nice to be distinguished, to be picked out like that for things like this."

Di'ba, who wears a headscarf, a distinct symbol of her Muslim identity, believes that she went through a lengthy immigration check because she was identified as a member of a group that was deemed "undesirable," whereas her friends had an easy time because they belonged to the dominant society. Di'ba recognizes the importance of security, but she also indicated that only specific people were being targeted; as a result, she faced racism. Di'ba's experience shows that she was viewed as "other" despite her Canadian citizenship. Constructs of Muslim identities make her feel discriminated against because of her religion.

Discriminatory policies are not limited to travelling; the *hijab*, often recognized by many Muslims and non-Muslims as an identity symbol of a *Muslimah*,[4] has become a sign of a "terrorist" woman in Canada. There were a number of incidents in Canada where *Muhajibh*[5] were harassed after September 11th,[6] and some participants mentioned that they also had encountered racist harassment. Pervin, for instance, reported that someone called her a "terrorist," and she thinks that it was because she wore the *hijab*: "Some guy came and he said 'terrorist' because I wear the *hijab*, I think so, that's what I did not like. Some people stare at me. I think that if you have the *hijab*, you are 'terrorist,' and really, some of them think so."

The media and September 11th

We are surrounded by the mass media. The media play an important role in suggesting to their audiences how to view the world around them. Said (1981) argues that "things like newspapers, news and opinions do not occur naturally; they are *made*, as the result of human will, history, social circumstances, institutions, and the conventions of one's profession" (45–46). Thus, people who write about Muslims, produce television or radio shows, report in daily newspapers, or circulate images in magazines or films do not work in a vacuum. A reporter, a journalist, a writer, or a producer of a show consciously decides what to write or produce and how to present it in ways that accommodate social, political, and economic understandings. Therefore, news or a piece of information "is less an inert given than the result of a complex process of usually deliberate selection and expression" (Said 1981, 46).

One of the examples that many participants mentioned regarding "deliberate selection and expression" of the media was the "fake video." Several days after the destruction of the Pentagon and the World Trade Center towers in the United States, a video was aired in which Palestinian people were shown celebrating the events of September 11th. Noreen, however, argued that it was a "fake video."

The media here are not honest. Like when September 11th attack happened, they showed forged, Palestinian people dancing in the street and we saw that on a satellite before, actually a few months before the attack…. It was faked and we called to the radio, my husband phoned, and … we told them that we have the tape and the tape has the date, the pictures has the date, it's an old footage and they just hanged up the phone…. They just brought it to show that we are terrorist and, I do not know, to show how bad we are, but it was not true and we tried to explain it, but…

White (2002) observes that "media reports promote fear and magnify the threat in the public mind" (260). Similarly, Noreen argued that the fake video was shown as a way to generate hatred against Islam and Muslims. The media not only shape personal and national identity, but are the lens through which reality is perceived (Henry 1997). North American media's consistent portrayal of Muslims as terrorists has shaped many Western people's views about Muslims, as evidenced in Noreen's experience. Noreen, for example, felt her identity made her vulnerable in a non-Muslim country.

Advantages of living in Canada

Most immigrants come to Canada in search of a better quality of life. The participants in this study indicated that even though their distinct identities often put them at risk and they encounter racism, their quality of life has improved. Having exposure to negative as well as positive experiences, the participants frequently assessed their lives in terms of what they lacked and what they attained by living in Canada. Many women mentioned that they view their residency in Canada as an opportunity to enrich their lives by combining the values of "back home" and the resources of the Western society. They feel that they "are the most fortunate people on this earth," because they have access to Canadian resources such as higher education and economic resources, of which they were deprived in their place of birth. Nabilah described the benefits of living in Canada and remarked that "if you step into my house, you will feel that you are living in a Canadian/Pakistani" home. By creating a home atmosphere that is a combination of her "home country" and Western amenities, she optimistically integrated both cultures. Rather than perceiving the West as a threat to her female Muslim identities, she altered her identities to include the best of both worlds – "Canadian/Pakistani."

Most Muslims who live in a Muslim society take their religion as a given, while those who live in a Western society are often more conscious of their Muslim identities because they are exposed to different values. Many participants pointed out that for Muslims in the West, the concept of quality of life includes the self-conscious integration of religion into their lives in new ways, and that living in a Western society has provided them with a chance to know about their religion in greater depth. Conducting their lives according to Islamic teachings is, they believe, part of crafting Muslim identities in a non-Muslim culture, but it is also a reaction to the questions about their faith that the participants are often asked by non-Muslim people. Farza'nah, for instance, remarked that as a Muslim woman she maintains certain values that are different from those of the larger Canadian culture. In order to present herself as reasonable in her beliefs, she feels that she should study Islam.

> The people that are living back home, you know, my cousins and everyone, they are less aware of Islam than us [who] are actually living in a non-Muslim community. It is just because I find it that we are forced [to] find out the reason, because it is so different here that, you know, if someone asks you why are you doing this, you have to have an answer to them, so you go and seek, seek an answer for that question that someone poses for you. Whereas for them, back home, they have it sort of inherited, and since everyone is doing it, it has become part of them.

Harris (1995) argues that "maintaining the integrity of one's identity is an ongoing struggle throughout adulthood" (1). Living in a multi-cultural society and being aware of different value systems, Farza'nah experiences an ongoing struggle in her life. Farza'nah's religious insecurity in a non-Muslim culture, then, appears as a threat to her faith, requiring her to take a defensive position. Farza'nah's commitment to her religion is a way of protecting her religion, but it is also an opportunity for her to seek knowledge about Islam. Living in Canada, therefore, has facilitated Farza'nah's search for her religion. Moreover, this knowledge, as well as her relationship with her religion, has become a mark of her identities in a non-Muslim environment.

Besides acquiring greater in-depth knowledge about their religion while living in a Western society, many participants indicated that life in Canada has provided them with a chance to grow individually, as women. The women feel a sense of autonomy, and they stated that they enjoy freedom in Canada that they may not have had if they were residing in a Muslim society. Comparing her life in Canada with that of Saudi women, Mali'hah stated that she "would never be able to live in Saudi Arabia," because in Canada she has the pleasure of living a relatively unrestrained life. She loves to live here because "I can just jump into my car and go wherever I want to and nobody is going to stop me; unlike, if I were in Jeddah, I would not be allowed to drive." Mali'hah perceives driving as a symbol of her freedom. In part Mali'hah's identities in Canada as a female Muslim are consistent and in harmony with Western standards.

The women's control over their lives is directly related to their relationships with their families, and some participants stated that their relationship with their husbands in terms of gender equality is more balanced in Canada than it was "back home." In many Muslim countries, men are expected to dominate women, and in maintaining the cultural traditions, most often men behave accordingly. However, human relations frequently modify as people's circumstances change, and Raheelah mentioned the change of gender roles within her family. She remarked that her husband is open-minded, but "he is open-minded here, okay, living in Canada. I don't think he would be as open-minded if we were just settled in Pakistan. It would be a lot different."

Where is home?

In discussing the advantages and disadvantages of living in Canada, the participants frequently referred to their country of origin as "home." James (1998) writes that "home" is "both a conceptual and a physical space. It is an idea that guides our actions and, at the same time, a spatial context where identities are worked on" (144). The participants in my study also identified "home" as an imaginary place, as well as a psychological concept that often shapes their identities. The participants' physical dislocation from their place of birth to their current land of residence has liberated them from a fixed spatial "home," and they perceive the concept as fluid. Mali'hah, for instance, stated that "home is wherever I am." Mali'hah has lived in a number of places inside and outside Canada, which has displaced her from a "typical home." She associates the idea of "home" not with her country of origin, but with her situated presence at a particular moment. "Home" is, for her, not a fixed entity to which she can make an absolute return because she views "home" as a psychological concept.

Rapport and Dawson (1998) state that "home" is "where one best knows oneself" (9), and most often the starting point of knowing oneself is one's place of birth. Therefore, although some participants do not relate the concept of "home" with their country of origin, they want to maintain ties with "back home." The reality of "back home," however, has made some participants aware that they do not belong there either. In response, one participant, Bilqis, has adopted an internal sense of home. She remarked, "I carry home inside me – wherever I go, it's home, yeah." Bilqis's concept of "home" is due to her visit to Guyana (her country of birth), where she thought her roots were. But her visit made her aware that she does not belong there.

> When you leave the place where you were born at a young age, it's funny; I went back expecting to find some kind of homing feeling, because I never felt like Canada was totally home. But I realized when I went back to visit Guyana that that was not home either. In fact, when I met Guyanese people on the street they would say to me, you are from outside. And it really hurt me at that time because I was wanting this homing feeling, but yes, I guess you create it inside.

Thus failing to connect herself with her homeland, Bilqis transformed the idea of "home" conceptually. The search for identity involves movement "in mind and body, within and between spaces of varying scales that are identified as home" (Olwig 1998, 225). Bilqis was a "foreigner" to her place of birth and she was a "misfit" in Canada. Thus, in her search for her identity, as Olwig says, she travelled within and between spaces, not only emotionally and psychologically, but also physically. Though she was hurt that she could not find "home," at the same time her journey enabled her to construct the feelings of belonging wherever she resided, and to "create home inside" rather than with reference to a particular place.

James (1998) states that most often *home* and *family* are virtually interchangeable terms. Similarly, my participants perceive the home with reference to the family, and many of them feel that Canada is a second home because they left their families behind.[7] Simultaneously, they also see Canada as a home because their children were born here. In both situations, the notion of home is strongly associated with the family. Ati'yah, for instance, remarked that if she had her family in Canada, it would feel more like home. However, she also stated, "Saskatoon is home, because my kids [were] born here and raised here."

For most immigrants, however, the experience of migration is not limited to leaving their families behind; they also depart from the idea of their country of origin as home. Hobsbawm (1991) states that when people are asked where they come from, they name "a city, a country, a province, not a house or a neighborhood" (67). Thus, very often, a country becomes a home for a migrant, and many of my participants also called their country of origin "home." Moreover, since most participants realize that their "back home" culture is different from their society of residence, they do not feel that Canada is a complete home. Many women commented that the kind of life that they lived "back home" could never feel the same in Canada because they have lots of memories of their country that cannot be reproduced in Canada, such as celebrations of Islamic holidays.

Although there are many cultural differences between the participants' country of origin and Canada, the informants also feel that they should try to make Canada a home. Sima, for example, stated that she will be living in Canada for the rest of her life; thus, even though "there are lots of differences, and it can't be like home, I should find a way of living in it." Sima realizes that being at "home" in Canada requires some adjustments, and in making those adjustments, she not only negotiates her idea of "home," but also creates a fluid notion of home based on situational needs.

Being here, being there: Constructed identities through space

According to Hall (1997), "histories have their real, material and symbolic effects ... [and they are] always constructed through memory, fantasy, narrative and myth" (53). The section on "home" above illustrates that the participants' pasts are vigilantly tied to the concept of "home." For them, "home" is a physical, imaginary, and emotional space, and the memories of "back home" are related to their sense of belonging and their identities. However, the participants have adjusted and negotiated their lives in their country of residence, and many informants realize that they have been uprooted from their "back home" culture. Therefore, although they have a strong association with their place of birth, they feel, simultaneously, connected with Canada and displaced from their country of origin. Nabilah, for example, commented, "When I go back home, I find things are harder to deal with. If the telephone system is not working well, you feel frustrated, while here the power never goes off." During the interview, Nabilah spoke about "back home" very enthusiastically; she admires her culture very much. However, having lived in Canada for a number of years, she has become accustomed to facilities like well-functioning telephone and power systems, which she views as a convenience of living. Thus, she finds it difficult to adjust to life in her country of origin without these facilities.

Some of the memories of the participants are fixed in time and place and their imagined "back home" cultures appear static. The women's occasional visits to their countries of origin shock them because both the indigenous people and the country have changed in their absence. Noreen, for example, stated that when she went to Jordan six months ago, "things were not the same as they were before. They wear tight clothes and when I went shopping for some clothes for me, I couldn't see anything that wide. I was really surprised." Noreen anticipated visiting the same Jordan that she left several years ago, but the effects of globalization on Muslim societies were evident. Wearing tight clothes was a sign of becoming "Westernized" as Di'ba called it, but Noreen was stunned that "back home" people were losing their Muslim values, including the traditional Muslim idea of modesty.

The dilemmas of two different worlds

The memories of "back home" and a commitment to religious values have led many participants to create a home atmosphere in Canada that is similar to that of their countries of origin. As a result, their home environments are different from the "outside world" and lead them to feeling that they are living simultaneously in two different worlds. Negotiating these two worlds generates tensions for the women, and a number of participants indicated that their originating countries' religious and cultural standards, particularly standards for women, are not in harmony with those of the "outside" world. The problems of crafting female Muslim identities in a culture where Muslim traditions clash with mainstream society can be exemplified by Bilqis's limited participation in social activities. Drawing attention to the cultural differences that cause difficulties for her, Bilqis commented, "As a child, yes, certain things were difficult.... When I was younger there was a mixed party or something, then I wouldn't be allowed to attend those things. There would be the fight at home, like could I go.... I suppose there are things that all teenagers and children struggle with to some extent...."

In most Muslim societies, it is not acceptable for boys and girls to participate in mixed parties, whereas in Canada, this is a common means of socialization. In most Muslim cultures, emphasis is placed on maintaining a young girl's chastity. Virginity, in many Muslim societies, is a prerequisite for marriage, and female sexuality is understood as a matter of family honour.[8] A woman who has sexual relationships outside of marriage brings shame to her family; consequently, unsupervised interaction between boys and girls is frowned upon. In Canadian society, although some restrictions apply, interaction between boys and girls is considered part of the process of growing up. At an early age, it was difficult for Bilqis to accept these kinds of restrictions, especially when most people did not share the same moral standard: she was caught between two different worlds. While her parents tried to keep their customs, it appears that Bilqis struggled to maintain Muslim cultural values and at the same time be part of the mainstream community. She recognizes that all youths often encounter difficulties, but as a young Muslim female, she thinks she faced more obstacles.

While exposure to Western standards and Muslim cultural values puts many immigrant Muslim women in contradictory situations, that exposure also provides a chance to enrich their identities. Hall (1992, 1997) writes about the development of identities and argues that since history intervenes, we cannot speak for very long, or with any exactness, about our experiences and identities. Identities rupture and discontinue; as a result, cultural identity is not just about who we are but also about what we have become. According to Hall, identities grow and change as people make alliances due to shared interests; thus, identities are not static. The participants in this study altered their identities in response to the changing environment, as school and home and social circumstances led them to adopt certain Western lifestyles while maintaining traditional cultural standards. The combination of two different cultures offered them an opportunity to enrich their identities. At the same time, however, they feel that they do not fully immerse themselves in either world and their identities appear to be very fluid. Bilqis, for example, stated that she incorporates into her identities Muslim culture as well as Western society's values, and as a result she cannot fit perfectly into either culture:

You are different in the Islamic culture and you are different in
the Western culture. Because you have – for me, I have some
of both. So ... you are out of place in both environments.... In
school, you know, you may be sitting beside a boy or in a mixed
class. But in a mosque, you are in the lady section with your
hair covered.

Stone (1962) argues that "to have an identity is to join with some and
depart from others, to enter and leave social relations at once" (94).
Living in two different worlds, it is important for Bilqis to adjust her
identities so she can fit into both conflicting places, the mosque and
school. Sitting beside a boy in a mixed classroom without covering her
head is common in her school, but in the mosque, it is not customary.
In her school, she proceeds according to Western standards, and in the
mosque, she behaves in the traditional way. Therefore, as Bilqis confirmed, this conflicting state of affairs leaves her neither Muslim nor
Western but "a bit of both." External forces shape her identities; her
building of new alliances is a sign that her identities are in a process
of change.

Crafting female Muslim identities in school

Said (1981) writes about the clichéd images of Islam and states that the
West and Europe have portrayed Islam, characterized it, analyzed it,
given instant courses on it, and consequently have made it "known."
The Western "known" version of Islam quite often, if not always, presents Islam as an extremist, brutal, and backward religion. One of the
main institutions for the transmission of these negative stereotypes is
the education system. Some informants mentioned that some university professors portray Islam according to the "known" description and
that often discussions on Islam reveal the teachers' biases. The women
feel that their teachers presented a distorted picture of Islam because
these instructors discussed the religion only from a negative point of
view and did not draw attention to the positive aspects of Islam. Sima,
for example, argued that "there might be some good stuff about this
religion too. If you are talking about the bad things, then why don't you
talk about the good things to the students?"

Islam and Muslim women's issues are very closely related, and when
sharing their classroom experiences, the students specifically indicated
that their teachers often homogenize Muslim countries, as well as the

situation of Muslim women. In particular, the informants referred to the women of Afghanistan. Sima, for example, remarked that her teachers often talk about the restrictions that Muslim women face in Muslim countries, and that teachers usually give the example of Afghani women. She feels that her instructors "look at the severe cases." Sima recognizes that the situation of Afghani women does not represent an average Muslim woman's life, and it is therefore not fair to generalize about Muslim women's conditions. By presenting a homogeneous view of Muslim women, Sima's professors ignore that more than half a billion Muslim women's lives are diverse and do not conform to the Western image of Afghani women.

The teachers' homogenizing views are not limited to Afghani women's situation; such views are associated, too, with the practice of female circumcision. Some participants stated that in many classes, their teachers talk about female circumcision and give the impression that it is an Islamic tradition and that Muslim countries practice it. Di'ba and Sima argued that "it is not an Islamic custom and it was even done before Islam." Moreover, Di'ba and Sima remarked that since the instructors do not specify which countries practice it, their professors homogenize the Muslim societies around the world and discuss the practice of female circumcision as if it were a universal Muslim custom. As educators, professors play an important role in shaping students' views. Providing inaccurate and/or partial information causes damage to the students. On the one hand, the non-Muslim students learn stereotypical ideas about Islam and Muslims. On the other hand, Muslim students experience racism in the classrooms, and Di'ba's and Sima's Muslim identities are compromised in a Canadian educational institution.

Conclusion

The stories told by my participants reveal that as non-European Canadian immigrants, they often encounter racism in Canada and that their identities are vulnerable in a non-Muslim culture. They are often viewed as "outsiders" or "foreigners" by the larger society, and ethnic and racial discrimination mark them as "other." The participants highlighted the negative stereotypes of Muslims perpetrated through the media and widely held in the population, arguing that the perception that Muslims are "terrorists" is perpetuated systematically. As a result of these biased images, my informants struggle with their Muslim identities while trying to craft distinct identities. The informants, however, indicated that they have had positive experiences as well and that their quality of life has improved both as individuals and as females in Canada. Their residency in Canada has enabled them to integrate the different cultures, seek knowledge about their religion, and live more autonomous lives as females than they might have done in Muslim states. But the aftermath of September 11, 2001 jeopardized these hard-earned struggles and profoundly affected the lives of my informants, both at a personal level and at the level of the broader Muslim community, the *Ummah*.

The memories of "back home" led the participants to position themselves as "outsiders" as well as "insiders." The feelings of "home" directed the participants to re-create "home" emotionally, spatially, and psychologically, and as a result, their sense of belonging is not restricted to their country of origin. They often perceive themselves as Canadian. Belonging to two different worlds, however, also puts the participants into difficult situations. In particular, Muslim values often conflict with those of the larger Canadian society. These tensions become most evident in discussions about female sexual behaviour.

In summary, since these Muslim women continually negotiate their identities in a non-Muslim country, their experiences reveal the fluidity of their sense of self as they adapt to the changing social and cultural context. All of the participants have held on to Muslim identities as a way of positively affirming who they are and as a defence against the racist attitudes that predominate in non-Muslim Canadian culture. At the same time, my participants have adopted elements of Canadian culture, which has enhanced their lives. In crafting their identities, all of the informants have demonstrated forms of agency in spite of tremendous constraints.

Acknowledgments

I would like to acknowledge the financial support of CUISR (Community-University-Institute for Social Research, University of Saskatchewan) for this project.

NOTES

1 By using the word "Western world or the West" I do not mean to homogenize it. "The West is as diverse as any other part of the World" (Mojab 1998, 25). However, the purpose here is to indicate the assumed superiority of the West that often underscores stereotypical images of Muslims.

2 Many factors contribute in shaping people's views, and it is not fair to limit them to the media images. Zulaika and Douglass (1996), however, state that "terrorism is essentially a media creation" (7). Similarly, Joy's mother specifically mentions the role of the media in determining Joy's perception about Muslims.

3 Currently, *hijab* is a popular term that refers to a certain standard of modest dress for women such as head-covering or loose garments, though the connotation of the word *hijab* is much broader and includes living unpretentiously.

4 The feminine form of *Muslim* is *Muslimah*.

5 A woman who wears the *hijab*, including a headscarf, is called *Muhajibh*.

6 See, for instance, Ajit Jain: *www.rediff.com/us/2001/oct/12ny31.htm*

7 For most of the participants, it was extended family that they referred to: that is, parents, grandparents, and siblings.

8 Islam does not permit premarital relationships, and it could therefore be argued that maintaining chastity is part of religious obligations. I, however, recognize that Bilqis's struggle here is due to culturally constructed views of female sexuality rather than religious restrictions. Islamic principles regarding sexual relations outside of marriage are the same for men and women. However, following the discussion in the interview, it was clear that Bilqis's parents, as well as many participants, view female sexuality differently from male sexuality and were not concerned about their male children having premarital relationships. I think, therefore, that Bilqis was not allowed to participate in the mixed parties for cultural reasons.

Chapter 3

'TRANSGENDERED' PERSPECTIVES AS A CHALLENGE TO SEX, GENDER, AND SEXUALITY

Coralee Drechsler

Introduction

In North American society, much is made of the differences between men and women, but for many, questions remain: are these differences as real and as rigid as the dominant perspectives suggest, and are 'men' and 'women' true and complete categories? These questions, and others, are at the core of my quest to understand the North American concepts and constructions of sex and gender, and how these concepts and constructions affect individuals. Rather than beginning with the perspectives and experiences of 'men' and 'women,' though, I wondered how people who do not fit neatly into the sex/gender system would interpret and communicate their own perspectives and experiences. The desire for this knowledge and for a way to challenge the concepts of sex and gender became the focus of my research, in which I have attempted to understand and convey the experiences and perspectives of individuals outside the sex/gender categories. In acknowledging the experiences and perspectives of transgendered people, I am challenging the curiously sanctioned categories of sex/gender.

For this discussion, it is necessary to define certain terms I have used and explain certain choices that I have made. In regard to punctuation, I have used double quotation marks solely to signify words and phrases provided by the research participants and to quote text sources. I have used single quotation marks to denote my discomfort with or a lack of concrete meaning of particular words and phrases, or to indicate a word or phrase for discussion. In addition, I have used single quotation marks around pronouns for certain participants who expressed no clear preference for a 'male' or 'female' pronoun. In choosing pronouns for participants, I tried to use pronouns that respect their positions in their sex/gender process at the time of the interview, while also signifying the challenge to the concepts of sex and gender. Of the seven participants, four would be considered "biological males" and three would be considered "biological females" according to dominant North American sex/gender identifications.

In relating their experiences to me, the participants used certain phrases that may not be familiar to some people. A number of participants referenced the "gender clinic" and the "Real-Life Test." The purpose of a gender clinic is to assist individuals experiencing 'gender issues.' At a gender clinic, an individual might access such services as counselling, support groups, clinical assessments for 'gender disorders,' hormone therapy, and approval for other body modification technologies, including 'sex reassignment surgery.' Any person who is interested in pursuing any surgery to change the appearance of 'his'/'her' body in terms of sex/gender must have the approval of a gender clinic to do so. In granting this approval, a gender clinic requires that the individual undertake a 'Real-Life Test.' The 'Real-Life Test' involves a person living, working, or attending school in 'her'/'his' 'target gender' for at least one year. The individual is expected to legally change 'his'/'her' first name and to ensure that 'he'/'she' is interpreted by others as a member of the individual's 'target gender.'

In further regard to vocabulary, I have used the term 'transgendered' to refer to those individuals whose perspectives and experiences I am interested in understanding and communicating. In this context, 'transgendered' describes a person who defies the categories of sex and gender in some way. Thus, 'transgendered' covers a considerable range of experiences that challenge the sex/gender system, including people who have been referred to as 'cross-dressers,' 'drag kings/queens,' 'masculine women,' 'feminine men,' 'intersexed' ('hermaphrodites'), and 'transsexuals.' However, it is necessary to note that the definition of 'transgendered,' particularly my definition, is neither stable nor universal.

Background

Any definition of 'transgendered' is dependent upon the organization of sex and gender that exists in North American society, since 'transgendered' is essentially that which is considered outside the sex and gender mainstream. The discussion of transgendered experiences and perspectives is difficult due to the various uses of the terms 'sex' and 'gender,' particularly with regard to their definitions and the distinction between them. 'Sex' is often used to signify bodies according to their biological characteristics. The dominant North American conceptualization of sex is that there are only two body types, male and female. The most immediate signifier of the sex of the body is most commonly visible at birth, at which time the body of an infant is declared male according to the presence of a penis (and absence of a vagina) or female according to the presence of a vagina (and absence of a penis). Because 'sex' is constructed as a dichotomy, any degree of confusion concerning the sex of a body, as occurs in an intersexed infant, must be overcome and corrected as soon as possible according to medical practitioners (Money 1986, 137). The sex dichotomy is thereby further justified. As a person matures past infancy, that person is expected to display characteristics believed to be congruent with that person's sex. For the most part, the definition of 'gender' compromises these characteristics. 'Gender' is understood, contemporarily, as the social characteristics that a given culture in a given historical time attributes to the two differently sexed bodies.

However, the separation between biological characteristics (sex) and social characteristics (gender) in North American society is neither complete nor perfect. For example, the presence of facial hair in males and the absence of facial hair in females is often cited as a secondary sex characteristic and, therefore, as a biological difference between males and females. Yet some adult males do not have noticeable facial hair, while some adult females do. This supposed biological difference between males and females is reinforced and perpetuated by the construction of this characteristic as a social difference. Adult females with noticeable facial hair are ridiculed, laughed at, and/or perceived as 'masculine' or 'male.' To avoid social sanction, adult females must ensure that they are free of facial hair through methods such as shaving, waxing, tweezing, and electrolysis. Thus, a characteristic constructed as biological is also social. These biological and social elements exist simultaneously, and both reinforce and influence each other. Therefore, what is constructed as sex is also gender, and what is constructed as gender is also sex. The impossibility of separating one from the other is signified by the use of the phrase 'the sex/gender system.' While I do not mean to imply that sex and gender are identical, I am suggesting that the reality of sex and gender should be open to question since the concepts of sex and gender, often presented as distinct in social science literature, overlap and interconnect in various ways.

The sex/gender system also affects our perception of sexuality. Through the regulation and prescription of sex and gender in all their binary forms (including male/female, man/woman, masculine/feminine), the sex/gender system establishes the categories of sexuality. For instance, the definition of a heterosexual person is directly dependent upon that person's own sex/gender as well as the sex/gender of the sexual and/or intimate partner chosen by that person. A person is only considered heterosexual if she or he chooses as a partner a person of the 'opposite sex.' Therefore, sex/gender is essential in the establishment of heterosexuality as the accepted and expected sexuality in North American society. Indeed, when a person displays a characteristic considered appropriate to the 'opposite sex,' that person's sexuality is questioned. However, it is also common to question the sex/gender of a person who is known to be non-heterosexual. Because of the heteronormativity prevalent in North American society, I have chosen to use the term 'sexuality' rather than 'sexual orientation.' The term 'sexual orientation' is predominantly associated with 'non-heterosexuality,' since 'sexual orientation' is usually only an issue when it is other than the established norm of heterosexuality.

Accordingly, then, North American society is organized in concert with certain beliefs about sex, gender, and sexuality, but these beliefs are not static. They change over time. One of these beliefs is that there are two sexes, male and female, and two genders, man and woman. A further aspect of these two genders is that they are each connected to certain behavioural presentations, masculinity and femininity, respectively. With regard to sexuality, the dominant North American belief is that heterosexuality is the normal and preferred orientation (Butler 1990, 23). The connections among sex, gender, and sexuality are presented predominantly as connections of coherence and continuity (Butler 1990, 17), which means that a male is a man and is mostly masculine in presentation, and a female is a woman and is mostly feminine in presentation. In addition, the "normal" man and the "normal" woman are also heterosexual. While the categories of sex, gender, and sexuality are presented as occurring naturally, they are in fact constructed through the "effects of power." It is through the power of the dominant culture in North American society that "certain bodies, certain gestures, certain discourses, certain desires come to be identified and constituted as individuals" (Foucault 1980, 98). Not only are the categories associated with the sex/gender system socially constructed, but they are constructed as dichotomies – an individual is a man to the extent that the individual is not a woman, and an individual is feminine to the extent that the individual is not masculine (Butler 1990, 22). Sexuality may also be interpreted as binary, with heterosexuality as the norm and 'non-heterosexuality' as the aberration.

The desired coherence of sex, gender, and sexuality is enforced through certain methods, including social sanctions and access to resources, but this coherence is also encouraged through established morality. Indeed, social sanctions and access to resources may be interpreted as the consequences of adherence or failure to conform to established morality. For the purposes of the sex/gender system, morality "refers to the real behavior of individuals in relation to the rules and values that are recommended to them: the word thus designates the manner in which they comply more or less fully with a standard of conduct, the manner in which they obey or resist an interdiction or a prescription; the manner in which they respect or disregard a set of values" (Foucault 1985, 25).

With morality thus constructed, individuals who defy the rules of sex, gender, and sexuality in some way are vulnerable to judgment as abnormal, perverse, and degenerative. Since transgendered people may be interpreted this way, they may be dealt with as a threat to the "social body," and may be subjected to "remedies and therapeutic devices" (Foucault 1980, 55). Through such remedies, transgendered people may be ostracized, subjected to violence, denied the right to work, refused standard medical care, referred for physical examination and/or psychological assessment, or made to feel the need to present themselves for such treatments.

However, the very existence of transgendered individuals who are interpreted as "the incoherent, that which falls 'outside,'" demonstrates the appropriateness of interpreting the categories associated with sex and gender as social constructions (Butler 1990, 110). Indeed, sex is not an apparent, fixed state of being, but rather an incomplete materialization of "regulatory norms" (Butler 1993, 1–2). Because sex is interpreted as a social construction, there is little to distinguish it from gender, particularly since gender has already framed "those biomedical inquiries that seek to establish 'sex'" (Butler 1990, 109). In other words, what is thought to be sex is also gender and extricating one from the other is impossible. The categories that result from sex and gender, 'man' and 'woman,' are consequently unstable identities not only because of the difficulty of definition (Butler 1990, 1; 1993, 218) but also because the individual's investment in one requires the denial or suppression of characteristics connected with the other (Butler 1993, 126). With the destabilization of 'man' and 'woman,' it is impossible to avoid the destabilization of sexuality, which is dependent upon the sex/gender system. If the individuals involved in an intimate relationship cannot be accurately categorized by the sex/gender system, then their relationship cannot be interpreted in the established terms of sexuality.

Destabilizing the social constructions associated with sex, gender, and sexuality enables individuals to both challenge traditional identities and question the criteria used in defining identities. Identification is not an event but an ongoing process (Butler 1993, 105) that involves both external and internal elements, due to the dynamics of power (Foucault 1980, 141). The identity of the individual is not simply the result of societal forces acting upon the individual, since the individual also has power to establish, assert, or acquiesce to an identity (Feinberg 1998, 89). Not only do transgendered individuals challenge the sex/gender system by confusing the categories through physical appearance, behaviour, and attitude, but they also challenge the system by refusing the identity established for them at birth. Moreover, the sex/gender system is also challenged by the insistence of some to be identified as "trans," or as another non-traditional identity. In this "resistance to categorization," transgendered individuals have some degree of freedom from the sex/gender system (Grant 1993, 131).

Information from 'transgendered' individuals

For the purpose of my research, I advertised for 'transgendered' participants in the Vancouver and Victoria area who would be willing to share their experiences and understandings with me. Seven people responded to the advertisement and agreed to speak with me. The interviews were held at a time and place convenient for each participant. One of the issues I was interested in discussing with the participants was how and when they noticed that their sex/gender identification was different from the expectations typical of North American society.

All of the people I spoke with recognized that there was something "different" about their experiences while growing up, but this recognition occurred to varying degrees at various ages. Of the seven participants, four related a feeling or behaviour in early childhood, specifically between the ages of four and six years. One respondent who was expected to be a 'girl' told 'her' family, at six years of age, that 'she' "wanted to be a dad" as an adult. Two other participants, both expected to be 'boys,' reported that they wanted to be 'girls' as children. One of these participants, at five years old, prayed that God would change 'him' into a 'girl,' while the other stated that while 'he' "felt entirely male," 'he' "didn't feel entirely 'boy.'" Another participant, who was expected to be a 'girl,' said that he has always felt male and has always expressed himself as such. Two respondents reported that difficulties with sex/gender occurred later in their development. One of these respondents, expected to be 'male,' stated that she experienced trauma during puberty as facial hair began to appear. The participant's father tried to interpret this situation as an experience of "male-bonding," but the participant felt that these pubescent changes were "wrong" and also felt envious of her sisters' physical changes. The second respondent with later difficulties experienced them as a result of sexuality. This respondent never really thought about sex/gender, and was a very 'successful' and happy 'girl'/'woman,' until the age of twenty-four. However, as a younger person with an interest in becoming sexually active, this participant felt that, while attracted to 'males,' it "wasn't right" to be with 'males' as a 'female.' In trying to reconcile this situation, the participant even tried dating 'females' since 'his' parents were particularly open-minded in terms of sexuality, but realized that, while 'he' "knew ['he'] was queer," 'he' was not attracted to 'women.' The seventh participant did not report any recognition of difference due to sex/gender during childhood and adolescence, but was distinctly aware that 'he' was "queer" and "freaky" as a youth, an identity that 'he' fully embraced. In this instance, however, this identity had to do more with punk culture and being unusual in a smaller community than with sex, gender, and sexuality. For example, this participant explained that the group of kids 'he' was in all thought of themselves as "queer" even though the participant was the only one in the group who had been sexually active with someone of the 'same sex.'

While conveying how the recognition of identity occurred, the seven participants all alluded to personal characteristics that have been constructed through the sex/gender system as 'masculine,' appropriately belonging to 'boys' and 'men,' and 'feminine,' appropriately belonging to 'girls' and 'women.' One participant in particular, who was expected to be a 'girl' but has always felt and identified as 'male,' expressed this point very clearly when he stated: "I've been studying men since I was a kid. I looked at them; I watched them. You figure out how to behave, how to stand, how to look, how to walk, how to talk, how to.... [You are] socialized."

While this participant encapsulated virtually every aspect of sex/gender socialization, the other participants specifically mentioned certain characteristics that distinguish between the established categories of sex/gender. Some aspect of physical appearance, particularly clothing and hairstyle, was mentioned by five of the seven participants, including the participant quoted above. Comments regarding clothing ranged from one participant's statement that 'he' was "cross-dressing" at the age of seven or eight years to another participant's report that 'she' wore mostly T-shirts and jeans all 'her' life, signalling what 'she' considered to be a more 'masculine' form of dress. Sex-/gender-typed clothing was also mentioned by a third participant who, when first "transitioning" at the age of twenty-four, shifted from the 'feminine' clothing of "skirts and dresses" to the 'masculine' clothing of "plaid shirts and jeans." This participant also noted that now 'he' is wearing more "gender neutral" clothing. In terms of hairstyle, this same participant also shared that, besides the change in clothing, the "transition" also involved the cutting of "almost waist-length hair." Another participant who was expected to be 'feminine' also mentioned short hair as the preferred hairstyle, which is linked, to an extent, with 'masculinity.' Two other participants referred to hair in their interviews as well. One participant, expected to be 'male,' relayed a story of cutting off her long hair as a child because people outside her family made her feel embarrassed about it. The participant then expressed feeling regret as a child for carrying through with the decision to cut her hair. The second participant, also expected to be 'male,' talked about 'his' current physical appearance. When assumed to be 'female' by strangers, the participant thinks this is due in part to "slightly longer fingernails," "earrings," and "long hair."

Other sex-/gender-typed characteristics mentioned by a number of participants concern interests and emotions. One participant who was expected to be a 'girl' expressed a childhood disinterest in "girl things," such as dolls, ballet, and makeup, and a preference for "boy things," such as sports and cars. Alternatively, a participant who was expected to be a 'boy' shared 'his' deep dislike and dread of sports, roughhousing, and competition. Likewise, another participant who was expected to be a 'boy' also mentioned 'his' attempts to avoid the ridiculing and teasing of "boy culture" in childhood. In addition, this same participant characterized 'himself' as "a very, very, very sensitive individual" who "always felt insulted by the typical macho comments and criticisms that already started at an early age on the part of the boys criticizing the girls or making fun of the girls. I always took it as a personal affront." Both of these participants who were expected to be 'boys' related that they found friendship, similarity, and solace in the company of 'girls' of their age. Another participant who was expected to be 'male' stated that she did try to accept "male expectations" but realized later that this was causing unhappiness. She also reported that she "has so many feelings that seemed to be really intense for a male. Like, guys aren't supposed to show their feelings."

All of the participants I spoke with directly or indirectly indicated that the formation of sex/gender identity is a process and a journey that involves change and fluidity. Indeed, all of the participants verbalized how their identities have changed over the years, even those who knew they were "different" from earliest childhood. It is important to understand that, in the experiences of all participants, identification did not strike like a lightning bolt. They did not see themselves as one thing and in the next minute realize they were actually something else. Neither did any participant give any indication that 'his'/'her' current identity is absolutely stable. Even the participant who had felt and identified as 'male' since earliest childhood indicated some degree of variance in his identification. While this participant sees and presents himself as 'male,' he has left some physiological changes until his forties, is questioning the nature of his sexuality, and identifies as queer regardless of his gender identity, the status of his physical body, or the identity of his intimate or sexual interest. One of the reasons why the people I spoke with demonstrate the instability of identity, besides the fact that they have chosen identifications outside the established sex/gender system, is that they challenge their own identities. Because they have all had experiences that are considered unusual by dominant North American standards, all seven participants indicated they have done a considerable amount of thinking and research about sex/gender. One participant in particular indicated that 'he' has thought about gender so much with such "intense scrutiny" and "intense analysis" that 'he' is now "bored" with gender.

While all of the participants responded to a request for transgendered individuals to share their experiences and understandings through qualitative research, only one of these individuals actually used the term 'transgendered' in self-identification, in addition to other labels. The other six participants expressed their identities through various words and phrases. In an effort to convey the uniqueness and the depth of each participant's self-exploration, I will present a sketch of each participant's experience, the identification of each participant, and the language that the participants used to express their identities.

The first participant explained to me that, although she experienced some difficulty regarding sex/gender while growing up, she did not address it until she was in her twenties. Instead, this participant fulfilled the expectations of the 'male' role, and even though she had achieved 'success' in this role in terms of education, employment, and marital status, she still felt that there was something wrong. The process of identification took her through different understandings of herself, including "bi boy" and "cross-dressing," until she realized that she wanted to alter her body. This participant was changing the appearance of her body from "male" to "female," but she also stated that her "headspace" is "androgynous." She stated that she is 60 per cent 'female' and 40 per cent 'male,' but added that these percentages fluctuate often. She is officially classified "on paper" with the gender clinic as transsexual because "that's what I'm doing." However, she does not like to use the labels 'transsexual' or 'transgendered.' Rather, this participant prefers the term "trans" as an identification because it "doesn't really say transsexual and doesn't really say transgendered. It doesn't even really say anything besides transgressing gender in some way." While she expressed an insistence to be recognized as 'female,' she also stated that she would like to be able to be/present as either 'male' or 'female' on any given day. In terms of sexuality, she reported that she is a "bi dyke," and that this sexual identification is based on her preference for "female" body parts, regardless of whether these parts occur "naturally" or are "constructed."

The second participant I spoke with did not identify as transgendered either. In fact, this participant did not use any label for identification. To a certain extent, this participant considers all people to be a blend of 'masculinity' and 'femininity,' but seems to understand 'himself' as so 'feminine' that "gender confusion" results. 'His' experience of sex/gender has been cyclical over the span of 'his' life thus far; at some points 'he' has been content, while at other times 'he' has felt extremely frustrated. At the time of our conversation, 'he' had not begun the Real-Life Test or changed 'his' name, but 'he' had participated in hormone therapy. 'He' also stated that 'he' was unsure what decisions 'he' will make about the process of his identification. While 'he' has been classified as transsexual at the gender clinic, 'he' avoids all labels of identification and instead simply describes 'his' experiences. In terms of sexuality, 'he' recognizes that 'his' identification is again ambiguous because 'he' is transgendered. In response to my question of how 'he' identifies in terms of sexuality, 'he' replied, "Well, if you want to call me a genetic male, then I'm heterosexual because I'm attracted to women. If you want to categorize me as a male-to-female transsexual, then you'd have to call me a lesbian."

When I asked the third participant how he identifies in terms of gender, he told me that he has always felt 'male' and that this feeling has not changed. After this statement, he led into a discussion concerning the identity of his sexuality, which he said is "queer." In response to why he identifies as queer, the participant said, "I guess because I'm not straight. And even if I was to be with a straight woman and live in a straight world, I'm still not straight." At the time of our conversation, gender, sexuality, and desire seemed quite entwined for this participant. Because he was in the process of physically changing his body, this participant was paying a great deal of attention to 'male' bodies. Even though he has always been sexually attracted to 'women,' he recognizes that "there's a fine line between like and desire." In addition, the participant also addressed the sex/gender dynamics present in a recent experience of mutual attraction with a "straight woman." He interpreted this as very different from his experiences thus far, which have all been with queer 'women,' mostly 'bisexual women.' He informed me as well of his refusal of the term 'lesbian' for himself because of the obvious connection of that term to 'female' or 'woman.'

Another participant also objected to the term 'lesbian' for 'herself,' but for additional reasons to that mentioned by the previous participant. When 'she' told me that 'she' identifies 'her' sexuality by using the term "dyke," I asked if the reason was because 'lesbian' is too connected with 'woman' or 'femininity.' The participant's response was that "a piece of it is that it's too woman and, for me, there is a difference between lesbian and dyke." This participant interprets 'lesbian' as based on a "middle-class, heterosexual model" and believes that lesbians are "closeted in their professional lives." "Dyke" is a more comfortable identification for 'her' because "dykes are very much more political activist, more in-your-face, radical, out there kind of people." When asked what 'her' sexual identity was based on, 'she' replied, "It's based on my physical attraction to women!" In terms of gender, 'she' was the only participant who actually used the term 'transgendered' to refer to 'herself.' This identity is appropriate for 'her' because 'she' does not classify 'herself' as either 'male' or 'female.' 'She' believes that most people, 'herself' included, are in the middle of a gender continuum that ranges from 'feminine' to 'masculine.' However, 'she' feels that 'she' is a little closer to 'masculinity.' This participant also stated that 'she' is trying to live the 'in-between' so that physical changes do not become necessary.

The fifth participant identified as "transman" rather than as transgendered. 'He' also stated that there was "no way to categorize my gender." The use of the label "transman" is connected to the participant's belief that 'he' is not a 'man.' The participant reported that 'he' was perceived as 'female' before 'he' had chest surgery, even though he was taking testosterone. Sexuality and gender were obviously connected in this participant's experience as well, since 'he' reported that 'he' does not mind how people perceive 'his' gender, but the perception of 'his' sexuality is important. 'He' related a story concerning a "dyke bashing" that 'he' and 'his' boyfriend experienced. This experience bothered 'him' because 'his' sexuality was misread – not only were 'he' and 'his' boyfriend interpreted as 'female,' but also as 'females' who are sexually attracted to other 'females.' This interpretation is contrary to 'his' identity, since 'he' presents 'his' gender "as a sexual orientation," and 'his' sexual identity is "fag." In addition, this participant stated that 'his' sexuality is based on gender: "I like men regardless of what their bodies look like."

The next participant did not identify as transgendered either, but did acknowledge that 'he' could be categorized that way periodically. When asked how 'he' does identify, this participant responded, "queer sissy." In an effort to gain a clearer understanding, I asked what 'he' meant by "queer" and by "sissy." For 'him,' "queer" indicates everything not 'normal,' and not necessarily in terms of sexuality. 'He' stated that an individual could be straight and still be queer because of appearance. "Sissy," for this participant, is both an attitude and an honouring of those people who have been labelled as sissies, punished for being sissies, yet are able to cope with this mistreatment due to their "resilience and brilliance." This participant has always embraced difference and has tried to use 'his' identity as a way to create awareness for other people. When I asked about gender and identity, 'he' stated: "I happened to be born with a penis. I'm happy about it. I don't have a problem with it. I'm not looking to get rid of it. I'm not looking to become a woman. Do I feel like a man, per se, based on what society thinks a man is? No, I don't. I'm clearly different than that."

'He' also mentioned that 'he' has always had more in common with 'women' and has had more 'female' friends than 'male' friends. While 'he' has a group of 'male' friends now, 'he' explains that they are "pretty nontraditional men. I mean, they're men that probably don't even identify as men." In terms of sexuality, this participant used "queer sissy" for 'his' sexual identity as well. However, 'he' noted that sexuality is "an ever-evolving process" in which 'he' varies 'his' identity, the roles 'he' plays, and 'he' is also mindful of the assumptions 'he' makes about other people based on sex/gender and sexuality.

This kind of self-awareness was also characteristic of the last participant. This participant did not identify as transgendered either, even though 'he' feels that 'he' fits that label. Like many other participants, this participant, too, did not define as a 'man' or a 'woman,' although 'he' said 'he' would put a check mark in the 'male' box when forced. 'He' also identified as "sissy" and for this participant, the term "sissy" means "failed boy," and is a challenge to what has been constructed as "appropriate gender." Like the sixth participant, this participant does not have an issue with 'his' physical body, but rather with the social expectations that are associated with that physical body. In regard to sexuality, 'he' used the term "gay" simply because 'he' is comfortable with the associated pronouns and because people understand it. However, 'he' understands sexuality to be socially constructed as static and intelligible, even though 'he' believes that sexuality is actually fluid and indefinable.

All of the participants I spoke with, each in a different way, found some sort of assistance in dealing with their 'gender issues.' Five participants have had some experience with a gender clinic, while the other two have had other forms of counselling, have had conversations with friends and acquaintances, and/or have taken academic courses. In order to provide a more complete and informative understanding of the participants' experiences, I will present the answers each participant gave to the question of what assistance, if any, 'she'/'he' has sought for 'gender issues,' and the participant's assessment and/or feelings about the assistance.

The first participant explained to me that she just reached a point where she realized that she wanted to alter her body. She achieved this realization through researching and talking with friends and other people going through their own processes. Sure of what she wanted, she approached the gender clinic with the attitude that she was not in need of counselling but only needed its approval to obtain the desired surgery. In terms of her process, this participant is receiving hormone therapy, has legally changed her name from a 'masculine' to a 'feminine' form, and is seeking approval for surgery. Her feeling about the gender clinic is ambivalent. She accepts that some people need the clinic to help them with the psychological aspects of gender, but she feels that she really had no need for the clinic's assistance in this regard. While she recognizes that some people who have used the clinic's services are entirely satisfied with how the clinic operates, the services it provides, and the expectation that they fulfill the clinic's requirements, this participant notes some negative and adversarial aspects in her experiences with the clinic. She explained that by asserting her 'feminine' gender identity, she convinced the clinic that she was not in need of counselling and felt sure of the appropriate course of 'treatment.' According to this participant, one can "pass" as a particular gender through assertiveness. For instance, she has successfully dodged the clinic's suggestions that she grow out her hair and dismisses the clinic's question of whether she is "feminine enough to be perceived as feminine, as female, as a woman by others." Despite rejecting, to a certain extent, the standards enforced by the sex/gender system, she does acknowledge her own "baggage" in terms of asserting identity, since she had to change her body "to feel comfortable" enough in order to assert her gender identity. Further, she stated, "theoretically I should have absolutely no need and want to change my body. If culture and society didn't mess up sex and gender as much as it does, I should be able to express whatever gender identity I want in whatever body I want."

Another participant critical of the gender clinic expressed his past inability to see himself as an old woman and his feeling that he therefore had "no future." He stated that the event of his father's death spurred him to make the decision to alter his body to 'match' his male identity. While he has dealt with the clinic, he also mentioned other sources of assistance, such as academia and studying gender, as well as discussion with other people. This participant was very straightforward in his dislike of the clinic, although having him share the reasons for this dislike was somewhat difficult. Some of the negative issues he addressed regarding the clinic include his impression that most of the workers are inappropriate in their interactions with clients, that the workers are overworked, and that the process is very time-consuming and frustrating for clients, who are subjected to "senseless rules" created by "non-trans people." Through my attempt to achieve further understanding, I asked the participant for an example and in response, he related the issues that he has with the Real-Life Test. He explained that "female-to-male transsexual[s] [are] supposed to live as a male for two years" and that they are expected to do so with their anatomy intact. Because of this situation then, people have to "walk around with a hairy face or a full beard and breasts as a male. And that's unsafe. You can get killed for things like that. Murdered. In New York a transsexual is murdered once a month."

The third participant who has dealt with the clinic and gives a negative assessment of the experience stated that 'he' bypassed the clinic as much as possible. In 'his' research about 'gender issues' 'he' learned how the clinic operates and was advised to avoid it. After realizing through reading that 'female-to-male transition' was possible, this participant decided to change 'his' body and approached a general practitioner about hormone therapy. The participant received hormones through 'his' general practitioner and only used the clinic to acquire 'his' "rubber stamp for surgery." In response to the question of what it is about the clinic that troubles the participant, 'he' mentioned the assessments in particular. From the participant's perspective, the clinic's assessments are "designed to drive you crazy, and if you don't go crazy then you're a true transgendered person because you'll stick through it." 'He' reported that his initial assessment was twenty minutes in length, and the subsequent two meetings were as short as five minutes in length. During the assessments, one of the purposes of which is to "look at your physical features and decide if you look masculine or feminine," the individual is asked certain questions that are understood to require specific answers. The process involves questioning the individual about 'his'/'her' history and experiences, and these answers determine whether or not the individual will have access to certain treatments. Therefore, the process is constructed in a way that encourages deception. Moreover, the participant also pointed out that the process leaves "no room for doubt." Individuals who need assistance in dealing with their 'gender issues' are not able to be honest about their feelings for fear that they will be denied certain treatments on the basis of their doubts. This fear concerns the alteration of bodies as well, as addressed by both this participant and the first participant, since any expression of grief is interpreted as the result of an inappropriate procedure, when in fact it is perfectly natural to grieve changes to the body even if they were and remain the desired result.

Some participants, however, expressed only positive opinions about the clinic. One participant told me that 'he' decided to present 'himself' to the clinic because the "level of frustration" was so extreme that deciding to take action was imperative. Through an assessment by the clinic, 'he' had been placed on hormone therapy and was currently in the process of 'transition.' At the time of our interview, the participant told me that if our conversation had taken place a few months earlier, 'he' would have informed me that 'he' was close to beginning 'his' Real-Life Test and changing 'his' name. Instead, the participant stated that 'he' has placed "road blocks" in the course of 'his' process because 'he' is unsure about what 'he' should do and considers surgery the "worst case scenario." This participant stated that 'he' is applying as much "rational thought" as possible, as opposed to "emotions," in 'his' approach to 'his' gender issues. 'He' indicated that the clinic has supported this approach and 'he' has felt very comfortable in 'his' experiences there. 'He' then added that although some people criticize the clinic, the reason for their criticism is due to their emphasis on their emotions rather than on rational thought.

The second participant who gave a positive assessment of the clinic began 'her' experience with the clinic after discussing the issues with a friend who is going through 'his'/'her' own gender process. However, this participant conveyed the importance of dealing with professionals rather than relying on personal relationships in addressing 'her' feelings. 'She' stated that 'she' preferred to discuss 'her' 'gender issues' on a professional level so that there were no personal consequences, meaning that 'she' would not have to be concerned about how the other person was feeling and how the other person was affected by what 'she' said. This participant stated that 'her' decision to approach the clinic was connected to 'her' need to be "somewhere where somebody would understand," and at the clinic 'she' has shared support and information with people with similar experiences. This participant feels that the clinic has been quite helpful to 'her' in 'her' attempt to "live in-between" genders.

Unlike those participants who have considered modifying their bodies or who have actually done so, the sixth and seventh participants did not choose to attend the clinic in dealing with their 'gender issues.' The sixth participant, whose gender is expressly connected to 'his' sexuality, began to deal with issues of sex/gender and sexuality through places of employment. 'He' noted that his employment in certain "queer organizations" provided a particularly open environment in terms of sex/gender and sexuality in which 'he' was able to think about 'his' own issues and listen to opinions and insights that one would not usually be exposed to at work. Since this employment, 'he' has also become friends with certain people who "challenge" 'him' on gender issues," and 'he' has had many conversations and has done a considerable amount of thinking about these topics.

Likewise, the seventh participant has also had conversations with others and done a great deal of thinking about these issues, but 'his' history of facing 'gender issues' is longer and more complicated. As a 'boy,' this participant experienced difficulty in terms of gender and reported feeling very ashamed, depressed, and withdrawn. Due to these external manifestations of 'his' 'gender trouble,' 'he' was sent to a counsellor in junior high school and was later "prodded" to see a "couple psychiatrists" in high school as well as a social worker. None of these professionals made any positive difference to this participant, and of the social worker, 'he' disclosed particular ineffectiveness: "His very language alienated me because he presumed that I was a boy, a regular kind of boy. He was trying to treat me or counsel me through depression and withdrawal and all these other things, but he presumed I was a real boy." Despite all these attempts to gain help, the participant reported being suicidal during most of junior high and high school, and 'he' did attempt suicide twice after high school. Continuing to search for some solace, this participant participated in fundamentalist Christianity and "ex-gay prayer counselling," but these forms of assistance also failed. The participant related that 'he' did not understand 'his' issues until 'he' participated in counselling at a gay and lesbian centre and in academic courses, particularly women's studies courses. Through these media, 'he' was able to gain a better understanding of 'himself,' 'his' personal characteristics and feelings, and the nature of the sex/gender system.

Conclusion

The most striking element that I found in participants' experiences was the conflict that seems to result from trying to reconcile their experiences of sex/gender and sexuality with the sex/gender system that structures North American society. The participants' language contained contradictions because of their unique positions in which they simultaneously reject and subscribe to the expectations and understandings prescribed by the sex/gender system.

In the attempt to discern when and how the participants recognized that their sex/gender identities were other than what was expected, I was somewhat surprised to hear so many mentions of social characteristics as opposed to physical characteristics. Contrary to popular perceptions about transgendered people, not one participant told me that 'he'/'she' knew 'he'/'she' was transgendered because 'he'/'she' disliked 'his'/'her' genitalia. Rather, the participants, including those for whom genitalia were an issue, conveyed that they disliked the social expectations connected to the body with which they were born. Indeed, most often participants mentioned clothing, hairstyle, body movements, statuses and roles, interests, and emotions as characteristics that indicated to them that they were not "normal" boys and girls, or men and women. While the participants recognized that gender is a fluid characteristic and that all people possess both 'masculine' and 'feminine' traits, they also attributed their knowledge of their different identities to the presence or prevalence of supposed 'opposite gender' traits.

The conflict present in identity formation was also indicated in the language participants used to label their identities. Since all the participants responded to a request for transgendered individuals to share their experiences with and perspectives on sex and gender, I was surprised to learn how few of them actually use that word to identify themselves. Despite the overwhelming rejection of the term 'transgendered,' though, none of the participants identified themselves as 'men' or 'women' either. Besides my concern that I was and am labelling people with a word that they do not use themselves, I am also aware that particular identities of certain participants contain the element of conflict. For instance, one participant who described herself as "androgynous" also insisted on being identified by others as 'female,' with specific reference to 'female' pronouns. However, she also shared her intention to present as 'male' or 'female' whenever she wishes after her 'transition' is complete. In addition, she states her sexual identity as "dyke," which may be difficult for 'gender conservatives' to understand when she presents as 'male.' This identification is destabilizing to all established, recognizable categories of sex, gender, and sexuality and yet, at the same time, is oddly dependent upon them. Another participant who has always felt male and chooses women as sexual partners stated, "When I'm sexual with a woman, I'm a male having sex with a woman and I always have been. Always. And I had my first sexual experience in grade 5." Despite this male identity though, this participant does not identify as a man, but as "queer." Another participant who identifies as transgendered labels 'herself' in terms of sexuality as a "dyke." When I asked 'her' what this sexual identity is based on, 'she' stated, "It's based on my physical attraction to women!" Since this participant does not identify as 'female' or as a 'woman' in the common understandings of those words, there is conflict present in 'her' identifications.

Despite these problems of accurately communicating and labelling experiences, perspectives, and identities, it is possible to understand that there are people who do not fit neatly into the prescribed societal concepts of sex/gender and sexuality. The variety of methods used by participants to deal with their 'gender problems' is one indication of how individual their experiences actually are, regardless of my use of the label 'transgendered' to categorize all the participants. Indeed, one of the important aspects of this project is that it clarifies the uniqueness of each participant's experience and challenges the connotations of the labels usually employed to describe them. For instance, the label 'transsexual' might be used to describe four of the participants, and these participants have been classified this way by a gender clinic so that they may access certain treatments. For those people who have not had personal contact with transgendered people, and I certainly belonged to this group prior to this project, the label 'transsexual' means someone who is changing or has changed from one sex/gender to 'the other.' This process implies a transition from one socially prescribed, concrete identity to the other socially prescribed, concrete identity. It is assumed that the transition itself is relatively meaningless and brief in terms of a person's lifespan, and that everyone experiences the same reality. This is not the case. While there are similarities among participants, their identity formation, the language they use to describe their processes, and the assistance they have sought are all different. Some participants were, at the time of the interviews, content just to discuss sex/gender issues with friends or in the context of support groups. Others were comfortable expressing themselves through clothing, hairstyle, body movement, and other easily changed aspects of physical appearance. Others participated in 'hormone therapy,' some ended this participation, and some modified their bodies through surgery. In their discussions of assistance, though, there were more examples of conflict resulting from living outside sex/gender "norms" in a society with quite rigid prescriptions. For example, one participant who is changing her body told me that she dealt with the gender clinic by "asserting" her identity and insisting that she needed only the clinic's approval for surgery and not its psychological counselling. I found it interesting that this person used a tactic usually associated with 'masculinity' to convince others of her 'femininity.' Moreover, this participant "asserts" her 'femininity' with a physical appearance that is contrary to the usual expectations of 'women.'

If one accepts or even entertains the idea that sex/gender may not be a concrete, rigid duality, one may also recognize sexuality as destabilized (Bornstein 1994, 32; Butler 1990, 128). Indeed, in my conversations with participants, all of them indicated a destabilized notion of sexuality, even when they were adamant about their identities. Those participants who presented a definite identity, such as "dyke" or "fag," were using criteria other than that established by the sex/gender system. In other words, their identities would be incomprehensible to people who subscribe to the definitions supported by the sex/gender system. The participants have established their own criteria and asserted their own identities, which simultaneously incorporate and reject elements of the sex/gender system according to each participant's desire. As some participants suggested, identity is not simply a case of how the individual interprets 'her'/'his' own identity, but also how others interpret that identity and what the individual believes 'he'/'she' should do to be interpreted according to 'his'/'her' desire.

The experiences and perspectives of transgendered individuals emphasize questions concerning the 'nature' of 'sex' and 'gender.' The transgendered individuals with whom I spoke recognized the 'differences' in their own sex/gender identities compared to societal expectations at various points in their lives and in various ways, but the recognition was most frequently connected to social characteristics. However, I do not believe that this should be interpreted as evidence against access to body modification technology or as an argument suggesting that 'gender trouble,' in its various manifestations, would be eliminated by restructuring the sex/gender system, should that be possible. Rather, I believe that it is important to challenge the sex/gender system as it exists in North America as a social construction and as one possibility for social organization. Regardless of the challenges to the sex/gender system itself, transgendered people must still exist and operate in a society that prescribes and makes real the social expectations of 'sex' and 'gender'; the conflict and contradiction in the information provided by the participants may indicate how they are able to reconcile their experiences and perspectives with the sex/gender system.

Part 2

RUPTURED SUTURES

Chapter 4

SILENCED, DENIGRATED, AND RENDERED INVISIBLE: MOTHERS WHO LOST THEIR BABIES TO ADOPTION IN THE 1960S AND 1970S

Sandra Jarvie

> "Though her soul requires seeing, the culture around her requires sightlessness. Though her soul wishes to speak its truth, she is pressured to be silent."
>
> — *Clarissa Pinkola Estés, Women Who Run with the Wolves, 185.*

Introduction

In Canada, during the 1960s and 1970s, record numbers of babies and children were surrendered for adoption. In the 1960s, the estimated total number of such children across Canada was 114,177, and in the 1970s, it was 144,445. A total of 258,622 children were surrendered for adoption in Canada within two decades, with the peak adoption period being the early 1970s (Griffith 1991). Rigid laws were structured to sustain adoption practices, secrecy, and control over the release of adoption information (Griffith 1991), and much adoption information and many records of the past are inaccurate and inconsistent. Caught in this web of statistics, laws, and secrecy were the mothers who lost their babies to adoption.

The 1960s marked a transitional period when the social restrictions of the past still had power to deny many unsupported mothers their babies. At the same time, these mothers stood on the threshold of an era when girls would claim their right to motherhood in female-headed households (Solinger 1992). Abortion was illegal in the 1960s, and the birth control pill was inaccessible for young, unmarried women unless prescribed to regulate menstruation or obtained from an enlightened physician.

A social critic of the 1960s, Clark Vincent, described the contradictory messages and expectations of society at that time by pointing out how young women were inundated by "sexual stimuli" and then admonished for acting on it; at the same time, they were denied contraception and knowledge about protection against pregnancy (1961). This incredibly complex and contradictory social phenomenon of the 1960s has been called the "sexual revolution." The number of pregnant young women soared, generating an increase in the efforts of "social engineers" to divert the flow of babies, which, if these single young women had kept, would have contributed to a major increase in female-headed households. Unmarried mothers were a threat to the patriarchal ideal of the two-parent family.

Historically, single, pregnant women have been the suppliers of newborn babies for adoption (Ferguson 1984). The majority of these mothers have been in their teens to mid-twenties, temporarily unsupported, vulnerable, and powerless. The reasons for their temporary dependent situations were "illegitimate" pregnancies and lack of support by families, the fathers of their babies, social institutions, and society. Although the myth is that these babies were "unwanted" and "abandoned" by uncaring, "unwed" mothers, the reality is quite different. The methods used over decades to separate mothers from their newborn babies for adoption have ranged from overt condemnation of pregnant, unsupported mothers to covert methods generating the expectation that pregnant, unsupported mothers should self-sacrifice out of love "in the best interests" of their babies. Some mothers believed they made a conscious, informed decision to surrender their newborn babies for adoption, but most mothers had very few options and/or little choice in their surrender. The discussion in this paper concerns the latter mothers.

Stigma and dehumanization

Adolescence is widely viewed as the transitional development period from childhood to early adulthood. During the teens to the mid-twenties, the adolescent moves from the dependency of childhood to the independence of adulthood (Santrock 2001). This transitional period is a particularly vulnerable time in girls' lives. Any traumatic event that disempowers them impacts upon and compromises their normal development and identity formation, and their gradual separation from their families and integration into the larger society. Any form of trauma also exposes them to the coercive violence of adult society (Herman 1992). For many girls and young women in the 1960s and 1970s, the trauma of an unsupported pregnancy disempowered them, leaving them vulnerable and defenceless against familial, systemic, and societal oppression, exploitation, and coercion.

In the 1960s, there was no greater "sin" than being an unsupported, single, pregnant woman. Pregnancy outside of marriage was acceptable if marriage followed, or if the father of the baby became a partner, or if the family enfolded the mother and child into its midst. Leontine Young, believed by those who facilitated adoption to be an authority on "unwed" mothers, summed up the plight of the unsupported mother in 1954: "[I]f one is to judge by what happens, it is not unfair to conclude that 'immorality' is bad enough but 'immorality' plus poverty is unforgivable" (12). It was the lack of financial, emotional, psychological, or physical support that forced many pregnant girls and women into the public arena to have their fate and that of their babies decided for them by those who held power and "expert authority" over them.

The full force of society's wrath against the unsupported mother and the envisioned burden she would impose upon taxpayers stigmatized her. In 1963 Erving Goffman suggested that those who have been stigmatized by society are considered not quite human. The societal expectation was that unsupported mothers should voluntarily surrender their babies for adoption. Unsupported mothers of the 1960s and 1970s were expected to deny the physical, emotional, and psychological human preparations for pregnancy that were the norm for supported mothers. Stigmatized young, pregnant women were discriminated against by medical and social agencies, which used "stigma theory" to explain the women's inferiority and danger to society (Goffman 1963). The label "unwed mother" was a stigma symbol, the kind of symbol that Goffman said draws attention to a "debasing identity discrepancy" that fragments the whole person. "Unwed" mothers were labelled morally deficient and unfit to parent, based on their temporary poverty, youth, and lack of support. Stigma theory named "unwed" mothers as inferior and a danger to society, thus demeaning, devaluing, and targeting a vulnerable group of girls and young women.

Stigmatizing affected the unmarried mothers' social identities and cut them off from society and self; they stood alone, rejected, and condemned by society (Goffman 1963). During the 1960s and the 1970s, there were thousands of unmarried mothers, and each stood in isolation against a vengeful society that meted out punishment for stepping outside the patriarchal boundaries of the traditional role of supported mother.

Furthermore, the stigmatizing ideology that emphasized the unmarried mother's inferiority and denied her status as a mother able to parent her newborn baby was echoed in the multitude of labels that mental health and social work professionals constructed about her. She was pathologized as promiscuous, unbalanced, neurotic, and unstable, and was believed to possess a myriad of other psychological disorders (Young 1954; Hartley 1975; Kunzel 1993; Vincent 1961).

But these young mothers became pregnant because they had sexual intercourse, just like other human beings do. Their mental and psychological capacities were no different from those of other members of their society. Being unsupported, stigmatized, and dehumanized as "unwed" mothers, however, they were at the mercy of the analysis of professionals whose agenda included the creation of, and the solution to, the socially constructed "problem" of the "unwed" mother and "illegitimacy." That solution was the rehabilitation of the "unwed" mother and the separation of mother and child "in the best interests of the baby."

In his study of unmarried mothers, Clark Vincent predicted, "[I]t is quite possible that, in the near future, unwed mothers will be 'punished' by having their children taken from them right at birth. A policy like this would not be executed nor labeled explicitly as 'punishment,' rather it would be implemented through such pressures and labels as 'scientific findings,' 'the best interests of the child,' 'rehabilitation of the unwed mother,' and 'the stability of the family and society'" (1961, 199). Vincent's predictions were realized.

Adoption facilitators

The power of social workers over the outcome for the unsupported mothers and their babies can be tied to the history of professionalization of social workers. Regina Kunzel (1993) documents the rise of and the claim to professional status through social workers' control and expertise in the area of "illegitimacy" and "unmarried" mothers. Social workers' "expertise" in the area of unsupported mothers and illegitimacy changed as unmarried mothers emerged out of each social class through the decades. The mothers were first considered "feeble-minded" and their children a "contamination of the gene pool"; middle-class mothers were labelled "neurotic and psychologically unbalanced" (Kunzel 1993). The solutions devised for the "problem" of "unwed" mothers and "illegitimacy" changed as the label for the unsupported mother changed. To ensure the quality of the gene pool, some social workers, during the period when unmarried mothers were considered feebleminded, believed that the solution to the problem was early detection, institutionalization, and sterilization (Kunzel 1993). The babies of working- and middle-class mothers became commodities for adoption promotion. "Illegitimate" babies became the "legitimate" babies of those who were deemed more worthy by virtue of marriage and greater wealth than the unsupported mothers.

Indeed, many social workers believed that unmarried mothers were unfit to be mothers. Kunzel says that the focus moved from a concern for both the mother and her child to the "best interests of the child" because the unmarried mother and her child were not considered to constitute a family: "[M]otivated by concern about 'family breakdown,' [social workers] tended to see unmarried mothers as 'mothers in name only,' unfit to raise their own children" (1993, 130).

The many varieties of negative assumptions about unmarried mothers are expressed in the words of Dr. Irene Josselyn, a psychiatrist of the time: "Too often the solution [to the girl's problem] depends on the function of the agency rather than on the needs of the unmarried mother. She may become a social problem, a statistic, a representative of a symptom of emotional disturbance, a resource for babies for adoption, a shameful disfigurement of society to be hidden from the public eye, or a punching bag upon which society can vent otherwise controlled hostility" (qtd. in Solinger 1992, 172).

"Scientific findings" and "scientific authority," constituted in the expertise and professional status of social workers, were used as rationales to implement solutions to the social problems of "unwed" mothers, "illegitimacy," and the personal need created by the infertility of other women or couples.

Homes and hospitals for "unwed" mothers

The two social institutions in which social workers were most influential were homes and hospitals for unmarried mothers. At a national conference on social welfare in 1963, the "unwed" mother was described as a "driven" and "trapped" client. Family members, doctors, lawyers, ministers, and others pressured her to surrender her baby for adoption.

"Unwed" mothers' homes of the 1960s were institutions of rehabilitation for unsupported mothers. Adoption was heavily promoted, with the expectation that it was to be voluntarily chosen "in the best interest of the baby" (Petrie 1998). The maternity homes silenced, isolated, and kept from public view the uncontrolled fertility of their residents. Isolated unmarried mothers were captive to a distorted reality that emphasized their dependence and inability to provide for their babies. The homes regulated the lives of the mothers with religious and psychosocial rehabilitation aimed at correcting what was really a socially and professionally created belief in the girls' and women's inferiority. On a personal and social level, many young unmarried mothers regressed to a form of "childhood," welcoming the control of "parental" authority toward the outcome of a desired behaviour. An environment that creates superficially kind or warm treatment promotes regression; it has been found in studies to be a very effective form of psychological control (Rickarby 1998). The dependent, dehumanized, and inferior status of "unwed" mothers made rational the social expectation that they give up their babies for adoption.

Petrie (1998), in her research on homes for unmarried mothers across Canada, quotes from a review of policies on adoption at the time: "[S]ocial workers and others serving unmarried mothers have arrived, as a result of experience, at the conviction that adoption is the best plan for most illegitimate children as well as for most unmarried mothers. This does not disregard the unmarried mother's right of choice" (147). However, the vulnerable and powerless had very little choice when those who held the power over them controlled the information and terms of the agenda. Many mothers were not even made aware of the services that were supposed to be available to them or of their legal and human rights in regard to adoption or alternatives to adoption that would have enabled them to raise their own babies (Carlini 1992; McColm 1993; Kelly 1999; Griffith 1991; Solinger 1992; Origins, Inc. n.d.).

Hospital staff, too, held power and authority over their often very young and vulnerable clients. Dr. Marion Hilliard, chief of obstetrics and gynaecology at the Women's College in Toronto in the 1950s, believed that an "unwed" mother should be punished by having her child adopted: "When she renounces her child for its own good the unwed mother has learned a lot. She has learned to pay the price of misdemeanour and this alone, if punishment is needed, is punishment enough" (qtd. in Little 1998, 137). Hilliard said this in 1956, but she expressed the mindset of many who echoed her harsh sentiments through the 1960s and beyond. The reality was that many unsupported mothers felt isolation, fear, and abandonment during labour and birth. Many were over-medicated, others not given any medication; some were left alone in a room or hallway, ignored, humiliated, and verbally abused (Origins, Inc. n.d.; Rickarby 1998; McColm 1993). For most unmarried mothers, the hospital experience provided little relief from psychic and physical pain (Petrie 1998).

These mothers were legally the sole guardians of their babies until they signed the consent-to-adoption form, and yet babies were routinely taken away from most of them immediately after birth. Many were denied the right to see or hold their own babies (McColm 1993; Origins, Inc. n.d.). Some were told it was best for them not to see their babies, but some demanded to see them. It was their legal right to do so, but most mothers were unaware they had any rights at all. The process of denying the mother contact with her baby intuitively suggests that hospital staff believed it would deter her from bonding with her baby. The logic was that such denial decreased a mother's resistance to signing the consent-to-adoption form (Rickarby 1998).

The practice of asking mothers to sign the consent-to-adoption form within hours or days of the birth of their babies does not recognize or take into consideration the physical, emotional, and psychological condition of the mother following birth. Girls and women were unable to defend themselves against the power of those in authority and in positions of supposed "expertise" while they were in a diminished capacity brought on by the physical crisis of labour, their dependency and any extenuating circumstances of birth, the immediate loss of their babies, and drugs used prior to, during, and after birth (Solinger 1992; Rickarby 1998). In the methods used to procure newborn babies for adoption, the condition and ability of the mother to make a rational decision seemed of no concern to adoption facilitators.

Adoption practices and adoption agents in their various forms appear to have been concerned in general with promoting adoption and meeting the needs of adopters rather than the needs of the unsupported mother and her child. Although literature of the time specifies the need for services to unsupported mothers, the underlying premise was the promotion of adoption as best for the baby and the mother. *Social Services for Unmarried Parents* (1957), for example, offers guidelines for services to mothers, but various passages remark upon the moral preference for marriage or openly promote adoption:

- In short, while avoiding a punitive attitude towards unmarried parents we must make clear the value of permanent and indissoluble marriage over any form of illicit union. (3)
- An important principle in helping the unmarried mother plan for her child is that the child has a right to the opportunity for normal growth and development, preferably in family group. (9)

- Adopting parents are now more willing to take the risks that any parent must take, knowledge of the value of the early parental relationship outweighs the worry about heredity that people used to have.... All these factors, plus the constantly increasing number of couples eager to adopt, underline the importance of unmarried mothers considering adoption not only as a good but a very feasible solution of her problem about the baby's future. (Appendix B)

The *Report of the Committee on Adoption in Alberta* (1965) summarizes the results of questionnaires sent to 2,167 couples who had adopted. Its authors were seeking input for changes to be made to the *Child Welfare Act*. But no questionnaires were sent to mothers who had lost their babies to adoption. The following excerpts from the report acknowledge the birth mother, but the focus is definitely on the adoptive parents, the great majority of whom "applied for white children" (29).

- Most adoptive parents ... wanted a new-born to 2 months old ... virtually none wanted a child over 4 years, indicating, of course, the desirability of placing a child as soon as possible after birth. Ideally, perhaps the child should be placed by the time it leaves the hospital. (29)
- It was argued on the one hand that she [the mother] should have the benefit of the most complete counselling both before and after the birth.... On the other hand it was argued that the baby should be placed with its adoptive parents as soon after birth as possible and for this reason the surrender procedure should be accelerated. (38)

In *Services to Unmarried Mothers: The Unwed Mother's Indecision about Her Baby as a Defense Mechanism* (Evan 1958), the following rationale for social workers' efforts is provided: "On a clinical basis it has been found that giving the baby up for adoption is the best solution for the majority of unmarried mothers and makes possible greater opportunity for their further development. Therefore, it is understandable that social workers have been oriented toward the achievement of this goal" (18).

Remarkably, though, in the context of all these reports purported to be about services to unmarried mothers, *Services to Unmarried Mothers: Generic and Specific Factors in Casework with the Unmarried Mother* (Leyendecker

1958) reveals that there was some awareness of the hypocritical attitude embedded within social service practices: "An attitude that seems particularly indefensible is the readiness, even eagerness, of social agencies to assist an unmarried mother to surrender a normal baby, whereas they expect her to be responsible for the planning for and insofar as possible for support of, a defective baby who is unadoptable" (3). Healthy newborn babies were in demand by adopters, whose needs were met through a "solution" to the social "problem" of "unwed" mothers.

Blaming the victim

The language of adoption in the 1950s and 1960s, and into the 1970s, eroded the self-esteem, self-confidence, and dignity of many mothers. The needs of the baby came first, but the needs of the unmarried mother were not considered as one of the baby's needs. The mother was expected to self-sacrifice out of unconditional love "in the best interests of her baby." That expression, which at one time was reserved for apprehensions in cases of child neglect and abuse, became a weapon against the mother. Proponents of the ideological approach summed up as being "in the best interest of the baby" assumed that the mother was unfit and incapable of acting in the best interest of her own baby. The combination of assaults at personal, systemic, and social levels against them contributed to mothers seeing themselves as having done something "wrong" for which only they were to "blame." Many believed that they deserved the "punishment" of social rejection and loss of their babies to adoption. It was the "unselfish sacrifice" that would redeem them socially and morally.

Once the babies were surrendered, the mothers were told they would "forget" their children, and they were advised "to get on with life." The mothers were often faced with the paradox of the distorted realities of adoption. They were led to believe that they had surrendered "out of love," "in the best interests of the child." Paradoxically, however, once the babies were gone, the mothers who had given them up were labelled "uncaring" mothers who had "abandoned" their "unwanted" babies. They were silenced, discarded, and rendered invisible. They had been victimized by their society and their social agencies and then they were blamed for their victimization.

William Ryan (1971), in *Blaming the Victim*, defines an ideological process that meshes closely with the social process used in blaming unsupported mothers, not only for their pregnancies but also for the surrender of their babies. Ryan purports that an ideology that blames the victim "uses a set of ideas and concepts deriving from systematically motivated, but unintended, distortions of reality" (11). The "distortions of reality" were enormous for the unsupported mother. Society told her that she did not deserve her own child, that she was incapable of raising her own child, that her sexuality was immoral, and after the expected surrender of her baby "in his or her best interests," that she could never see her child again. Then she was accused of "abandoning" her "unwanted" baby. The "distortions of reality" faced by the unsupported mother functioned on personal, familial, systemic, and societal levels. Ryan stresses that blaming the victim is an unconscious group or class function that maintains the status quo or class interests for those who practice it. This can be readily seen in practices that oppress and exploit women in a patriarchal society. In the case of unsupported mothers of the 1960s, blaming the victim provided a solution to infertility and to the threat posed by the growing numbers of unmarried mothers to the "ideal" of the male-headed household. By transferring the babies of many temporarily vulnerable and powerless unsupported mothers to, for the most part, childless couples, the blaming ideology supported the patriarchal "ideal" of the normative two-parent, adoptive family.

Trauma

The survivors of adoption practices of the 1950s, 1960s, and 1970s paid a heavy price in personal and social degradation, the loss of their babies, and continued blame for their victimization. Today some researchers acknowledge that many of these mothers were traumatized and that they continue to live with post-traumatic stress disorder (Rickarby 1998; Carlini 1992; Kelly 1999; McColm 1993). Many of these unsupported mothers were expected to make a "decision" that most had neither the life experience nor the information and resources to support. The trauma of their situations rendered many mothers unable to make decisions or rationalize beyond their experience and the socially constructed distortion to the reality that had created that trauma. The extent or existence of trauma for each individual mother depended on the context of her experience.

Judith Herman (1992) describes traumatic events as those that "overwhelm the ordinary systems of care that give people a sense of control, connection and meaning" (33). Traumatic events and the resulting reduced cognitive and emotional capacity for normal human functioning were the realities that surrendering mothers experienced (Herman 1992). Herman's descriptions of the effects of trauma on the individual provide us with insights into the experiences of surrendering mothers:

- Victims cannot take action because they feel that their actions will not accomplish a change in outcomes. For surrendering mothers, expert authority maintained an unchallenged view that adoption was in the best interests of the baby.
- A victim's self-defence is overwhelmed and disorganized; she is unable to protect herself against those who are not acting in her best interests. Many surrendering mothers could not discern beyond the distorted reality presented.
- Victims experience intense emotion but do not remember the details of the event, or they remember events in detail but do not feel emotions. Many surrendering mothers disconnected from self and their experience to avoid the unbearable pain of losing their babies.
- A victim feels that her sense of self is fragmented, not functioning as a complex integrated system. Many surrendering mothers' cognitive and emotional functioning could not work in concert to enable them to make rational decisions.
- Victims experience numbing to escape what they cannot change by action in the real world; they alter their states of consciousness for survival. Many surrendering mothers experienced numbing and a disconnection from emotions and reality.

The mothers who surrendered had no means to escape their situations. In varying ways, they accepted the distorted reality created by family, social institutions, society, and adoption facilitators who told them their babies were "better off" without them.

Adolescence is a time of identity formation and growth toward autonomy. The trauma of the reactions to her pregnancy and of familial and social ostracism shattered this growing sense of self in the unsupported teenage mother. The labels of "tramp," "slut," "whore," and "unwed mother" distorted her identity and sexuality. Her value in society was questioned because of the denied natural humanity of her motherhood. Her capabilities as an adult were questioned because she was deemed incapable of providing for and raising her own flesh and blood. Others were promoted as better than herself as mother.

The need for resolution to post-traumatic stress in many of these mothers may not have surfaced for six to eight years or even decades (Soll 2000). Some mothers may not even have begun the process of reliving and resolving their trauma, grief, and loss until there was a crisis or a reunion with thier adult children lost to adoption (Carlini 1992; McColm 1993; Rickarby 1998; Origins, Inc. n.d.; Herman 1992).

Accountability

Society laid the blame for surrendering babies for adoption solely on the mothers, but no action of theirs in their vulnerable and powerless position condones the action of those who had the power, ability, and resources to help the mothers provide a home for themselves and their babies. Nothing the mothers did condones a society that stigmatized, dehumanized, and victimized powerless vulnerable pregnant girls and women and then blamed them.

The closed system of adoption information disclosure and contact denied the mothers for decades any knowledge about the fate of their babies lost to adoption. That information is still difficult to acquire in many jurisdictions today. If the mothers were expected to self-sacrifice out of unconditional love so their babies would have a "better life," it is not logical that they should be penalized for making that sacrifice.

Accountability for and acknowledgment of the actions of the past that created the untenable paradox which silenced and denigrated the mothers who lost their babies to adoption is the only way to end the social blindness that perpetuates the myths and illusions of adoption practices. Our society condoned the practices of the past and still refuses to acknowledge that many of the babies were not "abandoned" and "un-wanted." It is not only the mothers who have been affected by trauma, re-pression, dissociation, and denial. These same phenomena are expressed in our social consciousness as well (Herman 1992). The lies, myths, and illusions that deny the past continue into the present. The label "birth mother," for example, continues the stigma in the dehumanizing term "unwed mother." Society continues to marginalize these mothers.

Conclusion

The opening paragraph of *Death by Adoption* by Joss Shawyer (1979) reads as follows:

Adoption is a violent act, a political act of aggression towards
a woman who has supposedly offended the sexual mores
by committing the unforgivable act of not suppressing her
sexuality, and therefore not keeping it for trading purposes
through traditional marriage.... [T]he crime is a grave one, for
she threatens the very fabric of our society. The penalty is severe.
She is stripped of her child by a variety of subtle and not so
subtle manoeuvres and then brutally abandoned. (3)

These words succinctly sum up the attitudes and actions toward and the environment lived in and survived by many unsupported pregnant girls and young women in the 1960s.

The 1960s, however, are only one period of time in the history of promoting adoption to pregnant girls and young women, though that era was a crucial transitional period for women and their right to motherhood within female-headed households. A longer period, at least from the 1950s to the early 1970s, laid the foundation for the adoption industry and the commodification of babies. Adoption during this period was focussed on the interests of the adopters in providing a child for a home (Davies 1997).The social engineering employed in the past to transfer babies from many unsupported, vulnerable, and powerless pregnant girls and young women to create families that were purported to be psychologically, physically, and economically better placed is still promoted in more subtle ways today. Such social engineering reacted to a change in societal concerns: no longer was the focus on finding a home for a homeless child, but rather on finding a child for prospective parents. The practices of stigmatizing, traumatizing, and blaming the victim, which occurred in the separation of mothers and their newborn babies, were violent actions taken against the powerless and defenceless. Under conditions beyond their control, girls and young women were bound by a legal decision that many were not emotionally, physically, or psychologically capable of making. In most legal situations, these conditions would be considered exploitative and coercive. Girls and women were subjected to acts that were "terrorizing violations," but other people, even those who were closest to them, did not necessarily perceive such acts that way (Herman 1992).

Today, surrendering mother survivors are sharing their stories through studies, books, and the Internet. They are forming consciousness-raising groups and affiliations, both in real space and online, that acknowledge and validate their experiences and name their experiences for what they were and are. The actual experiences of these girls and young women were "an appalling disjunction" from the social construction of that reality (Herman 1992). Those who benefited in some way from the separation of mothers and their newborn babies and who did not experience the stigma, dehumanization, trauma, victimization, and unbearable loss of their children created the terms and realities of adoption. The surrendering mother survivors are deconstructing that distorted reality. The silence and invisibility imposed on mothers who lost their babies to adoption during the 1960s and 1970s is ending. Mothers, in ever greater numbers, are reclaiming their voices and their denied motherhood, sharing their stories, voicing their truths and realities, and acting on their right to know the fate of the now-adult children whom they lost to adoption.

Chapter 5

tell-me-what-I-want.com:
ADOLESCENT GIRLS, CONSUMER SOCIETY, AND INFORMATION TECHNOLOGIES

Ellen Whiteman

Introduction: Societal influences and the Internet

Societal expectations undoubtedly influence adolescent girls. However, the extent to which teenagers are influenced depends on both the media through which girls see the message and the way each individual reacts to the message. Adolescent girls are not a homogeneous group and they do not react to every social message in exactly the same way. Roberts (1993) argues that "the appropriate questions ... do not ask whether mass media affect adolescence; rather, they ask which messages (or parts of messages), under which conditions, affect which perceptions, beliefs, and behaviors" (635).

While I realize that there is an interconnection among the messages created by television, music, print, and information technology cultures, I focus here on teenage girls' responses to information technologies. I interviewed eight adolescent girls over a period from May to October 2001: seven were fifteen or sixteen years of age, and one was eighteen. In this chapter, I look at what these girls discussed and at the artefacts they demonstrated during our interviews, attempting to identify and interpret the influence of some of the social messages they receive through information technologies. The girls' identities have been protected by pseudonyms.

Consumerism

The theme of consumerism ran not only through all the open-ended interviews I conducted with the participants, but also through almost every site they demonstrated during the interviews. One of the main ways in which society influences the participants in this study is through advertising. Advertising is everywhere, both on the Internet and in actual space. While theoretical work has been done on advertising, it has generally focussed on print, television, and, to a lesser extent, radio. Berger (1973) concentrates on print and defines the purpose of publicity (or advertising) as making "the spectator marginally dissatisfied with his present way of life. Not with the way of life of society, but with his own within it" (142). In other words, Berger suggests that advertising exists to tell us that all we need to be happy/satisfied/content is the particular product the advertisement promotes. Happiness is not found through changing the world but through changing our spending habits. Berger argues that advertising is not even about selling a product, but about selling an image. In order for the image to be *desired*, it must create envy in the viewer (1973, 147-48). He calls the image that creates envy "glamour," but for adolescent girls, this image is associated with being "cool," with fitting in. Kilbourne (1999) builds on Berger's ideas, adding that some advertisements go so far as to suggest that while people may let you down, products never will (84-85). Advertising carefully cultivates an image of self that adolescent girls must reflect and then offers them the products that promise to result in this image. However, the products never quite deliver. The image remains unattainable, and another product is always needed.

Klein (2000), who focusses on the Internet as well as on print media in her analysis, takes this argument a step further and points out that advertisers have hired younger-looking people to go out and find the image that adolescents already have in their minds so that they can market that image and sell it back to consumers worldwide (72-73). In the mid-1990s, advertisers became aware of the importance of the adolescent global market, and they have been targeting teenagers ever since. Teens' own alternative cultures have been mainstreamed and sold back to them at inflated prices. Brand name labels determine the essence that gives teens an identity. A brand name does not sell a product so much as a lifestyle or a culture to which adolescents, for all of their supposed rebellion, conform. A company that makes a particular kind of jeans wants not only to be known for making the jeans that teens wear, but more importantly, to make *the* product that defines teens as teens (Klein 2000, 72-73).

Kilbourne (1999), who also focusses primarily on print media but who has done some work on the Internet, does not look so much at how advertisers market to teenagers as at how children are inappropriately targeted by advertisers who want to make them "brand-loyal" for life. She says that "children are especially vulnerable on the Internet where advertising manipulates them, invades their privacy and transforms them into customers without their knowledge" (43). Kilbourne fears that the interactive medium combined with little or no regulation will have a profound effect on the future of advertising. Gone are the rules about targeting children with inappropriate material. For example, on the Internet, advertisers no longer have to obey rules about advertising tobacco products.

Advertising on the Internet

The Internet has taken advertising to a new level that other media cannot achieve. The Internet is interactive, pervasive, and, for the most part, unregulated. Advertising is everywhere in the form of banners, pop-up text boxes, and linked pages that force a user to click her way through a predetermined sequence in order to escape. There can be moving images as well as text, photos, and other information. Banners and pop-up ads are on most commercialized sites, as well as some of the sites that started out as non-commercialized but became popular enough to be sponsored. Sites create "cookies," chunks of information that can be used to track users as they surf virtual space. General sites such as Yahoo or Sympatico display general advertising, while more specific sites allow for "niche" advertising similar to that found in specialty magazines or specific television shows.

On the Internet, advertisers are no longer limited to the traditional spaces between the television shows or the articles. Furthermore, while advertisers have always been able to pay for product placement in television shows and magazines, for the first time with the Internet, the advertisement can become the entertainment rather than simply being alongside the entertainment. A good example of this blurring of the lines comes from Kilbourne's discussion of the Budweiser frogs. The frogs first appeared during the 1996 Superbowl and then made their way to the computer desktop. The frogs did nothing but sit on lily pads and croak "Bud Wise Er," but they became a common desktop theme (Kilbourne 1999, 157–58). The creators of the Budweiser frogs wrote both an advertisement and a children's cartoon. The advertisement itself became a sought-after, visible product.

Games are another way in which online advertisements are viewed and shared. The Web site at *www.candystand.com* is a good example of how online games are created and distributed for the purpose of advertising a product. The site contains a number of different children's games that integrate candy, cookies, gum, and other products aimed at children into the workings of the games. Two of the participants in my study took me to this site and played the games while I was observing them. A third participant mentioned the site, but told me she used to play these games but she has become too busy. The games are different from normal advertisements because they allow the player to interact with the products in ways television or print media cannot. In a television commercial, the products can dance or even speak, but in virtual space the surfer can control the movement and actions of the product, at least within the set parameters of the game. In the candystand games, chocolate cookies become "mud" traps for mini-golfers, Lifesavers become tee-off points, and Teddy Grams become golf hazards. The products are so effectively integrated into the games that Amy mentioned them as part of the fun rather than as part of the advertising. On the other hand, Lori, the other participant who demonstrated candystand to me, was annoyed by the advertising, but she felt that it was the price of "free" games.

Advertisers are also using games and making "free" offers as a way of getting access to e-mail addresses and other personal information about the people surfing their sites. To download "free" material from most Web sites, a user must first register with the site. E-mail addresses are usually required, but the sites may also ask for optional information about age, income level, sex, and personal interests. This information forms a "cookie," which is accessed by the site every time the person signs on to that site. But more importantly from the advertisers' perspective, the "cookie" allows Internet sites to track who visits, and it allows advertisers to have personal information about a particular user. The sites then either use the information themselves to send out advertising or they sell the lists to other advertisers. Free Internet sites such as Yahoo and Hotmail are good examples of this online marketing strategy. A user gets free e-mail access from any computer connected to the Internet. Yahoo then uses a user's e-mail address to send advertisements to her from online companies. All of the participants in my study except one use these free e-mail sites in order to ensure privacy within their homes, and all of them receive advertising "spam" as the cost of free e-mail. Like private television or radio broadcasts, e-mail is not free even though there is no user fee.

Other game sites incorporate the acceptance of spam e-mails as part of the online game. One of the sites to which Lori took me was *www.neopets.com*, a free virtual pet site (Neopets, Inc.). Here players can choose from a variety of virtual pet options which they can play with, feed, and "love," and for which they can buy things. However, food and all other items for the virtual pet must be bought from an online store. Players build up credit at the store either by playing advertisement-laden games or by agreeing to have advertisements sent to their e-mail addresses. Lori has accepted advertisements from online travel companies, online credit card suppliers, and other products in order to get credit to feed and amuse her virtual pets. While Lori uses one of her many personal e-mail addresses, I suspect the site relies on younger children sharing an e-mail address with their parents. Companies can then reach people with the money to respond to their online offers. Even if the advertisement is read only by children, they are potential consumers developing brand loyalty with each e-mail that they accept. Children creating imaginary pets is not a new phenomenon, but in the past they did not have to provide personal information to a global system of advertising to do so. Ravetz (1998) expresses concerns about virtual pet sites that go beyond a concern with advertising. While the user can spend as much time as she wants with the virtual pet she creates, a pet much more "real" than imaginary pets have been in the past, there are no consequences for abusing the pet through neglect: "Of course if you don't feed them and they metaphorically 'die' you are not going to face charges of cruelty to an animal. No real commitment is necessary" (119).

One step beyond the virtual pet sites is *www.gurl.com*, where visitors can create virtual boyfriends. The site states that "you will get to customize your model to suit your tastes and let the romancin' begin" (Drill, McDonald, and Odes 1995-2005). Like the virtual pet, the virtual boyfriend is a sample commodity: "[G]url members will be able to visit their cybersweeties, find out more about them, gaze adoringly into their eyes, let them whisper sweet nothings all day long ... and introduce them to friends." While none of my participants mentioned creating "cybersweeties," *www.gurl.com* is linked to *www.seventeen.com*, which they frequented. The participants may have been too old to be interested in creating virtual boys, or they may have been too embarrassed to admit that they had created romance online.

At the *Seventeen* Web site, *www.seventeen.com*, girls are encouraged to request samples of products offered by advertisers. Candy and Ginger told me that they often get free product samples. To receive these products, however, they must give their home addresses online. The giving of personal information on the Internet raises many questions about security. All but one of my participants seemed in no way worried about giving out e-mail addresses or even their home addresses. The exception was Lynne;

she was extremely worried about security and never gave out personal information or signed up for products or services that required it. Interestingly, at fifteen, she was one of the youngest of the girls. All of the other participants gave out personal information without a second thought if they thought there was something to be gained from doing so.

Information on the Internet

While advertising is obviously aimed at the buying and selling of products, information has also become a commodity that is bought and sold on the Internet. Webmasters pay search engine providers to privilege their sites on the search results; sites are constructed in ways that give T1, DSL, or cable users access to information that users with dial-up modems cannot access. Cyberspace itself is sold to consumers through monthly access fees or by the hour in cybercafes. My participants both recognized and accepted the commodification of information on the Internet. Lynne helped me to understand that there are four ways in which information is commodified.

The first way is by direct sale of information to consumers on popular Web sites. Lynne lamented the fact that many of the sites from which she had in the past obtained information were no longer accessible unless the user paid. Lynne can not afford to purchase information, so she has started to access some of those sites at school because the school pays for a subscription. As Lynne pointed out,

> There are certain things I'd like to do but because of restrictions for access or, like, some sites you have to pay a fee to go on to get access to information, you know. If I had more time and more money ... I might go and check out a few more Web pages than I do right now.... I like this one; I used to be able to check phone numbers on this Web page and, like, if somebody phoned me and all that was left was their number but I didn't know who called, I could check it here, but now they've changed it so there's a fee, so I use this Web page a lot less.

Lynne is well aware that the user fees restrict her access. She also demonstrated that security itself has become a commodity to be bought and sold. She was checking a name out of curiosity, but she could not gain that information unless she paid a fee to the supplier of that information online.

The second way that information is being commodified on the Internet is through the sale of personal information. Since Lynne is security conscious and afraid of how her information could be used, she refuses to give out personal information. However, some of the participants in the study who are not as cautious "sell" their personal data to receive information.

In response to my question of what criteria she used to determine if information was credible, Lynne replied,

> I can ... compare it to a book or newspaper or I try to use official government Web sites and if they supply links – when I was doing my research paper, one of the interviewers actually recommended a couple of Web sites, so I used those. I try to use research Web sites like *worldbook.com*.... You have to be very, I guess, picky about what is there and if it's something that you can prove or compare or you know to be fact, then I can kind of say, okay, if I get something at this Web page again, then it's probably true, but there is also a lot of junk out there.

Her criteria for judging information seemed to be to use only information that was state-sponsored or that she could validate through another source. In Lynne's model of authenticity, the government was seen as an authentic or legitimate source. This assumed authenticity gives the state a more visible presence in students' lives than it has had in those of previous generations because they can access it virtually anywhere. However, Lynne knows that she needs to sort through the massive amount of information on the Internet. She knows that information has value to her only if it is correct, and she is learning how to sort through the "junk" on the Internet to find the information that she needs.

In his discussion about advertising, Berger argues that advertising points out to viewers that they are lacking something that can be bought in order to bring happiness or satisfaction. Information can also be the one more thing, yet another commodity, that people "need." Since the Internet has almost unlimited potential as a repository for information, the search for the "perfect" or most up-to-date information can be constructed as a need that is never satisfied. Lynne said of her time spent on the Internet, "If I'm interested in something I will spend a ridiculous amount of time, like I could spend two hours just looking for one specific piece of information." In Lynne's case, the needed piece of information is typically a soap opera update that will allow her to participate fully in discussions with her friends, or an update on the 9/11 tragedy. In the latter case, she has sought information to make her feel knowledgeable and more secure.

The other participants also consume information in an attempt to feel secure or happy. All but one of my participants talked about going to *www.seventeen.com* and taking quizzes designed to help them with some aspect of their lives, and all but one participant said they read their horoscope regularly online. These are all ways in which information is being consumed in much the same way as other products. As with other forms of infomercials, or perhaps even more so because the Internet makes acquiring information feel pro-active in ways other popular media do not, the creation of an insatiability for ever-new, ever-more information is distressing. While she was not talking about the Internet, Sawicki's (1991) explanation of Foucault's concept of docile bodies is applicable to information technologies that exercise a form of "disciplinary power ... exercised on the body and soul of individuals. It increases the power of individuals at the same time as it renders them more docile. In modern society disciplinary power has spread through the production of certain forms of knowledge" (22).

My participants have the power and readily available space to look for and find virtually any kind of information they want. However, the information that adolescent girls find through online magazines and other forms of advertising can result in self-surveillance and concern about meeting Western cultural expectations. Such advertising feeds the narcissistic attitudes and desire for peer connection that Klein (2000) talks about in the opening quotation to this paper. The online quizzes and open-ended questions can be blueprints for girls for the performing of their femininity (Currie 1999). Such self-regulation and self-surveillance renders adolescent girls vulnerable in Western culture even as they acquire knowledge about their bodies and become proficient in information technologies.

Relationships

I found it somewhat disturbing to discover that the participants seem to be commodifying their online relationships in much the same way as information is commodified for them online. Their e-mail activities can produce meaningful conversations, at least when the participants know their correspondents. In ICQ and MSN, however, they do not necessarily know the people with whom they are chatting, and this allows them to take on identities. When Candy and Ginger ordered a conversation through ICQ with a young, single Saskatoon man, it seemed more like ordering fries with a burger than any attempt at real human contact. But of more concern is that the person with whom they were talking could have been anyone ordering up adolescent girls for conversation.

I believe the danger in segregating people into specific groups and categories such as young, single, and male, as do ICQ and MSN, is that the conversations are limited by a specific focus that defines the chatroom. The conversation, or indeed, the virtual relationship that might result, is forced into these particular parameters. While this categorization enables people to find online conversational partners who share their interests, it may result in people isolating themselves from the rest of the world and from face-to-face human experience. While virtual relationships have advantages in allowing fantasy conversations, they are not a substitute, or even a good preparation, for a face-to-face human relationship.

On the cybersweeties Web site discussed earlier (*www.gurl.com*), girls can opt out of real relationships and project all of their romantic fantasies onto an image they create in cyberspace. This is another example of how relationships themselves are being consumed rather than actually experienced. The girls creating cybersweeties are not learning how to negotiate in a real relationship; they are simply projecting their own ideas of an ideal boy onto a computer screen, ideas they are getting, in part, from the sites they are visiting. How will any regular boy with all of the faults of a regular human being ever measure up to a perfect cybersweetie? "Made-to-order" boyfriends are not a new idea: bands such as "The BackStreet Boys" project the image of the perfect boyfriend to sell compact discs. Cybersweeties, the next level in creating a girl's "prince charming," takes the fantasy a step further: the girls can not only create their perfect guys, but they can also get computer-generated responses. Instead of only imagining that "prince charming" will love them, the girls are told by a computer that the fantasy is true.

www.gurl.com also reinforces the overwhelmingly heterosexist messages that Web sites like *www.seventeen.com* perpetuate. The site is aimed exclusively at girls, but site visitors cannot create a female version of the cybersweetie to whisper sweet nothings in their ears. As long as a girl's fantasies fit the heterosexual norm, and she is satisfied with living only in fantasy, this site will give her everything her heart desires.

This site could be enjoyable for a pre-teen or young teenager who is just beginning to explore her sexuality. Considering the rate of violence against girls in dating situations, a virtual romance may be safer than a real relationship. However, this site may be setting girls up for disappointment and even safety risks because in the fantasies the girls are in complete control. The virtual boys on the sites I was taken to are never violent, never push for sex, and never drink or do drugs. Girls who practice on virtual boys are not learning about the hazards of meeting "real" boyfriends who might not be sweet, kind, and romantic. The virtual experience may actually result in girls projecting their fantasies onto real boys with devastatingly unsafe results.

The influence of the Beauty Myth

While relationships are influenced by consumerism, nothing affects relationships and girls' understanding of their place in relationships more than the Beauty Myth. The Beauty Myth in Western culture defines how girls are supposed to look, how they are expected to treat each other, and how they will be treated by boys and men.

The Beauty Myth is a term popularized by Naomi Wolf in her discussion of how standards of beauty and body image are used to control women. Wolf (1991) describes the Beauty Myth as the last patriarchal hurdle placed in front of women's and girls' true equality. For Wolf, the Beauty Myth is "a story: the quality called 'beauty' objectively and universally exists. Women must want to embody it and men must want to possess women who embody it" (12). In other words, a universal standard of beauty has developed that few, if any, women can meet. In Western society, the current standards include whiteness, unnatural thinness, and perfect skin, bodies, and hair. Anyone achieving less than this perfection is a failure. Women must strive to live up to this standard and men must reward only the women who succeed at "universal beauty." Advertisers and mass media control and define the standards of beauty and can use this control both to sell products and to tell women and girls what they should think. As Currie (1999) states, "[B]y encouraging women to believe that they are unacceptable as they are, media representations set a standard to which women strive" (33). Some of the messages about beauty to which adolescent girls are exposed through information technologies contradict the positive messages they are receiving from friends and parents. These less tangible but more pervasive technologies of discourse create an environment that tells adolescent girls to be pretty and sweet, and to take up as little space as possible, both literally and metaphorically.

The participants in this study were getting messages about feminine beauty from countless different sources, but especially from *www.seventeen.com*. The homepage of this Web site is mostly advertising, but several of the links on the side lead to articles and other information. The articles fall into five main categories: beauty, fashion, sex and body, boys, and real life. All of these categories contain articles that maintain and reinforce the Beauty Myth for adolescent girls in three main ways: 1) they define a universal standard of female beauty; 2) they assume compulsory heteronormativity and relationships with boys; and 3) they create the parameters for competitive relationships among women.

Defining universal standards of beauty

Advertising and articles about appearance are the most obvious ways in which the Beauty Myth is promoted at *www.seventeen.com*. Throughout the site, countless articles emphasize the importance of beauty. One entire category is filled with articles with titles such as "candy color for your nails" and "want to change your look?" Subheadings such as "when skin deep is enough" imply that the girls need not worry what is under the skin as long as the skin is beautiful. Adolescent girls who access this site are reminded continually that if they are not beautiful, they are nothing. The demand for thinness is reinforced by articles in the "Sex and Body" section. For example, one article has large prominent print, as well as a colour photo, shouting out the question to girls, "will the pill make you fat?" The important acknowledgment that adolescent girls are already making choices about sexual intercourse and contraceptives is undermined by a concern about weight gain. Fat is clearly the worst thing that can happen: the other possible side effects of the pill or sexual activity do not get the same large headlines that weight gain does.

Another important element of defining beauty to adolescent girls involves demonstrating which clothes are fashionable. Many articles at *seventeen.com* focus on fashion and have subtitles such as "stuff you'll love to wear right now,", reflecting the fickle nature of fashion. Girls have to wear the clothes "right now" because by next month there will be new fashions for them to covet. The titles of many articles, such as "go behind the mini" and "turn up the volume on a white blouse," also have definite sexual overtones. Even a more practical article, "we live in jeans," emphasizes the importance of maintaining and showing off young women's perfect bodies. Having perfect hair, skin, and nails does not define an adolescent girl as beautiful without the correct clothing to wear. Advertising reinforces the Beauty Myth with images that conform to and define it, and with the message that the correct fashions and products are necessary to create beauty. Beauty is not a natural state but an illusion that must be created and bought.

Compulsory heteronormativity and relationships with boys

Another vital element of the Beauty Myth is the understanding that all women and girls are heterosexual and interested in finding and keeping a boy or man. The point of achieving the universal standard of beauty is not to feel beautiful within oneself but to attract a member of the opposite sex. While the article "are you ready to go all the way?" attempts to demythologize sexual intercourse, it assumes heterosexuality. Specifically, the article points out that while sex will not suddenly make a girl a grown-up, as many young women are led to believe, it could "transform you into a parent." Nowhere in the online magazine is there any mention that adolescent girls may be struggling with issues related to defining their own sexuality. Like the universal standard of beauty, the assumed standard of heterosexuality is the only identity discussed.

The Beauty Myth also has clearly defined standards for how adolescent girls are to relate to boys. Adolescent girls who do not have boyfriends, or at least boys who desire them, are failures. To this end, the magazine devotes a great deal of space to explaining how to understand and "catch" boys. The first heading that caught my attention was "test your boy IQ." Here, girls are not testing their boyfriends' intelligence, but rather how much girls know about boys. Then, in case girls do not know much about boys, the magazine helps clue them in with the story "sweet or slimy: true stories of boy behaviour." Finally, if girls find out about boys and do not like what they see, they can, as already mentioned, create their own cybersweeties at *www.gurl.com*.

The message that a girl must have, or at least want, a boyfriend is continually reinforced at these Web sites. According to the Beauty Myth, imbibed through adolescent-targeted discourse more accessible through the Internet than ever before, a girl has only succeeded if she has a boy to admire and desire her. Furthermore, adolescent girls learn through popular sites such as *www.seventeen.com* that to get and keep a boyfriend, their own needs and sexual desires must be secondary to those of boys.

Under the terms of the Beauty Myth, girls learn that they need boyfriends to be complete; they also learn that other girls will always be out to steal their boyfriends. One prominent article on the *Seventeen* site that reinforces competition for boys is entitled "Trauma Rama: he saved the last dance for her." The story tells how a girl's best friend stole her date at a dance. The competition between two girls over a boy is reinforced, and the story implicitly states that even close friends are suspect if there is a boy involved.

The participants in my research have certainly bought into the Beauty Myth to a certain extent. The three participants who were comfortable enough to use ICQ while I was observing them chatted only with boys. When I asked Ginger and Candy how they found people to chat with, Candy replied, "You can type in, like, male." These girls believe that being liked by boys is extremely important, and they use information technologies in their quest for male attention.

The participants in my study were caught up in the messages developed and sustained through the Beauty Myth and the overwhelming pull of consumerism

Resistance—is it futile?

While the participants in this study are clearly affected by the overwhelming cultural messages of beauty and consumerism, spending hours online pursuing what I would describe as stereotypically feminine sites, they may be trying to resist dominant societal messages, particularly in their computer usage. Resisting social pressure is a challenge for anyone, but it is especially difficult for adolescents who, as Klein (2000) points out, are the most heavily targeted market for advertisers. Can teenagers resist? Klein argues that increasingly, individuals are taught to become passive consumers of culture rather than participants: "[T]he underlying message is that culture is something that happens to you. You buy it at the Virgin Megastore or Toys 'R' Us and rent it at Blockbuster Video. It is not something in which you participate or have the right to respond to" (178). The participants showed some signs of resistance. One girl does not go online much, partially because she does not have access at home, but also because she feels that she would rather create programs than waste her time surfing. Another participant said she is careful about where she goes online and what she signs up for because she is aware that the so-called free merchandise requires that she pay the price of her privacy.

In addition, a number of participants take part in the common underground economy that provides young people with music at a cost less than they would normally have to pay. Four participants access music files on Napster, and two have found, through their younger brothers, ways of continuing to access music even beyond Napster's restrictions. While they are not completely resisting the message of consumerism – they still want to access the latest music – they are resisting paying inflated prices for music. There are other ways of sharing music that are more localized than the online Web pages.

It is worth remarking, however, that some of the ways of sharing music which the girls see as forms of resistance may instead represent their buying in to consumerism in the name of individualism. One of the participants shares music within her peer group. When any one of the group buys a new compact disc, she copies it for the rest of the group. The participant said, "One of us will buy a CD and then just make copies for the rest, so we pay her for the CDs and if they have dial-up connection, we pay a little more, so that balances out the cost and we all get to enjoy the same music, though without having to spend a ridiculous amount of money." The girls may think they have more control over their music because they choose the order of the tracks on the disc and make their own "mixed" discs to reflect their own tastes. And they may think they are avoiding paying inflated prices. But they appear to be oblivious to the fact that musicians count on the selling of their music to make their livings.

Five of the eight participants said they watch less television because they are spending more time on the computer. Information technologies give users more control and more choices than passive watching of television, allowing the participants to choose more specific entertainment than television can offer. Amy said, "I don't watch barely any TV now and I did before. Television is boring." Lynne uses information technologies to enhance her television watching. She watches music videos on her computer because she can pick the videos she wants to watch and there is less advertising. Ginger finds that having a computer in her own home has "totally taken over my TV watching time." I wonder, though, if there is reason for concern about the effects of information technologies on attention span if these participants find television uninteresting.

The participants check out *www.seventeen.com* before or instead of going out and buying the magazine. If girls do not find enough material that they are interested in, they simply do not buy the magazine. In addition, they find sites on the Internet that allow them to get the same kind of information that *Seventeen* offers without paying for the magazine. Candy pointed out that she goes to "teen sites teen stuff, where there is, like, stories and stuff." While the *Seventeen* site is clearly intended to encourage girls to buy the magazine, it sometimes has the opposite effect. While they may be astute in knowing how to find the material they seek in other sources, they are not necessarily resisting the commodity that *Seventeen* is selling, female beauty.

Finally, the girls seem quite conscious that the mediation of the technology allows them to try on other personae, bodies, or faces in ICQ or MSN or chatlines. Some of them see this as a form of control or even of resistance to societal messages about what they should look like. They can form community and ask questions even as they create fantasies about themselves. But is their ability to remain unseen, so essential on the one hand to their safety, keeping them from asking more important questions about the commodification of beauty?

Conclusions

Both Beauty Myth messages and consumption messages are prevalent on the Internet. The sites frequented by the participants of my study are laden with advertising and information on beauty, body image, and fashion. The interconnection of consumerism and Beauty Myth reinforcement results in powerful messages aimed at adolescent girls. However, as Roberts (1993) points out, adolescent girls are not one mass market that passively absorbs these messages without question. They are individuals with different values, needs, and desires, and each of them has the potential to take and accept different messages from the advertisements and images. They are, in general, accepting some of the messages of consumerism and ideal beauty, but the fact that they may also be trying to resist some of these seemingly overwhelming messages may be a positive sign now and encouraging for their futures. They are searching online for the narcissistic reasons to which Klein alludes, but they are also searching for a sense of community and forms of communication that will meet their individual and collective needs. Threads of consumerism, and especially advertising, run through this medium of communication, and the sense of community and belonging that adolescents are seeking is used as one more means to sell them products, images, and, most importantly, belief systems. But the current world protests against capitalism and economic globalization, led largely by young people, demonstrate that the capitalistic system that requires mass consumerism in order to function still has a long way to go to ensure that adolescents will simply "buy in," "turn on," and "tune out."

Chapter 6

THE IMPACT OF PALLIATION ON FAMILIAL SPACE:
HOME SPACE FROM THE PERSPECTIVE OF FAMILY
MEMBERS WHO ARE LIVING (AND CARING) FOR
DYING LOVED ONES AT HOME

Allison M. Williams

Introduction

Changes in health care services delivery have encouraged a movement of care from formal spaces such as hospitals and institutions toward more informal and sometimes diffuse settings such as "community" and home. It is increasingly important for geographers to explore the impact, experience, and meaning of these changing geographies of care in order to highlight and understand the effect of particular individuals and places, as well as to help direct changes and trends in health care policy. This is in keeping with Kearns' (1993) observation that there has been neither an adequate analysis of the role of health care, illness, and caregiving in the experience of place, nor sufficient work in health services research that adopts a place-centred theoretical perspective. Given that the changing geographies of care has been a recent phenomenon within contemporary society, little is known about the role of health care, illness, and caregiving in the experience of the home environment, and vice-versa. The home presents a complex and rich site for study, since it not only designates a dwelling but also represents a multitude of meanings (such as personal identity, security, and privacy), which likely vary according to class, ethnicity, and family size, among other socio-demographic variables. This complexity is compounded by the numerous political-economic issues raised by care in the home setting, such as burden of care and the placement of pharmaceutical and equipment costs.

An emerging body of work on the new health geography, which is irrevocably embedded within the larger traditions of social and cultural studies, has begun to develop the necessary epistemological and conceptual tools, such as the concept of therapeutic landscapes, to address such issues as the nexus of place (Kearns and Gesler 1998). Places (broadly termed "landscapes") associated with treatment, healing, and/or care may be called "therapeutic landscapes" (Gesler 1993, 171). Therapeutic landscapes are those changing places, settings, situations, locales, and milieus that encompass the physical, psychological, and social environments associated with treatment or healing; they are reputed to have an enduring reputation for achieving physical, mental, and spiritual healing. Although the literature points to the use of therapeutic landscapes in the healing and recovery of illness, the concept can also be used in the maintenance of health and well-being (Williams and Forbes 2003).

Within a broad critical political economy approach, I have used the concept of therapeutic landscape as a framework to examine the perspectives of family members living and caring for dying loved ones at home. These caregivers are assisted by formal (publicly provided) palliative home care services. In the first year of my multi-year project, I examined one household unit. That examination has provided initial insights into the issues of home-based palliative care.

I begin this chapter by reviewing the reorganization of health care services from institutional environments to the home. I introduce the concept of therapeutic landscape as a framework to explore the impact, experience, and meaning of the changing geographies of care on informal family caregivers. Next, I review the literature that addresses the meaning of "home" to round out the context for my research. Finally, I present the purpose, methods, and results of this first stage of my research. My conclusions highlight how research on home space can allow a better understanding of the impact that care in the home has on particular places and individuals, specifically informal caregivers. Such research can also inform desperately needed changes and trends in health care service policy and eldercare policy (Keating *et al.* 1997, 1999; Williams and Forbes 2003).

Changing geographies of care

In Canada, hospital beds have been reduced in number, and there is increased fiscal pressure for patients in need of care (even if diagnosed with an advanced terminal illness) to be cared for in their own homes until they die. Although the home has been designated as providing a "care system" in contrast to the "cure system" provided in institutional care (Sahlberg-Blom, Ternestedt, and Johansson 2001), advances in technology have allowed what in the past was generally considered in-hospital treatment to now be conducted in the home. The growing number of in-home patients in Canada is also influenced by the rising proportion of elderly people in our population (McWhinney, Bass, and Orr 1995). In addition to its potential for cost reduction, in-home care has the potential to improve patients' quality of life (Lubin 1992; Mercadante *et al.* 1992; Ajemian and Mount 1980). Due to the history of institutionalization of health care in Canada, the provision of home care is a contemporary and novel experience for family members who often become informal caregivers. As Kearns (1997) notes, health care restructuring takes place not only in places but also in the lives of individuals.

The home continues to be stressed by the state as the primary setting for care, where the needs of the patient, seen as a whole person, are met through the promotion of "family-focused care" (Gradine 1995). "Family-focused care" is commonly known for placing more of the responsibility for meeting patients' needs in the hands of informal (unpaid) caregivers within the home environment. One of the main obstacles to in-home care is the absence of a willing and able caregiver (Lubin 1992; McWhinney, Bass, and Orr 1995). The availability of family caregivers able and willing to provide care, together with access to adequate caregiver support, is essential to prevent hospitalization of the person needing the care (McCorkle 1988; Brown, Davies, and Martens 1990). Clearly, there is a critical role to be played by publicly provided home care services. But the provision of public health care in the home is a key policy issue that has yet to be thoroughly examined or addressed in Canada (Keating *et al.* 1997, 1999), particularly for informal caregivers who are not only carrying out their caregiving tasks but also living in the caring home environment even after the deaths of their loved ones.

Although the home is understood to be a therapeutic environment for the palliative patient, whether the home environment is therapeutic to family members who also operate as caregivers has yet to be comprehensively determined.[1] Research suggests that families, like palliative patients, prefer the palliative home environment to the hospital environment (McWhinney, Bass, and Orr 1995; Seamark *et al.* 1995). The home has even been understood as providing an opportunity to minimize the disruption to a family's routine, thereby improving the family's, and specifically children's, adaptation after death (Schater 1992; British Paediatrics Association 1966). Brown, Davies, and Martens (1990) found that both patients and family members preferred palliative care at home to the hospital because the home environment facilitated "being there," normalcy, self-direction, sustenance relationships, and reciprocity. Subjects indicated, however, that these benefits of home care occur only when there is a willing and able caregiver, when the patient is not "too ill," when the physical environment of the home can be adapted to meet the patient's needs, and when public home care services are provided to the extent required.

An emerging body of work on "caregiver burden" or "caregiver distress" has begun to clarify the increased demands on family members in a community-based health care system (Aranda and Knight 1997; Statistics Canada 1997). Research has recognized the multi-dimensionality of a caregiver burden, which suggests that stress and coping models must include numerous variables such as age, gender, socio-economic status, and relationship of the caregiver to the patient. Primary stressors and secondary strains on the caregiver are a result of directly caring for the impaired person and of the "spillover" effects into other domains of the caregiver's life, such as family and work (Aranda and Knight 1997). Little research has been conducted on the burden experienced by caregivers in palliative care situations (Dundgeon and Kristjanson 1995), and the examination of the home environment as it is impacted by the dying process has yet to be examined as one of the variables affecting caregiver burden. In addition to exploring the meaning of "home" across the caregiving process, what also warrants study is whether family members experience a change in their "sense of place" (Relph 1976) or attachment to home throughout both the dying and the bereavement processes. The therapeutic landscape concept provides the framework for examining the impact of palliation on home space.

Therapeutic landscape

Academics, public health practitioners, medical professionals, and the general population are increasingly recognizing the importance of place as a dynamic element in health and healing. Places, together with the health care services that characterize them, are increasingly being seen as contexts for the development and maintenance of the health of populations. Although the important relationship between place and health/healing is increasingly being embraced by social and health scientists, the examination of this relationship is only in its infancy (Kearns 1993). Health/medical geographers are interested in exploring the links among landscape, health, and healing as they move away from viewing place as a physical landscape and toward a relational view in which space is implicated as human activity or vice versa. Meaning is the key to the importance of places, and it is the subjective experiences that people have within places that give them significance. Places not only provide an identity and satisfy a human need for roots, but they are also locations of social networks, providing settings for essential activities such as caregiving and often sought out for their aesthetic qualities (Gessler 1992).

Through adapting theory and field approaches from the wider social sciences, health/medical geographers who have long been interested in place have recently extended their spatial analytic approach, which formerly viewed space as insignificant in character. While being exposed to theoretical positions outside of the traditional realm of positivism (Litva and Eyles 1995; Eyles and Litva 1996; Kearns 1993; Mayer and Meade 1994), health/medical geographers are actively engaging in contemporary social theory and in the new frontiers of cultural geography. Humanist and structuralist theory have been commonly used in exploring the meaning of place; both perspectives seek to identify the subjective view of place experiences. Consequently, health/medical geographers have revealed and enhanced the understanding of both the meaning and nature of place with respect to health and health care (Gesler 1993; Jones and Moon 1993; Kearns 1995; Kearns and Joseph 1993). This "reformed post-medical geography of health" (Kearns 1993) has opened up opportunities for research in the area of therapeutic landscape (Gesler 1992).

Contemporaneous with the shift in the subdisciplinary emphasis from "medical" to "health" concerns (Kearns 1993), health/medical geographers continue to show interest in the socio-ecological model of health (Kearns, Taylor, and Dear 1987; Hayes *et al.* 1990), which involves an interactive set of relationships between people and their social, cultural, and physical environment (White 1981). Implicit in the adoption of a socio-ecological perspective is a redirection of goals from treatment to prevention (Rootman and Munson 1990): elements that constitute a place ultimately have a bearing upon the health of residents, whether patients or family caregivers/members. A positive sense of place is strongly associated with a healing environment because it is "deeply relevant to the basic need for internal cohesion, mental health, a sense of security and direction, and a feeling of relationship with the world around one" (Jackson 1989, 13). Abel and Kearns (1991), together with Williams (1998), discuss home as a therapeutic landscape, where a strong sense of place is maintained, both in the physical environment and interpersonally. Maintaining the health of family caregivers/members in the palliative home environment – where complete physical, social, and mental well-being are (normally) maintained (Lee 1982) – implies a soundness of place identity. Understanding these relations is the first step in developing a healthy home environment, or therapeutic landscape, for family caregivers/members living through the dying and bereavement process.

The literature points to the use of therapeutic landscapes in healing and recovering from illness (Gesler 1992; 1993), but the concept of therapeutic landscape can also be used in the maintenance of health and well-being. If a healthy, definitive fit exists, then the environment is deemed therapeutic because it contributes to well-being:

> Like any other cognitive system, place identity influences what each of us sees, thinks, and feels in our situation-to-situation transactions with the physical world. It serves as cognitive backdrop, or perhaps better said, as a physical environment "data base" against which every physical setting experience can be "experienced" and responded to in some way. Broadly speaking, what is at stake is the well-being of the person. That well-being, in turn, requires not only maintaining and protecting the self-identity of the person but in making adjustments in that identity as the person, and his or her physical and social worlds change slowly over time and more rapidly because of sudden, significant events. (Proshansky, Fabian, and Kaminoff 1983, 66)

The application of the concept of therapeutic landscape follows the recent work about the meaning of place, illustrating a shift away from understanding places in themselves and toward an appreciation of place as a social and cultural category; the ideas of both individuals and collective subjects and of self play important roles in these discussions.

Meaning of "home": A review

Homes are central in the lives of most people. Examining the home as a site of shared symbolic meaning draws upon humanistic ideas that reconstitute landscape (Relph 1976). Home, in its modern conception, is a non-traditional health care setting (Abel and Kearns 1991), where health-promoting properties represent focal centres for unique healing properties and reputations found in, but not out of, place (Kearns 1997). This approach is informed by and draws together a number of strands in the recent work on the relationships between healing spaces (where the focus on place involves an interest in the context of an experienced place) and the broader processes of health care restructuring.

Through personal attachment to place or geography, a person acquires a sense of belonging and purpose that gives meaning to his or her life. This affiliation or identification with place is often experienced as a sense of being "at home," of being comfortable, familiar, and "really me" (Relph 1976; Rowles 1983; Seamon 1979). Without exception, the home is considered to be the "place" of greatest personal significance in one's life, "the central reference point in human existence" (Relph 1976, 20). Because home is usually the foremost place in people's lives, home has received considerable attention (Tuan 1974), but only recently has this attention been in connection with health care (Abel and Kearns 1991). In addition to being a geographical location, home is also the crucial setting through which basic patterns of social relations are constituted and reproduced (Walmsley and Lewis 1993; Werner, Altman, and Oxley 1985; Rubenstein 1990). According to Buttimer (1980), place identity, or the sense of belonging, is a function of degree to which the activities important to a person's life are centred in and around the home. Buttimer implies that a particular balance between "home" and the surrounding geography, or "horizons of reach," is necessary for the maintenance of self-identity and emotional well-being. This sense of "rootedness" or "centredness" is an unself-conscious state. In describing the essence of place, Relph (1976) states that

> the essence of place lies in the largely unself-conscious intentionality that defines places as centres of human existence. There is for virtually everyone a deep association with and consciousness of the places where we were born and grew up, where we now live, or where we have had particularly moving experiences. This association seems to constitute a vital source of both individual and cultural identity and security. (43)

Those environments that bring about a strong, positive sense of place for individuals can also be described as authentic landscapes, just as those associated with placelessness are described as unauthentic (Relph 1976). Meaning, value, and experience are found in those environments that have a strong sense of place. Sense of place defines the identity, significance, meaning, intention, and felt value that are given to places by individuals as a result of experiencing those places over time

(Pred 1983; Relph 1976; Tuan 1976). Through lived experience, moral values and aesthetic judgments are transferred to particular sites that, as a result, acquire a spirit or personality. It is subjective knowledge that gives such places significance, meaning, and felt value for those experiencing them. The field of care (Tuan 1974), or appreciation of such places through non-visual senses – smell, hearing, touch, and taste – is also associated with the unique placefulness given to them. Tuan describes "topophilia" as the affective bond between people and place or setting (1974, 4). Similarly, Relph describes this bond as existential insidedness: "the most fundamental form of insidedness ... in which a place is experienced without deliberate and self-conscious reflection, yet is full of significance" (1976, 55). Cosgrove surmises that "home is perhaps that place where most of us experience true existential insidedness" (1978, 69). Just as some environments have negative connotations, experienced environments that have a strong positive sense of place have a therapeutic effect "on human attitudes and behavior" (Jackson 1989). Gesler (1992) describes landscapes endowed with a strong sense of place as being known only from within over long periods of acquaintance. This knowingness is exemplified in the home, where "networks of interpersonal concern" have existed for an extended period of time (738).

One health application of strong sense of place is psychological rootedness, usually achieved through a longstanding and possibly ongoing relationship with a certain place. Somerville (1997) is one of many psychologists who have explored the role of home in human experience, arguing that home is physically, psychologically, and socially constructed as a place where individual meanings of home, such as privacy or identity or familiarity, can be internally explicated as physical/psychological/social construct (Casey 1993; Doyle 1992; Ahrentzen 1992; Fogel 1992). Home is associated with those environmental features endowed with meaning that are related to one's life course. Implicit in this multi-faceted view of home is the assumption that home allows person–environment transactions that satisfy basic human needs (Lawton 1984). Sixsmith (1986) describes home as an emotional reference point for a sense of self. Rowles (1978) goes so far as to state that the need for home is a fundamental human imperative. Others have referred to the need for community and sense of personal history (Shumaker and Conti 1985), and the need for personal autonomy and ability to effect desired change (Lawton 1984). These needs continue throughout life, despite changes in age or life stage, or even changes in place of residence. Clearly, home has special meanings, meanings that are important to one's feeling of well-being.

Although knowledge of the home as a therapeutic environment for the palliative patient has been well documented, due to the feelings of identity and belonging that the home engenders, the question of whether the home environment maintains its sense of place for the family members as a result of a loved one dying at home has yet to be determined. A number of social scientists have suggested the need for such research, noting that the role of material aspects of housing and of societal and individual forces in the production and reproduction of the meaning of home has been neglected in the literature (Depress 1991; Rubenstein 1990; Somerville 1997).

Purpose of my research

The purpose of my multi-year research program is to examine how the reorganization of health care services specific to palliative care[2] – from institution to home – is reshaping the experience of the familial home environment. By studying the views of family members who are living and caring for dying loved ones at home, assisted by formal (publicly provided) palliative home care services, this research will determine whether or not the home is a therapeutic environment for *family members*.[3] The results of the first year of data collection provide insight into the issues surrounding this phenomenon through the examination of one household unit. Because rural areas have poorer access to formal, publicly provided, in-home palliative care services than urban centres (Williams *et al.* 2001), a comparative rural-urban research design will be employed within the remaining research sample (three rural family units and three urban family units). Through examining family members' perspectives across rural and urban locales, responses to the dying and bereavement process by individuals, households, and locales will be determined.

Method

The two methodological approaches simultaneously employed are a series of semi-structured in-depth interviews and videography.[4] Ethical approval to conduct the research was granted by both the University of Saskatchewan Ethics Committee and Saskatoon District Health. Because the household is the primary unit of analysis, entry into the family household was facilitated by a palliative case manager affiliated with Saskatoon Home Care. Purposive sampling (in which subjects are selected for certain characteristics) was used by case managers to select a household unit defined as being comfortable with the research process.

The household selected was made up of a caregiver daughter and her palliative mother. Given the parameters of the sample frame, where the family home is specified as the setting for fieldwork, data was collected in the thirteen-week time period when the palliative patient was living in the Saskatoon home with the caregiver daughter. Although the methodological objective of my research is to meet with each family member living in the home six times, the caregiver daughter in this case study was interviewed only twice due to the ongoing institutionalization of the palliative patient after being admitted into a long-term care facility (for caregiver respite).[5] In addition, the home was filmed only once, shortly after the first interview, due to the minimal changes evident at the time of the second interview. The first interview took place on November 15, 2000, ten weeks after the palliative patient moved to the Saskatoon home to be with her daughter. The second interview took place one month later, before the palliative patient was transferred from the long-term care facility (for respite) to a hospital palliative care unit.

Each interview took approximately two hours and was audiotaped. The interview schedule used includes questions about residential history, family formation history, household demographics, locational history of the palliative patient, health care services, intra-household adjustments (physical and task changes), social adjustments, community activities, self-assessed health, meaning of home, sense of place/attachment to home, and privacy. Transcribed interviews were analyzed using grounded theory, due to its suitability for research questions that deal with experience over time and change as well as with experiences that have stages/phases (Morse 1994). Grounded theory methodology is conceptually dense. Conceptual relationships, stated as propositions, describe patterns of action and interaction between and among various types of social and environmental units, in addition to describing process, such as reciprocal changes in patterns of actions/interactions over time and place. Preliminary analysis of the two interviews is presented here. The distinguishing features are highlighted.

Results

Locational history and family structure

The family has roots in Battleford, Saskatchewan (approximately a 1.5-hour drive northwest of Saskatoon), where both sides of the family farmed for many years. At the time of her diagnosis with various types of cancer on June 6, 2000, the sixty-seven-year-old palliative patient had been widowed for some time and had been living alone in Battleford. She was a mother of two; both the married son (aged forty) and the single daughter (aged thirty-six) had been involved in the caregiving process. Together with a close friend of the palliative patient, the son played the primary caregiver role until the daughter arrived from overseas (approximately seven weeks after the diagnosis). The daughter had been living and working out of the country for close to five years and consequently was unable to arrive until some time after the diagnosis due to the need to complete her affairs overseas (providing notice to her employer and landlord, etc.). The family decided that the daughter would operate as the primary caregiver, given that the son was a full-time professional and married with eleven-year-old twin boys. The daughter caregiver began working as an aquacize instructor when she moved to Saskatoon, teaching an average of ten hours a week. She also began a master's program at the University of Saskatchewan in September but withdrew early in the term; she decided that due to her caregiving role, she could not meet the time commitment required. The caregiving daughter has FMS (fibromyalgia syndrome) and a weak back, which is treated regularly by a chiropractor.

As illustrated in Table 1 below, the palliative patient was moved many times after being diagnosed. Although numerous reasons were identified, the three main reasons for moving were the following: 1) to access informal care, 2) to access better services, and 3) for caregiver respite. The move from Battleford to Saskatoon (via Dalmeny) was made so that the palliative patient could access the caregiver daughter's doctor and the "overall" higher quality services available. The range of services in Saskatoon include a palliative home care program, a university research hospital (Royal University Hospital), and the only hospital palliative care unit in the city (at St. Paul's Hospital).

The thirteen-week period in the Saskatoon home is when the research took place. Following this, the palliative patient moved to a long-term care facility (for caregiver respite), where she experienced a fall. She was then admitted to Saskatoon's only hospital palliative care unit and subsequently moved to a long-term care home. According to Pattison's (1978) three clinical phases, she was, at the time of the last move, in the "chronic living-dying" phase. The caregiver daughter continued to live in the Saskatoon home together with the palliative patient's cat. She moved out on March 1, 2001.

Table 1: Moves experienced by palliative patient.

MOVE	PLACE	APPROXIMATE AIME
1	Battleford home	3 weeks from diagnosis (June 6, 2000)
2	Battleford Hospital	1 week
3	Dalmeny – son's home	3 weeks
4	Friend's home in Battleford	1 week
5	Battleford home with daughter	1.5 weeks (daughter's home July 28)
6	Saskatoon Hospital (RUH)	3 weeks
7	Saskatoon home (Victoria Place Apts.)	13 weeks (Sept. 1–Dec. 10)
8	Respite care	1 week (Dec. 10–Dec. 16)
9	St. Paul's Palliative care unit	4 weeks (Dec. 16, 2000–Jan. 18, 2001)
10	Saskatoon Convalescent Home	Jan. 18, 2001

Home place

Although the palliative patient was not familiar with Saskatoon, the caregiver daughter knew the city well because she had spent five years completing her undergraduate degree at the University of Saskatchewan. Saskatoon was also closer than Battleford to the palliative patient's son, given that he and his family lived in Dalmeny, a bedroom community approximately fifty kilometres outside of Saskatoon.

Victoria Park Apartments is one of many rental apartment blocks that could have been chosen as the Saskatoon home. When asked why Victoria Park was chosen, the caregiver daughter answered that it had "an elevator and there were mostly old people living there. There is about half to three-quarters that are all retired, old ladies. They have a community room; take Mom for coffee there, they chat. It is very nice." The neighbourhood was also considered in the choice made: "Right by the river, quiet, lots of parks, you can go outside. And Broadway is close and I particularly like the Broadway area, too. So I did it for that, for me being selfish, but the main reasons was the elevator, huge apartment, the view, the cost, and the people in the building."

The advantages of the apartment as home were defined by its being "very quiet, no yard work, self-contained." The negative characteristics included the small kitchen and the doors: "It is hard to push your wheel-chair through them. The doorframes need to be a little bit wider, but other than that it is a great place."

Furnishings and other household items in the one-bedroom apartment were partly owned by the palliative patient and partly by the caregiver daughter. They were what were left of both parties' "cleaning and sorting" processes from each of their previous homes. The caregiver daughter had completed her own sorting before arriving in Canada and had her most treasured belongings shipped from overseas. In the case of the palliative patient, the fifteen years of accumulated belongings in the Battleford house, together with the previous thirty-five years' worth of belongings from the family farmstead, were roughly sorted through with the caregiver daughter's help before her mother moved to Saskatoon. The Battleford house was repainted by friends living in the community and sold. Much of what was in the house was given to the local charitable second-hand stores. The treasured items that were taken to Saskatoon were those that had sentimental value: "Grandmother's dishes.... They are, like, hundreds of years old. Mom's photographs of when she was a child.... It is the old, old things that Mom holds dear, like her collection of rosaries. Those are very important, some Bibles. Those are the important things. The furniture, it doesn't matter, it is unimportant."

The palliative patient's cat, Dempsey, was brought to Saskatoon as well. She had been with the palliative patient for ten years, never leaving her side, even when her owner was sleeping.

Intra-household adjustments (physical environment)

Changes made to the apartment after moving were minimal. In the first interview, the caregiver daughter discussed the bathroom as having experienced the most change. In addition to support bars on either side of the toilet (used together with a hand cane by the patient), a hydraulic bath lift had been installed. In the bedroom, the bed faced the window, providing a view of the river and the sky: "[Mother] likes to see the sunsets and the sunrises. That is very spiritual for her. And for us too, another spiritual one for both of us is looking at the sky. 'You know,' she says, 'if I see the sky, I know God is there. When you see the sky, you know God is happy ... you know, coming from the farm....'"

An electric condenser with twenty-five feet of hose (for mobility) was also in the bedroom for the palliative patient, who slept sitting up due to her condition. As a result of her limited mobility due to paralysis on the left side, she spent most of her waking hours in a wheelchair (with her legs propped up in order to prevent her sliding off the chair). Transfers were made solely by the caregiver daughter.

At the time of the second interview, two additional items of equipment had been brought into the home: a wheelchair tray and a Hoyer lift. The tray made a huge difference for the caregiver daughter, given that the palliative patient spent most of her waking hours in the wheelchair. According to the caregiver daughter, the Hoyer lift had only been used once because it was extremely clumsy: "It is a very cumbersome, clumsy machine used for lifting people. It is not practical in the house.... It takes longer to hook it up and everything than to just pick [Mother] up. If she was a lot heavier okay, but she is heavy but not heavy, sort of, so it was just pick and drag. And so if she has to go to the bathroom, the Hoyer lift ... you know, takes five minutes to set up.... You need a big room to maneuver it into."

At the time of the second interview, the palliative patient was becoming increasingly cognitively impaired and was having difficulty sleeping during the night. As a result, some adjustments had been made to the physical set-up of the home.

> We took the rocking chair out of the living room and put it in the bedroom because sometimes at night Mom would decide, "Well, I am not sleeping anymore, I am going to sit over there." So she would go sit in her rocking chair and sleep in her rocking chair for three hours. You know, so I would sleep in her bed, and then she would know I was there. She just liked to sit in there, too. Just made a huge big area [in the bedroom] for the wheelchair because she would sit in her wheelchair and then she would sit in her chair, back and forth. [We] kind of pushed everything away to make a big space.

Due to the short period of time in the apartment, the caregiver daughter appeared to have little attachment to the Saskatoon home. When asked what her present home meant, she replied, "The apartment is just a building, it is what is inside, this energy inside. You can have a home anywhere, we can be living on the street, but if it doesn't have good energy and happiness, it is not home."

When asked to define good energy, she replied,

I do not like people in the house with negative energy. People coming to visit Mom, if they are going to cry, we just say, excuse me, you have to leave because this is a home of happy energy ... and they have to respect that. If they don't, then they don't come back, and we have had to do that with a few. They just say, "Well, you are not allowing us to grieve." I am, like, "Well, you have to respect the dying person here. She doesn't need this and she doesn't want this. It brings her down, it destroys her energy and it destroys energy in the house."

Maintaining the home as a "sanctuary" for both her mother and herself was a priority for the caregiver daughter. At the time of the first interview, the home represented "comfort, privacy."

Sanctuary is a place where we can go and be whoever we want to be. It is a place where we don't have to change our hats. When I go outside, I have to do this. The fitness instructor has to wear this hat, you know, have to be like this. When I go to my job I have to be this or I have to be that, but in our house, if you want to sit, fine. You want to have coffee, fine. You just want to relax; you can feel like you can sit on the floor, sit on the couch, and just be. We don't have to whisper, she is dying, or oh my God, she has got cancer. We don't say the C word, you know! Sanctuary allows you to be honest with what you are and with what we have.

At the time of the second interview, the meaning of home had not changed for the caregiver daughter: "It is still the same.... It is still where the heart is. Still where the heart is, still where the cat is very important."

What had changed was the degree of tidiness. Because the caregiver daughter was spending a great deal of time with the institutionalized palliative patient, she had not maintained the apartment since her mother had gone to respite care.

Services

Other than the pharmacists, the occupational therapist, and the doctor, who was a general practitioner to both the palliative patient and the caregiver daughter, the caregiver daughter was not at all impressed with any of the services her mother received. While living in the Saskatoon apartment, the palliative patient was seen by a nurse once a week for about one hour. When discussing the home care services, the caregiver daughter noted the lack of continuity, which she suggested was because many of "these people are only working half-time.... With the ... coordinated assessment people. One is only in the afternoons, one is in the mornings. It is so confusing ... it is frustrating."

Although homemaking and personal care services were provided without charges, the caregiver daughter decided to try a paid visit. The daughter found to her disgust that the paid visit was a disaster: "When I got home the cat was in the hallway, the door was wide open. Mom was propped up on the couch. There was a lot of water all over the bathroom and I am just, like, it took me two hours to clean up the mess that she made. I am not doing this. Ten bucks for this? I don't think so.... [Mother] couldn't even reach her water or her pills."

In addition to the cost of the home care visit, the caregiver daughter defined the additional costs of caring for the palliative patient as the following: pharmaceutical costs, chiropractor fees, and the costs associated with the food required by palliative patient's special diet.

Finding a respite bed in the city was difficult. A waiting period of two weeks was required. The day after the palliative patient was admitted to a long-term care facility (for respite care), she had a fall that caused substantial deterioration in her physical and cognitive abilities. The incident caused a great deal of anguish for the caregiver daughter because she felt it could have been prevented. She believed the palliative patient had fallen out of the wheelchair because her feet were not propped up. She was also disappointed that the doctor was not called. As a consequence, the caregiver daughter felt a great deal of mistrust for the facility, and she spent most of her week of respite at the facility: "I was just scandalized. I was just, like, oh my God! How could this be? And nobody will take responsibility [for the fall]. Like, I don't want to sue them, I just – what happened? Was there a lack of communication? I need to know this. So because of this, I thought I would have a week of respite where, no, I had to go every day: three to four hours in the morning and again in the afternoon ... just checking to make sure things were going all right."

Ongoing extended visits by the caregiver daughter continued after the palliative patient moved into the hospital palliative care unit, and again to the long-term care facility. The caregiver daughter describes the health care system as discriminatory against both her mother in its ageism, and herself, as a single woman. Although aware of the caregiver daughter's FMS condition, the hospital staff at the palliative care unit, together with the conditional assessment unit, suggested that the caregiver daughter take the palliative patient home. The caregiver daughter resisted their suggestions: "I said, what am I supposed to do? Tell me ... I bring her home and struggle and basically kill her myself.... I said, I can't do these things. It doesn't matter ... married folks have more power than single people too. If you are married, oh, you have a family, we understand – you can't really take care of Mom with kids in the house.... But if you are single, look out."

Due to previous informal home care experience, the family had come to the decision to keep the palliative patient institutionalized if she became cognitively impaired.

> Mother said too, like she said if anything ever happened to her that she could not reason, she couldn't think, she says don't – because my grandfather [Mother's father] had Alzheimer and I remember her father was seventy-three. I was maybe ten and nobody would take him, so [Mother] had him in our house. It was awful. She says, do not let me get the way my grandfather was.... He couldn't go to the bathroom anymore; he would pull out his catheter all the time and it was just – and so Mom says, "No, no, no. I don't want you to go through that. I don't want you to go through that."

The caregiver daughter's experience with the health care system caused her anger and distress. She spoke to the office of her Member of Parliament and planned on writing a letter to the local paper.

Caregiver role (intra-household tasks)

At the time of the first interview, the task adjustments were identified by the caregiver daughter as minimal. She saw cooking for two as a good thing because it meant she had to prepare nutritious meals. The task of sorting the material possessions brought from Battleford was mentioned numerous times: "We're finding these little treasures now, an old love letter. My grandfather's boat ticket from overseas to come to Canada, those sorts of things.... And things that my mother had packed from when her mother died that she hadn't gone through. Like for thirty years, just kind of packed in a box." The countless boxes seen throughout the house, particularly in the dining/living room and bedroom of the Saskatoon apartment, confirmed the amount of sorting that was planned.

The tasks related to personal care were not discussed as adjustments at the time of the first interview. This may have been due to a number of life experiences that contributed to the daughter's training as a caregiver. In addition to lifeguard training, first aid instruction, and her mother (the palliative patient) having been a nurse, the caregiver daughter had experience working with L'Arche, an intentional community that cares for the physically and mentally challenged. The feeling she had about either being or not being a caregiver – "It is either in you or it isn't" – was reflected in her perspective on her caregiving role at that time:

> Mom and I were chatting and she said, "Do you want to be here?" … She said, if you don't want to be here then go because I don't want to be a burden to you. That is a very important question. Do you want to be the caregiver? Because if I didn't then there would be this constant friction and that just destroys everything. It destroys the environment…. There is no question: *I do want to be there because there is no one who could take care of my mother like me, there is nobody*. Nobody knows my mom as well as I do – her little quirks, the little things…. The quality of life in the last few months, that is a form of respect. The idea is dying with dignity, and if you are continually being bombarded with new people, there is no healing energy, there is no saving grace from God because you are continually trying to change to meet … other caregivers' expectations. …
>
> You need to have this quality and I know I can give it to Mom, at least the consistency…. That is the thing, so we decided she is going to die living. You know, every day is going to be a new day, a fun day, a laughing day. Every time, before she goes to bed, I say, "Did you have a good day? What did you like, what didn't you like?" And we talk about that so that in the morning we start fresh. The thing is never go to bed angry.

At the time of second interview, the caregiver daughter was clearly suffering from burnout as a result of the increasing demands on her. When asked how she was feeling, she replied, "Caregiver. It has been the Stephanie role, the Stephanie role is just empty. Like I am just totally exhausted – mentally, physically, spiritually ... threw out my back, my sacroiliac joint; my second vertebra in my neck goes out all the time. Severe tendonitis in my hips, from lifting. No sleep, fibromyalgia flare-ups, hell. You know, severe headaches. Headaches, headaches, head-aches...."

Her degree of fatigue was due to various factors related to the palliative patient, coupled with her own ill health and the lack of good quality respite care.

> I needed a break and Mom needed a break.... About three weeks before needing respite, we were looking at it. Mom never slept in the evening really. She would get up every hour and a half, two hours; all reaction to her tumours. I was getting really tired. It was just getting more difficult and I noticed there was a bedsore forming as well.... Mom and I were both getting on each other's nerves. It was driving me crazy. A lot of stress ... because you are not sleeping. Mom would get up, she would yell ... I would go in ... oh, nothing. It is from medication and her tumour, she was sort of like talking in her sleep, and she really wasn't aware of where she was. It was, like, an Alzheimer type of thing. So that was getting really, really frustrating and then just her general weakness was getting very debilitating for me to do all those transfers and stuff.... I was getting really crabby, really crabby.

The decision to get respite was made with the help of the caregiver daughter's general practitioner, who also decided that the palliative patient would not be going home after the accident that took place while in respite. The caregiver daughter understood the decision in the context of her own limitations.

> I understand my limitations ... I know that if Mom was here [in the home] I couldn't lift her up. I can't roll her anymore.... Like, by knowing my limitations, I am also taking a lot of respect for my Mom too. What is comfortable for her in her last weeks.... Do I want her to be at home and just be pulled and dragged and pushed and shoved into things, or would I rather have her lifted by two people, rolled by two people, rolled properly, having the right medications, this and that?

The most difficult part of the whole caregiving experience was the caregiver daughter's lack of knowing what would come next. This was discussed at both the first and second interview:

> Like, I know what the future will bring, but I don't know what it will bring in two hours from now. I know the end result will be death, and that is cool – I can handle that, but it is between now and then is what I can't control. (Interview 1)
>
> You can see the end and you want the end to come but you don't want it to come. Sort of trapped like ... it can go this way, it can go that way.... Sort of, like, you want the end to finish but you don't want it to finish. (Interview 2)

This "lack of knowing" was a source of great stress because the caregiver daughter defined herself as a person who needs a good deal of control in life: "I have no personal control. I don't like that.... I am not spontaneous anymore. I don't like that at all. Big stress." When the caregiver daughter left for a two-week holiday, stating that the lack of control was making her crazy, the palliative patient's son agreed to take a more active caregiving role.

Conclusions

This research has provided an elementary understanding of the impact of palliation on familial space. The data collected illustrate that the structural and social aspects of the home environment do impact on the caregiving experience. The increased medicalization (in the form of equipment) of the home environment assisted the caregiver daughter somewhat in her role, while the conscious definition of the parameters of acceptable social behaviour in the case of visitors maintained the health of the social environment. At the same time, an unhealthy intra-family social environment evolved due to the increased cognitive impairment of the palliative patient. This resulted in sleep deprivation and fatigue on the part of the caregiver daughter, diminishing her ability to cope, and created tension in the caring relationship within that home.

This case study confirms the need for access to adequate caregiver support if family caregivers are able and willing to provide care at home (McCorkle 1988; Brown, Davies, and Martens 1990). The caregiver burnout experienced by the daughter in this research illustrates the need for more home care services of better quality. Better quality auxiliary care would recognize the importance of both continuity and better training for the personal care provided. The research also recognizes the shortcomings of the long-term care system as a whole, evidenced by the minimal respite services and questionable quality care in long-term facilities.

While this research contributes to the continuing development of the "new" health geography, specifically the concept of therapeutic landscape, it also informs the ongoing debates in the human and social sciences on the meanings of space and place. In addition, this work provides a contribution to the analysis of the role of health care in contributing to the experience of place, and vice versa (Kearns 1993), while furthering knowledge about the minimally researched area of in-home care and adding to the growing literature on the caregiver burden. I hope that this work in its completed form will also be of potential practical importance for furthering our understanding of the ways in which households, however geographically differentiated, deal with the in-home caring and bereavement process, a phenomenon that is increasingly common in these times of health care restructuring. Informal (unpaid) and formal (paid) caregivers alike will then be better able to work toward adjusting the home environment in a sensitive manner, making it a therapeutic environment for all familial members sharing the household with their loved ones. For example, by better understanding how the physical environment can be best manipulated, family caregivers will be less overburdened in sharing the living environment with their dying loved ones.

Simultaneously, research results can potentially contribute to eldercare policy through identifying environmental factors that influence family/caregiver discomfort. Factors contributing to psychological or physical burnout for family caregivers need to be identified and effectively dealt with (Paquet 1995). Wells and Dendig (1996) have determined that poor caregiver health is a factor in the loss of the caregiver's capacity to care. Governments at all levels have recognized that one of the challenges in implementing a community-based care model is the pressure that care in the home can sometimes place on family members or other informal caregivers (Ontario Gerontology Association 1997; Coutts 1997; Niagara District Health Council 1997). Finally, although the patients and their family caregivers have been, and will likely continue to be, the focus of the study in home environments, a third group needing to be examined are formal health care providers.

NOTES

1 In the case of palliative care, the mandate includes meeting the physical, psychological, and spiritual concerns of both the patient *and family* (Canadian Palliative Care Association 1996; Dundgeon and Kristjanson 1995).

2 Palliative care is understood to mean the management of patients whose prognosis is limited and for whom the focus of care is quality of life.

3 Family members include people who perceive themselves as having an enduring commitment and set of mutual obligations to one another; the term does not necessarily imply a blood or legal relationship.

4 Although the death trajectory (Glasser and Strauss 1967) defines the length of time over which the dying process takes place, Pattison's (1978) three clinical phases (*acute crisis phase, chronic living-dying phase*, and *terminal phase*) define three of the six interview times planned with each family member. The last three of the series of six interviews for this particular case study took place during the bereavement period, more specifically at the *avoidance phase, the confrontation phase*, and *the accommodation phase* (Rando 1995).

5 In both cases, the palliative patient was diagnosed to be in Pattison's (1978) *chronic living-dying phase*.

Chapter 7

SPINNING YARNS OF WOMEN'S ACTIVISM IN SUPPORT OF INDUSTRIAL FORESTRY ON CANADA'S WEST COAST

Maureen G. Reed

Introduction

With this title, I try to relay two signals. First, I align myself with long-standing feminist scholarship that has used tapestry and weaving metaphors to denote the colour, texture, variety, and richness of women's lives (Aptheker 1989; Diamond and Orenstein 1990). Second, I intend to "spin yarns" in the vernacular sense of telling a complex story. In this latter context, I consider how best to retell and relay stories of rural women in communities on Canada's west coast who support industrial forestry.

I have structured the chapter as follows. First, I provide background to the study and personal profiles of three (of fifty) research subjects who exemplify contradictions of purpose, perspective, and action in relation to forestry and land-use practices. These stories provide a stark, yet rich, backdrop for the theoretical discussion I advance. Second, I examine possible ways to interpret these stories by considering feminist scholarship in ecofeminism and labour studies. Third, I outline my own framework of social marginalization, which I use to analyze women's stories. Finally, I question this framework and examine the possibility of new stories and actions using the concept of embeddedness.

I recently completed a study set in temperate rainforest communities of British Columbia's west coast. Here, challenges to environmental sustainability are derived from economic restructuring of the forest industry, ecological change and increasing public demands for environmental protection, and changes in relations with First Nations. The 1990s marked several changes in the allocation of land use and the regulation of forestry practices that reduced lands available for harvest and altered requirements for forest management. Many women living in these communities continue to actively support the forest industry, its workers, and general community viability. Yet while much attention has been given to women's pro-environment positions (*e.g.*, Shiva 1989; Mies 1986; Seager 1993; Berman *et al*. 1994; Boucher 1998; Sturgeon 1997), women who support industrial forestry have received far less attention (but see Switzer 1996). In this study, I combined policy analysis with an interactive research methodology involving depth and peer interviews (with fifty women), a focus group (with twelve additional women), interpretive workshops, and community feedback sessions (Reed 2000). To relay some of the threads of these women's lives, let me begin by telling three stories.

Tales of women

"Betty" is forty-four years old.[1] She has lived in northern Vancouver Island for five years but spent several years in other logging communities. Her partner is a professional forester; they have three teenage children. Betty describes herself as a housewife and mom, and she is perhaps the classical stereotype of the logger's wife. Trained as a registered nurse, she has followed her husband's[2] career through small logging camps, back to Vancouver, and then to the Island, where he holds a senior position with a major company. She quit working early because "there was nowhere to nurse." At the time of the interview, she was the chair of the parent advisory committee for both the school and the district. And, she reports, "I've always been a member of Canadian Women in Timber" (cwit).

cwit is a pro-industry group that supports fairly traditional interpretations of appropriate roles for women in forestry and family settings. Groups in British Columbia formed after similar chapters of the American-based organization Women in Timber warned of the social dislocations that women experienced in the logging communities of the American Pacific Northwest. cwit does not challenge gender relations in the home or in society, but was rather born out of a desire to protect those traditional norms and the places that practice them. Its activities also reflect a conventional separation of education and politics. Long-term members of the group consistently classify their activities as educational, not political. These activities focus on providing leaflets in booths at trade fairs, letter-writing, and speaking in elementary schools about "the working forest" (*i.e.*, where harvesting takes place).[3] When asked what sparked her involvement, Betty says, "I've always been interested in forestry and logging because that was my husband's job. So, I don't know. You just sort of slide into things, I guess. Family. I would say family involvement. Things that touch your family."

Betty is in a financially secure situation. Her husband has a salaried position with enough seniority so that they would simply move if the need arose. They live out the "traditional" family life.[4] Betty has been active in a range of activities for her children, ferrying them from skating to swimming lessons, involved with the parents' committee, and so on. Recently, her activism has turned toward issues other than forestry. In her work, she says, "I think my energies have been [going] into other directions instead. So that you start frothing at the mouth at the education and the health ministers instead." In a traditional configuration of appropriate activism for women, then, forestry work is one part of the building of community, in which education, health, and other commitments are also constituent.

"Donna" lives in the same town as Betty, but in a different community. She is forty-two years old, with a daughter in her twenties. Since 1972, she has had two relationships with loggers. She has held several low-paying full-time jobs in different businesses in the past several years. She has made her current relationship and household dynamics the site of activism in addition to her more "public" work.

Donna gives a very long and detailed picture of the history of logging in the north Island. She discusses the huge profits and waste of the early years, as well as the fact that the old growth is declining and that logging companies are only grudgingly changing their practices. She talks at length about the fears and concerns that loggers have for their jobs, their health, and their local environments. Her partner has a grade 10 education. He sits on the environmental committee within his company. She says that the loggers support or initiate most environmental practices and are concerned that loggers have increasingly been forced by their companies into adversarial positions with environmental activists. Yet she is also sickened by the evidence of stark "redneck" anti-environmental attitudes in some individuals: she shudders as she recalls the "bugger a hugger" T-shirts some people wear. However, she does have compassion for loggers. She discusses the generational expectation placed on male youths to "go to work in the woods like a man," corroborating sociological studies showing that gender and class are learned in institutions of community and family (Dunk 1991; Carroll 1995). She also speaks of the loss of a social contract between company and worker – the bosses are now accountants and do not look out for their men. Consequently, she believes that loggers work under increasingly dangerous and stressful conditions, with few options or incentives for retraining. She talks of men who have tried training options outside of the forest industry but have returned to logging for the money.

Despite living most of her adult life within the culture of forestry, Donna describes that culture as profoundly negative for women. She provides many examples: drugs, alcohol, physical and emotional abuse, and sexism and inequality, both within the household and in public spheres. In confronting some of these issues publicly, she has feared for her personal safety. However, she believes that communication – both literacy and public speaking – are important elements of empowerment; for this reason, she has established a writing club for women, believing that women will become empowered if they tell their own stories. In addition, she became a member of North Island Women, a very active organization dedicated to promoting education and training for women in the North Island region. Her interests also lie in promoting women's entrepreneurship as a means out of financial dependence.

Donna states that women's traditional roles at home have been re-inforced by economic practices that keep men working long hours and by community services that shut down early. For example, men's shift work schedules make it impossible for them to be able to share equally in child care, home maintenance, and financial arrangements. For the past couple of years, she has, in her own words, "gone on strike" from being errand-runner and housekeeper, refusing to continue to be the "wife-secretary-support worker-mother" for her partner. As a further act of defiance, and to her financial loss, she has separated her bank account from her partner's and lives with her daughter in Nanaimo for part of the year. She credits her ability to remain in a relationship with her partner to her decision to live apart.

Donna is someone whose allegiances conflict. She supports her partner, a logger, on a personal level, although with increasing hesitation. Much of her activism has taken place in the "private" domain of the household and the restructuring of familial relationships. She sees workers caught between expectations handed down over generations and new realities, so that the culture of forestry no longer serves male workers particularly well. But if the culture of forestry is not always positive for men, it has been profoundly negative for her. After working against sexist, racist, and violent attitudes that she has experienced toward women and environmentalists alike, she has realized that she can stay no longer in the community.

"Ferron" is thirty-seven years old and has lived in the North Island region for seven years. For the most part, she is an "outsider." She was university-educated in Vancouver, as was her husband, who is a professional forester. She bucks the (social) community norm of early parenthood, with two preschool children. She is committed to breastfeeding her children for periods longer than most women do. In outlining her daily tasks, she allocates three to four hours a day to breastfeeding her nine-month-old son. Seeing that I am pregnant, she engages me in a discussion of the benefits of natural childbirth and herbal teas suitable to prepare me for the birth.

Ferron is a strong, unambiguous supporter of the forest companies. Articulate, outspoken, and committed, she has become a community spokesperson. But it is not motherhood, family, or community values that motivate and support her attachment to forestry. She comes to this position as a registered professional forester with several years of work experience. Her training comes from a school and a time period in which the "scientific expertise" of professional foresters was largely unchallenged. Her attachments come from professional training, work experiences, and the abilities and knowledge she brings to local issues. Her targets are external to the community, as she puts together public education programs through Knowledge Network[5] and undertakes countless media interviews.

While she has adopted unequivocally the practices and vision of professional forestry, she speaks candidly of the sexism within the forestry profession. She believes that as a woman, her prospects for promotion were exhausted before she quit. Nonetheless, she has been active across a range of activities that promote the interests of forestry and forest-dependent communities. She is frustrated that companies must now engage in "political" forestry as opposed to "scientific" forestry, and she argues that the blanket requirements of new forestry regulations do not fit local ecological conditions. She speaks of the increased stress on professional foresters, of the fear of new legal sanctions if they make mistakes, of the increased paperwork, and of the decreased ability to undertake proper field analysis. She notes the irony of foresters who were attracted to the profession by their desire to work outdoors but are now stuck in their offices completing ever-proliferating government forms. She has worked hard in mentoring and public education, and describes with pride how community members have seen her as a spokesperson for their interests despite her relatively short residency on the North Island. On this basis, she was asked to be a speaker at a protest rally held on the steps of the

British Columbia provincial legislature in March 1994, to which fifteen thousand forestry supporters came. At that time, she was six months pregnant with her first child. Who would have thought she wasn't "just" another logger's wife?

Beyond these three women, many others who were interviewed had appeared on protest lines at Clayoquot Sound or other places on the island. Yet their support was not a blind and unstinting one. Some women who were involved in protest activities expressed to me acts of violence and oppression in their home lives that they attribute, in large part, to "a forestry lifestyle." They opposed these acts on the domestic front by leaving the abusive relationships and supporting other women who faced similar circumstances. Yet they continue to serve on local committees that support conventional forestry practices and workers. Other women support loggers and foresters with whom they have loving relationships, while simultaneously engaging in individual and collective acts that challenge local forestry culture. Some women undertake letter-writing campaigns (both for and against environmental activism); they engage in stream rehabilitation; they attend pro-logging rallies; they aid displaced forestry workers. My troubles begin when I try to "fit" these women into an appropriate theoretical framework to explain their situations.

A fitting framework? Telling tales of forestry-town women

Feminist scholars have been appropriately preoccupied with studying marginalized women. This preoccupation with marginality stems from a genuine and appropriate desire to engage and support people in understanding and overcoming unjust social relations. In my digging, I found that marginality is sometimes attributed to groups that are racially or ethnically marked (Collins 1990; Seitz 1995). In labour studies research that focusses on women in resource towns, marginality is attributed to women because of the class positioning through their partners' labour, their geographic and social isolation, their lack of job opportunities, and so on (Egan and Klausen 1998; Gibson 1992; Hall 1986; Marchak 1983; Maggard 1990; National Film Board 1979). In ecofeminist writings, women as a whole have tended to be considered marginal. The critique of "difference" that has been writ large within feminist scholarship in other contexts has only begun to emerge in environmental writing. In both types of research, women who are politically active are seen to mobilize around practical-domestic concerns that affect safety, security, and welfare of family and community, focussing on specific issues such as public health, education, morality, and community environment (West and Blumberg 1990; Garcia-Guadila 1995). I call this "social mothering," wherein women's traditional Western role in the family and home is extended to notions of community care and management.

From these roots of community management, two stories can be told. The first is an ecofeminist story of women's roles in environmental protection; the second is a labour studies story that tells of women's roles in protecting social class and community culture. Both labour studies work and ecofeminist work first identify women's marginality from mainstream society. They describe women in rural communities as dependent, conservative, materialistic, regressive, and/or exhibiting politics borne of their positions as victims of exploitation within systemic power relations (*e.g.*, Hall 1986; Boucher 1994; Gibson-Graham 1994).[6] Traditional forms of femininity and community care dominate; women overcome these traditional roles when they become politically active. Politics is viewed through public acts of protest. In environmental protests, if women are connected to their communities, they will act in favour of environmental protection (Seager 1993; Liepins 1998). Labour studies interpretations do not anticipate that politically active women will necessarily demonstrate to protect the natural environment (Sachs 1994). Instead, women overcome their "traditional roles through public acts in which they 'stand by their men'" (*e.g.*, Hall 1986). Labour studies scholars maintain a rather rigid interpretation of gender identity and class positioning that has generally been read from the assumed socio-economic positioning of the male partners, which has usually been viewed as working-class.[7] In short, neither ecofeminism nor labour studies theories have accounted for the multiple layering that shapes women's lives or the multiple forms or sites of women's political activism. Instead, they have reduced the scope of visible activities and perspectives associated with women's activism. My efforts have focussed on conceptualizing and illustrating social marginalization.

A tale of social marginalization?

Since World War II, Canadian forestry workers and families have enjoyed high wages, good benefits, and access to a publicly supported social safety net that includes employment insurance, universal health care, and old-age pensions. Notwithstanding many axes of difference within communities, many of the women within forestry communities are clearly not marginal in the conventional sense. Nonetheless, I do consider them to be socially marginal. Drawing on work of political theorists and geographers, I define social marginalization as the inability to exercise both the formal and substantive rights of citizenship in civil society (Prior, Stewart, and Walsh 1995), as well as exclusion from centres of decision-making and popular values. As environmentalism has emerged as a dominant or core value in land-use debates on the Canadian west coast, women living in rural regions are located at the margins of social and political discourse that surround policy-makers, activists, and scholars dealing with contemporary environmentalism.

My framework is heavily influenced by the work of Iris Marion Young (1990) and others (Pulido 1996; Proctor 1995, 1999; Sibley 1998; Fraser 1997; Kobayashi and Ray 2000).[8] I have identified four facets of social marginalization: exploitation, social exclusion, powerlessness, and moral exclusion.

Exploitation includes the appropriation of the labour of one group to the benefit of another. For my study, I considered exploitation in terms of women's labour in the paid workplace and in unpaid activities in the household and community organizations. It is easy to illustrate how the "work" of forestry and forestry communities has been attributed to male workers in primary resource sectors, exploiting women by using their labour without adequate acknowledgment of their importance. Both Donna and Betty illustrate this empirically, although Betty likely would not agree with this interpretation (see also Reed 2001).

Beyond exploitation, I considered the *social exclusion* of certain people from useful participation in society: for example, the elderly, disabled, or unemployed. It remains a fact of these forestry communities that opportunities for full-time, secure, (well-)paid work for women are more limited than for men. Hence, I examined the restructuring of forestry policy and social services in the North Island region. As in other parts of the country, women are more likely to use social services and less likely to qualify for employment insurance. Women face multiple barriers to training programs, from structural hurdles (*e.g.*, only those who are insurance recipients are eligible) to logistical ones (*e.g.*, the lack of adequate and affordable child care). Women are also more likely than men to be delivery agents and clients of social services. The restructuring of social services in British Columbia throughout the 1990s was particularly burdensome for residents of rural areas. Women in these places felt the brunt of these changes – both as clients and as service providers – by virtue of their social and geographic locations.

Powerlessness refers to the lack of respect accorded to groups other than professional workers. The powerless often have little or no work autonomy; have little opportunity to exercise little creativity or judgment in their work; often have no technical expertise or authority; may express themselves awkwardly, especially in public or bureaucratic settings; and are not accorded respect. By contrast, professionals have often had the opportunity for progressive development of their personal capacities, are awarded greater decision-making authority and greater respectability in society.

Powerlessness may be identified in relation to divisions of labour in workplace settings, the ways in which decisions about environmental policy are made, and how outstanding issues and protest events are orchestrated and reported, both locally and beyond. Women living and working in forestry communities have little control over how they are perceived by bureaucrats or the public within and outside their communities (see Reed 1997, 2000).

Last, I tackled the issue of *moral exclusion*. Moral exclusion takes place when the views and experiences of some groups become stereotyped and used to construct them as "other." This construction then serves to exclude these groups through processes that consider the experiences and culture of the dominant group as the norm or standard against which others are judged. In the battle of woods and words, both environmental organizations and rural residents have been complicit in stereotyping and marking the "other" in their battle for moral high ground. But at present, the tide is turning to favour environmental organizations. On B.C.'s coast, environmental organizations are far more successful in generating public support among urban, professional, middle-class citizens than are those from rural communities, whose voices are heard as "whines" from a geographic, political, and cultural periphery (Prudham and Reed 2001).

In this framework, social marginalization works in many ways. It is a multi-faceted concept that does not require conscious and intentional oppression of one group by another. Rather, social marginalization can take place as a consequence of institutional, structural, and cultural features of well-intentioned liberal democratic society. Furthermore, while I suggest that multiple elements may be at work, I do not suggest that they operate evenly within or across landscapes. Some women in this study were decidedly more privileged than others. But beyond these observations, I have become concerned about using the discourse of marginalization at all. I raise two questions.

In this chapter and elsewhere, I have been critical of the collective studies of women's activism from labour studies and ecofeminism because they have created a dualistic perspective on women's motives and activities, where sometimes these motives and activities are valorized (*i.e.*, in labour studies) while elsewhere they are ignored (*i.e.*, in ecofeminism). In developing this framework of social marginalization, I wonder if I feed the preoccupation with marginality that has reinforced the dualism of pro- versus anti-environmentalism.

I also bear the burden of criticisms contained in gender/development studies where "women in development" represent women uniformly as victims, unable to overcome their disadvantage except with outside assistance (*e.g.*, Braidotti *et al.* 1995; Chowdhry 1995; Parpart 1995; Marchand and Parpart 1995). Victimization discourses that are focussed on individual and liberal solutions have promoted minor corrections to existing practices rather than necessary changes to underlying social structures. In this context, I wonder if a focus on social marginalization operates similarly by using the discourse of marginalization to re-inscribe, if unintentionally, familiar stories and solutions.

Embeddedness and other stories

How, then, might I conceptualize the perspectives and activism of women in forestry towns? Here, I offer the concept of embeddedness to describe political activism. Embeddedness refers to a sense of rootedness of place and social life – in one sense, a growing up together of space and place. Hanson and Pratt (1995, 18) suggest that "gendered identities, including aspirations and desires, are fully embedded in – and indeed inconceivable apart from – place, and different gender identities are shaped through different places." I suggest that women's activism is embedded within local, social, and spatial contexts. In my case, details relate to local effects of restructuring of the forest industry, changing ecologies, affirmation of the rights of First Nations, reorganization of government environmental and social policies, the availability of physical and social infrastructure, local labour practices, and community social norms. These factors inscribe women's identities and shape their motivations for, and choices about, forestry and political activism. When these elements of women's lives are explicitly documented, women's support of workers, forestry practices, and forestry culture is not unified, conservative, progressive, or crassly material. Rather, women's activism, both individual and collective, is heterogeneous and contingent, complex, contradictory, and embedded.

I have argued for the need to move away from simple dichotomies and away from our desire to explain women's activism in simple terms of social mothering and community management. These kinds of explanations reinforce rather static perceptions about forestry-town women as well as preconceptions about what characteristics constitute progressive and conservative politics. Embeddedness can help explain multiple motivations, perspectives, and activisms of forestry-town women and avoids classifying activities into static dichotomies of "pro" versus "anti" environmental actions. This is critically important as a means to generate a dialogue between people (including researchers) who frequently stand on opposite sides of high-profile public policy debates. Embeddedness also tempers a potential tendency to overdetermine women's victimization or agency in undertaking particular actions. Women's identities and activist agendas are continually open to choices but are also shaped by how partners, co-workers, community members, policy-makers, academics, and/or other women delimit and constrain them. Women's identities and activist strategies may also be "dealt" them within the confines of households, workplaces, communities, policy debates (such as environmentalism), and research agendas (Reed 2000).

The notion of embeddedness also serves another important priority of feminist research. Embeddedness may help to maintain an engaged and sympathetic understanding of the complex and contradictory nature of women's lives that is encouraged by feminist research methods (Reinharz 1992; Moss *et al.* 1993; England 1994). As feminists, we need to listen for the differences, despite the potential for significant ideological disagreement. The concept of embeddedness allows for a sympathetic portrayal of women's lives, suspending judgment about the substance of political debate. In effect, it avoids re-inscribing exclusions that feminists have worked so hard to dismantle.

Acknowledgments

This project was funded by Forest Renewal B.C. I would like to thank my research assistants, Maija Heimo, Janice May, and Mary Pullen. In addition, I received technical support from Paul Jance (University of British Columbia) and Keith Bigelow and Elise Pietroniro (University of Saskatchewan). I am also grateful to the Women's Studies Research Unit for sponsoring the conference "The Lived Environments of Girls and Women" (July 2001), in which this paper was presented, as well as for supporting its publication in print form. And, of course, the research could not have been done without the candour and concern of the research participants. Finally, I appreciate my family, including Bruce, Louis, and Michael, as always, for the time, space, and creative outlets they provide. All errors and omissions are my own.

NOTES

1 All names have been changed.
2 I have alternated the terminology of "husband" and "partner" to respect the terms used by women interviewed.
3 I am not defending the substance or procedures of these activities. The interpretation of sustainability and the determination of appropriate political activities by CWIT would probably be contested by environmental groups that advance very different notions of community, forestry, and sustainability.
4 Gibson-Graham (1994) considers whether or not "traditional" denotes longstanding and prevalent gender roles or ones that are relatively recently instituted or locally naturalized as hegemonic. Here, however, I use term "traditional" to denote the concepts described in the text.
5 Knowledge Network is a non-profit organization dedicated to "distributed learning." In addition to other ventures, it provides public education programs that are available on cable television.
6 Ironically, the act of labelling itself has marginalized these women (at least within eco-feminist depictions), making them ripe subjects for a new generation of feminist research agendas such as my own.
7 Current analyses of class by feminist scholars now attempt to disrupt these categories (Sachs 1997; Gibson-Graham 1994).
8 My framework draws liberally from, and adapts extensively, Young's (1990) five faces of oppression. After careful consideration, I chose the term "social marginalization" to refer to Young's concept of "oppression." Young uses "marginalization" to describe one "face" that I call "social exclusion." I use her ideas with gratitude and apologies for errors of interpretation that this adaptation may demonstrate.

Part 3

HABITATS *for/of* HUMANITY

Chapter 8

CRAFTING SELVES: THE IMPACT OF IDENTITY ON
INTERCULTURAL FRIENDSHIPS AMONG WOMEN

Kim Morrison

Introduction

Friendships among women are complex relationships embodying many dimensions and affecting identities and lived experience in many ways. The women of Intercultural Grandmothers Uniting (IGU) come together in friendship, building bridges across race and generation. Their group mandate includes identity descriptors such as "Grandmother," "older," "First Nations," "Metis," "other," "Canadian," and "women." These terms relate to issues of age, race, culture, nationality, parenthood, and gender and clearly ground the grandmothers in identity-based standpoints. While the list of descriptors and the use of self-definitions creates the appearance of discreet identity units, traits claimed as identity-defining are complexly interwoven into the individual women's lives.

Historical context

Intercultural Grandmothers Uniting (IGU) is a network of Saskatchewan First Nations, Metis, and other Canadian older women. IGU has focussed its efforts on the Treaty 4 area, with activities centred near Fort Qu'Appelle, which was the site of the treaty signing. Treaty 4 was signed October 13, 1874 with the Cree and Saulteaux, and the land affected by that treaty extends from just east of what is now the Saskatchewan/Manitoba border to just west of what is now the Saskatchewan/Alberta border in southern Saskatchewan; it includes the city of Regina and several other cities and towns.

Intercultural relationships in Saskatchewan have a complex history, and I sketch out only the contours of that history here. In *Skyscrapers Hide the Heavens* (1989), Jim Miller describes early relationships between Europeans and First Nations as co-operative, but by the nineteenth century, European settlers were taking more and more of the resources and began viewing the First Nations as an impediment to expansion (268–73). In order to facilitate expansion, the British Crown entered into treaties with First Nations, providing them with treaty rights in exchange for the use of the land that aboriginal peoples had traditionally occupied.

While harmonious intercultural relationships were presented as an integral part of the treaty's purpose, these objectives have not been consistently realized because racism has marked intercultural encounters since early contact. Increasing pressure as a result of growth in European settlement overshadowed the importance of intercultural harmony. The need for more land for settlers led to a "coercive policy of land acquisition and directed cultural change" (Miller 1989, 273–74), including the use of forced residential schooling for First Nations children. Indeed, Constance Deiter (1999) has found that the Canadian government's assimilation efforts caused, among other things, a loss of parenting skills, identity and self-esteem, as well as the "vilification of [First Nations] culture and language" that has lasted many generations (78–79). The women participating in my study of intercultural grandmothers repeatedly used the word "segregation" to describe how disparity in social power manifests itself in the daily lives of Saskatchewan residents.

Segregation, along with other social factors, makes choosing intercultural friendships difficult. For Paula Gunn Allen, a history of mistreatment by settlers meant that generations of Aboriginals have been "reared in an Anglophobic world that views white society with fear and hostility," and that today they feel "fear of and bitterness towards whites" (1986, 224). This fear can keep First Nations individuals from associating with Euro-Canadian people as much as possible. However, First Nations are forced to interact with dominant social institutions and therefore have to develop skills that allow them to navigate in this hostile cultural territory. The choices about where, how, and even whether to "build bridges" and to challenge segregation differ for the dominant Euro-Canadian and for marginalized Aboriginals. For example, all First Nations grandmothers in my study have had experience with the European culture and have endured some form of forced acculturation in their schooling, while most of the Euro-Canadian grandmothers had no exposure to Aboriginal cultures prior to their involvement with IGU.

My exposure to interracial and intercultural relationships while growing up in Saskatchewan has certainly increased my research interest in intercultural friendships. I was born and raised in North Battleford, a small city in northwest Saskatchewan with historical significance to Euro-Canadian and First Nations relationships. In the words of the grandmothers, I am an "other Canadian woman." The grandmothers seemed to be most interested in the fact that I am of German and Dutch descent, that I am a parent, and that I grew up in predominantly Euro-Canadian working- and middle-class neighbourhoods.

While generalizations are difficult to make, it is fair to say that Euro-Canadians do not like to think of themselves as racist. In fact, denial of racism has been put forward by Sherene Razack as an integral part of white Canadian identity (1998, 11). However, a review of Canadian history by Constance Backhouse (1999) shows that racism is indeed a fact of life here. The legacy of systematic and legalized racism is evident in Saskatchewan today, resulting in schisms that, at times, seem too great to bridge. Yet bridging them is of increasing importance, given changing demographics in Saskatchewan and Canada and the need for justice and equality. Aboriginal populations in Canada are expected to grow rapidly (Canada n.d.), with the "Registered Indian" (the legal term for First Nations people associated with reservations) population projected to increase from about 500,000 in 1990 to 900,000 by 2015 (Canada 1995). Saskatchewan is expected to experience the largest proportional gains, with an increase from the current 15 per cent of the general population to 17 per cent by 2015 (Canada 1995).

Intercultural friendships

While changing demographics in Saskatchewan make the development of intercultural friendships increasingly important (Federation of Saskatchewan Indian Nations n.d.), one of the organizing concepts in friendship theory is homophily, or the idea that people will befriend those similar to themselves. Aristotle conceptualized the urge to befriend similar others as finding another self; Western thinking is built upon this concept (Hunt 1991; Raymond 1986; Stern-Gillet 1995). While traditional views of friendship often consider homophily a natural phenomenon or a core characteristic of friendship, more recent findings suggest that the norms and ideologies of the larger social environment act to either prevent the formation of interracial friendships or to bring existing intercultural friendships to an end (Hewitt 1986; Quadagno, Kuhar, and Peterson 1980). These factors further complicate intercultural friendships among women. The women of IGU draw on their common identity as grandmothers to build intercultural friendships.

Motherhood and grandmotherhood

Mothering and motherhood have commonly been represented as one uniting aspect among women, supposedly bringing the diverse experiences of most women together in one discursive and experiential realm. Such thinking must be tempered with the recognition that it can lead to an essentialist reduction of women to their mothering role. But because mothering has indeed been so central to women's constructed identity, exploring the ways in which women unite in friendship under this auspice is significant. Claiming authority to act on the basis of socially understood and accepted motherhood concepts provides access to areas often restricted to women even though oppressive systems are built upon the very same concepts. According to Evelyn Nakano Glenn, therein lies the paradox:

> In order to claim positions of power and influence, women
> have to accommodate prevailing notions that women possess
> special knowledge or moral qualities by virtue of being mothers.
> Such claims reinforce the ideology that justifies women's
> subordination, that is, the notion that women are essentially
> different from men and thus should be relegated to specific
> functions in society. (1994, 23)

Similarly, according to Colette Browne, the role of grandmother is a further source of women's oppression, prescribing a domestic role that limits alternative choices (1998, 205). While aligning oneself with essentialist notions of womanhood and mothering poses risks for women, social constructions of motherhood have been used as common ground to organize and as justification for engagement in political action (Fiske 1993; Naples 1998; Pardo 1990). The participants in this study negotiate this paradox by expanding the definition of grandmother beyond the biological to encompass "any loving and caring person" who maintains a focus on the well-being of themselves, their children, and their grandchildren.

Perspectives on identity

While grounding my research in feminist notions of fluid and constructed identities rather than essentialist and static views, it was important for me to examine how identity concepts have been developed by the grandmothers and how they draw on such identity categories in developing their friendships. The terms for identity used by the members of Intercultural Grandmothers United (IGU) carries with it layers of meaning. Terms of commonality, such as "older" and "grandmothers," are used to bridge differences in cultural identities, while at the same time the cultural identities are maintained and prioritized as "First Nations, Metis, and other." Operating within broader social ideologies that characterize such categories as mutually exclusive and segregated, it is paradoxical that the grandmothers simultaneously occupy a categorical identity space and highlight the interconnectedness of the categories through their friendships. Acknowledging and valuing commonalities and difference simultaneously, the grandmothers celebrate their diversity while bridging differences with those concerns and life experiences they do share.

Wilma, a First Nations grandmother, had been telling me how much she enjoyed meeting women from other reserves and previous classmates at the grandmother's gatherings, when I asked her the following question: "And how do you feel about meeting the white women at the gatherings and getting to know them?" Wilma replied, "I think that there's no difference really. We are all the same only we are, you know, different. Like they're white and we're Natives and they're all different nationalities themselves, you know? There I think it's the friendliness. And [being] willing to share." The individuality of each person's experience is respected and learned from, so that while factors such as friendliness and willingness to share are seen as commonalities, each woman's experience is valued as unique. They are the same, only different.

Issues of identity are an intricate part of the friendships that the grandmothers create and the work that they do, as well as how they do it. The women come to the group with their own culturally based ideas about what a grandmother is, yet they build upon a perceived commonality to create friendships. Wilma draws on personal experience as a grandchild to describe what a grandmother is:

> A grandma. A grandma to me is a most important person. Other than, besides your mother. Because, to me, she meant so much and she taught me so much. And she was always there for me.... She brought up, she raised up a lot of children.... Children that were homeless, you know. Even before that, I think that's, like with us Native people, that's why most of us grandparents have got their grandchildren [living with them]. Because we don't

want 'em raised by strangers. They're our responsibility and they are family and we'd sooner have 'em with us.

Lee, a Euro-Canadian grandmother, draws on her experience as a grandmother rather than as a grandchild to describe what a grandmother is:

> Probably a – now this is general – I'd say a grandmother is probably someone who, whose body is telling you that she's getting older [laugh]. Plus the fact that she's had a lot of experience in life and is willing to share it. And children love grandmothers.... And I know the reason.... And my own children [chuckle] say, "we have to get them away from you before you spoil them!" Actually, you don't, you're just not on their back all the time [laugh].

Cultural diversity in the grandmothering role is apparent. As with Wilma, the issue of grandmothers raising grandchildren was a common thread among the Aboriginal women's stories. Full-time responsibility for a grandchild can clash with the notion of the indulgent grandparent reflected in Lee's response when she mentions "spoiling." Even the luxury of "not [being] on their back all the time," perhaps in the form of discipline, can be the result of temporary visitations versus the long-term responsibility experienced by grandmothers who are primary caregivers. Across these differences, the recognition that grandmothers are an important part of life and learning, with responsibilities for the future of their grandchildren, provides a strong starting point from which these women can come together to build and maintain bridges of friendship.

Competing conceptions of aging also come into play with the varying views of the grandmothers, the traditions of the First Nations, and the ideologies of the dominant culture. Simply put, there is a big difference between thinking of someone as elderly and as an elder. Respect for aging and different abilities is demonstrated at a gathering when the grandmothers "walk the hill." IGU gatherings are often held at a retreat centre nestled in the hills of the Qu'Appelle Valley. Lee relates this story:

> In the spring or fall when there is less snow on the ground we would go out and say, walk the hill. As a break. And if you could only go half way, that's fine. No one was trying to push you and say, "Come on!" ... Our physical abilities were respected and

some of them were limited because of illness and accident. But they're always welcome.

Use of the phrase "but they're always welcome" could be misconstrued as a situation where ableist norms and barriers to participation are ignored under the pretence that the activity is theoretically open to all, but my observation of just such an outing revealed a different connotation. Grandmothers of all abilities headed outside to "walk the hill." Some were assisted to the bottom or a little way up until they felt they had had enough, and others went right to the top. All were encouraged to do what they could and enjoy the outdoors. No one was considered the winner and no one was cajoled into going further. All had "walked the hill" even those with canes who had rested at the base and shared laughter with those continuing on. Each was respected for who she was and what she could do. This is not to say, however, that the grandmothers do not struggle with labels of identity, for, as I will now discuss, they do.

IGU is described as a group for "First Nation, Metis, and other Canadian women." However, it became clear during interviews that women were uncertain how to properly refer to each other in a racialized context. There was often a pause while a grandmother selected a term to describe a racial group. Often they would ask, either directly or with an "uh?" if I was uncomfortable with the term they chose. Sometimes it seemed the grandmothers were using one term for lack of a better one. For example, Mary, a First Nations grandmother, said, "I'll call them whites, uh?" when beginning to discuss her relationship with the Euro-Canadian grandmothers. Lee informed me that the group struggled with terminology from the beginning, and that the label "other Canadian women" was hard to decide upon. The Project Working Council wanted to prioritize the Aboriginal women as a direct statement against the dominant culture, but could not agree on how to refer to the "other" women. As Lee said,

> Yeah, we get lost in terminology, don't we? We sure do. And unfortunately, I guess when we first went in there they were calling us "non-Native" and I objected to it. I said, "I was non-Catholic, I was non-French" [pause] and I was a non-Everything, you know over my lifetime, and I said, "This has got to be positive," and that's why we make it "other Canadian women" [in unison]. Mhm. Because I objected to that [use of "non"].

The group did not want to use "white" because it wanted to be open to all races and the initial choice of non-Native seemed to be an attempt to invert the often used non-white. However, Lee, who grew up in a Protestant and English minority in Montreal, felt that her nationality was being neglected yet again. Often, there is a tendency for those of the dominant group to see themselves and their identities as neutral or a baseline from which "others" are then defined. Use of the term "other" to apply to those women not of First Nations or Metis descent inverts socially constructed hierarchies by recasting those of privilege as "the other." In the case of IGU, the privileged are defined with reference to the colonized; subject and object are inverted. However, by avoiding the use of the prefix "non," those grouped as "other" are not negated and remain part of the overall category of "Canadian women." Ostensibly, all remain subjects. Furthermore, the ordering encompasses First Nations and Metis women within the category "Canadian women," placing further diversity of experiences within the identity of Canadian women. However, despite the IGU's intentions at inclusion, the grandmothers who fit into the "other" category tend to be Euro-Canadian.

IGU has held workshops on racism and has examined white privilege and colonial history, but, it seems, issues of immigration and a further deconstruction of whiteness and the multiple misunderstandings of it are lacking. Lee and I discussed the diversity of the group during our interview: "Well, we have – Laverne is Metis. We've had them from Greek background, we've had them from other colours, too. But the stress seems to be on the Native Indian and the white community. But everybody's welcome. We don't, you don't see so many [women of colour], and maybe I shouldn't say that because they are in the inner city."

Lee seemed slightly flustered by the direction her response was taking and quickly changed the topic. The focus of the grandmothers has been on how well they are doing to foster intercultural relationships, yet the possibility became apparent to Lee that the group could be excluding people of colour who were not Native, as well as limiting access to Metis women. Lee then resorted to the defensive responses of "everybody's welcome," which ignores the structures that prevent people from joining or returning, and "you don't see so many," which is meant to absolve the group by minimizing the number of people excluded.

There also seemed to be confusion about what "other Canadian women" might mean around the notion of whiteness. In reviewing our interview transcript with me, Lee added these words to this section: "We've had ladies from Germany, and other European countries from Iceland, and a few who have spoken French. They are all Intercultural Grandmothers, as are the Natives and whites. *Some Europeans ≠ whites!*" [emphasis in original conversation]. Lee seems to have an imperialist definition of white that goes beyond pigmentation to culture in a manner similar to early colonial times in Canada when white was equated with British and other "suitable" cultures. Lee uses this conception to broaden the category of "other" beyond "white" and to make the group seem more inclusive, even though virtually all the women in the other category would self-identify as white and the Aboriginal women regard them as such. Thus the further complexities of race and identity are revealed.

Lee fails to interrogate why non-Aboriginal women of colour do not return to the group and why there is limited involvement by Metis women, and she is not alone. While the "other Canadian women" are from a variety of cultural backgrounds, this may obscure the fact that they are various shades of white. Further work could be done to examine whether the discursive construction of "other Canadian women" is flexible enough to allow women from cultures not based in Europe and whether simply listing Metis creates an inclusive space. The inversion of dominance that occurs when white women are included in the "other" category does not hold true for women of colour who are constructed as other throughout the discourse of Euro-Canadian culture. Perhaps inclusion in the category "other" is a way of creating a space that is neither affirming nor safe for non-Aboriginal women of colour. (I attempted, through the coordinator, to make contact with previous members no longer attending the group in order to explore this issue further, but this was not possible.) For now, the women draw together around their shared identity as grandmothers.

Claiming the identity of a grandmother enables the women of IGU to bridge their differences. During our interview, Mary, a First Nations grandmother, told me that being a grandmother is "like, it's no, it's no nationality, you know. You are a grandmother, you're a grandmother. You know! You all have something in common." The friendships the grandmothers form occur within pre-existing constructions of cultural selves and power structures, all of which influence what it means to be a grandmother. Yet their development of friendships across cultures destabilizes existing subjective categories and makes clear their interrelatedness. Working with IGU provides the opportunity to bring into focus the complex intersections of gender, age, race, and family affiliation and to examine how these are produced and reproduced in each woman's life and her relationships.

Conclusions

Operating within a homogeneous, overwhelmingly powerful social structure that encourages segregation and separation, the grandmothers have come together around the identity "grandmother" to build bridges of friendship across cultural differences. In a complex interplay of ideology and experience, their friendships began with each person carrying with her not only her own identity but also ideas about other women built on myths and stereotypes. Through their friendships, they come to learn and understand more about themselves and the other women, recognizing commonalities and building upon them, while at the same time naming and respecting differences. These women construct humanity and grandmothering as overreaching commonalities, yet each remains a unique individual grounded in her culture. The group appears to have some work to do to become more inclusive to those women neither Aboriginal nor Euro-Canadian. Nonetheless, IGU has succeeded in building bridges of friendship between cultures and women that colonization constructed as irrevocably separate.

Culture, class, and age interact in complex ways to influence identities. A construction of identity as fluid and multiple makes possible the reconsideration of self, recognizing the permeability of self so that the "other" need not be constructed as opposite and a friend need not be constructed as exactly the same as another self. Influences of culture, class, and age are expressed in distinct ways through experiences and discourses of friendship. Friendship facilitates the sharing of perspectives, a respect for differences, and the ability to consider self and others equally valuable in the commonalities and differences.

The grandmothers maintain the importance of unique life insights while remaining grounded in identity categories. We are all the same and we are all different, but because we all share in this difference, this difference becomes a similarity. In other words, one of the similarities emerging from the interviews is an appreciation of the shared differences among the women. Modern day feminists can learn from the grandmothers' ability to celebrate difference from the foundation of a common identity while acknowledging that that identity still means different things to different people. Respecting each other as the same and different, self and other, but of equal value, destabilizes hierarchical social constructions and creates a space for the development of intercultural friendships among women.

Chapter 9

WOMEN'S PROFESSIONAL MENTORSHIP IN
PSYCHOLOGY AND THE ACADEMY:
ONE GROUP'S STORIES OF QUILTING AND LIFE

Denise J. Larsen and Jennifer A. Boisvert,
with Jocelyn Lock, Tikker Percey, Diane Priebe, and Linda Vaudan

Introduction

How we choose to mentor and support one another in the profession of psychology and the academy speaks volumes about the values we hold in our chosen practice. This paper highlights the experience of six women who chose to form a professional group based on mutual support, mentorship, and common professional interests. In writing this story, we are both authors and members of this group. Our experience reveals unanticipated individual benefits and a unique shared journey to building a healthy professional community. In addition, the experience described herein offers a positive alternative to the professional climates of academia and clinical practice as they are often experienced and described in literature.

The paper begins with a brief description of the members of our group. This is followed by an abbreviated review outlining literature directly related to some of the common foundations of our group process. Our collective experience is subsequently highlighted through individual writings, a description of the group process, and the research methods used. Common experiences are noted through themes and discussion. Finally, conclusions regarding the experience are drawn.

Who we are

At its inception, the Women in Psychology group comprised six women, aged twenty-four to fifty-five (the average age being thirty-five years). Two members were master's degree graduates, one was a Ph.D. candidate, and two were bachelor's degree graduates. All group members had trained at the same university, though not in the same faculties. At present, of these six members, three are graduate students and three are chartered psychologists. In terms of employment, two women are private practice psychologists, two women are involved in research, one woman works in parole supervision, and one woman practices as a psychologist in a medical setting.

How the literature relates to our experience

We begin the literature review by highlighting briefly a model of mentorship that shares a vision common to our group ethic. Following this description, literature related to the professional climate of psychology and, more particularly, the academic climate is addressed. In addition, we present developmental models that highlight the need for lifelong professional learning and support. Perhaps unusually, we also include literature that reviews quilt-making, as well as literature that reviews group support. This literature is included because, as a group, we decided to employ quilting in order to facilitate group process and the sharing of individual and common visions in the profession.

Mentorship in psychology

Though we might not have called it that from the outset, mutual mentorship was an ethic that evolved naturally from the beginning of our group meetings. Mentors have been variously defined (*e.g.*, Gray 1998), but a description that resonated well with our group members describes mentors as "those who gently guide the growth of others during various stages of development" (Huang and Lynch 1995, xi). The distinction between mentor and mentoree blurs when we begin to realize that in the teaching/helping relationship, the mentor or teacher not only provides direction but also benefits from the encounter. A cyclical relationship between the mentor and mentoree is formed in which, at various points during the process, the teacher becomes the learner, the learner becomes the teacher (Huang and Lynch 1995). This model of mentorship fit particularly well with our group process: a group formed at the initiative of the members, lacking any formal leader, and functioned as a forum for discussing ongoing career and personal discoveries.

Professional development in psychology

Though our group varied in educational levels and professional experiences, we could all be described as being early in our careers. Well aware of our relative inexperience, and perhaps still willing to reveal our "growth edges," it was clear that developing into our careers was an ongoing task before all of us.

Within the literature, counsellor development has been an object of theoretical formulation and research for over thirty-five years. As early as 1964, Hogan made hypotheses regarding the professional development of student counsellors. Since then, several stage models of counselling student development have emerged (e.g., Loganbill, Hardy, and Delworth 1982; Nelson, Johnson, and Thorngren 2000; Stoltenberg and Delworth 1987). In addition, a handful of researchers and clinicians describe professional development beyond counsellor training (e.g., Kottler 1995). Skovholt and Ronnestad (1992) identify lifelong professional development issues based on a large qualitative study of counsellors at differing career points. Our group experience supports the notion that career development continues long after graduation. It has been interesting to witness the rich environment that women with various training levels and work experience can provide for one another – a point we address below.

The chilly climate in psychology and the academy

From the inception of the Women and Psychology group meetings, a common theme emerged around overcoming difficult experiences within academic and professional environments. The women in the group had hoped for nurturing, supportive educational environments. Instead, university training was often experienced as harshly competitive, and the climate as unnecessarily aloof. These experiences resonate with research, which highlights the difficulties that women experience while involved in Ph.D. programs, regardless of area of study (Kerlin 1997). In addition, research into the academic experience as described by professors also points to a harsh academic climate. According to Mintz (1994, 77), "[F]ew would dispute that the academy is rife with conflict and contradiction. Conflict is greatly valued in higher education." Within the field of psychology itself, research highlights the experience of some long-term professors who find the academic environment very difficult (Larsen 1999). Consider the following: "[O]ftentimes, depending on the circumstances as a graduate student, and as a faculty member for that matter, you have to become fully adept at biting bullets. Except that some bullets are too hard for you to bite. You just can't do it" (Larsen 1999, 102).

The history and meaning of quilting

Carrying the individual legacies of our training and our work experience, seeking a foundation of respect for one another, and with a strong desire to learn to mentor and support, our group embarked on a unique endeavour. We decided to use quilt-making as a way of giving voice to our experiences and our visions, as well as a way of facilitating group process. Though we had only limited awareness of the rich history of women's quilt-making, we were to learn first-hand the potential richness held within the process. Only later did we learn that in pioneer societies, quilting provided rich and often rare occasions to engage in "women's talk" (Horton 2000). Quilt-making also provided women with a means of self-expression and a way to depict the events of their lives (Gunkel 1996). Today, it continues to serve the same purposes. Quilting is a means of depicting one's identity, of revealing pieces of oneself in the choices made about fabric, colour, pattern, and so on (Hilty 1980; Lithgow 1974). On a social dimension, quilts provide insight into the prevailing culture and reflect the times in which they are made (Horton 1985). The same can be said of the quilt created by the Women in Psychology group. As explored below, the quilt reflects our personal views and experiences in psychology. It also makes a collective statement regarding the current atmosphere of the academy and the profession of psychology.

Women in the group context

Previous social research points to the effectiveness of a group such as ours in improving the quality of life for its members through mutual support, voluntary assistance, and the creation of a caring community (Dalton, Elias, and Wandersman 2001). Women's group participation has demonstrated an increase in hope, support, and sisterhood in a number of circumstances as members share information, experiences, and solutions (*e.g.*, Boisevert, Jevne, and Nekolaichuk 1997). Hence, women's group involvement may enhance personal and professional development and growth through the experience of mentorship, support, and connection (Jordan, Surrey, and Kaplan 1991).

The process: Our methodology

While this chapter does not claim the rigours of a full research study because this was not the intention of the group participants, it does evolve out of a knowledge of feminist research practices (*e.g.*, Richardson 1997) as well as narrative methodology (Polkinghorne 1995). Most notably, the "data," our stories, are told in our own voices through individual vignettes included in this document. Given the ideographic nature of narrative research methodology and the value that voicing our own experience may have for others, excerpts of four group members' stories are shared, along with descriptions of their quilt squares. Finally, we do not claim that our experiences, either individually or collectively, represent a universal truth; rather, they represent a way of looking at the world and a way of attempting to place relationship and support within the context of our professional lives.

Our written stories and quilted squares

The four stories and descriptions that follow were written by members of the Women in Psychology group. Each story, in the voice of its author, highlights aspects of the individual group member's experience and the meaning of that experience for her.

1) *Diane's story: "Trusting the process"* –
   Developing and nurturing a women's talking circle

I have often been blessed with opportunities to learn important lessons in my life. One of these lessons is about trust, both in myself as a person and in the process of life. To trust that things will unfold as they should has been a struggle for me because I believe in self-determination. The last few years have presented several challenges to further my learning of this lesson.

When I began my journey to graduate school and the career of psychologist, I was filled with hopes and expectations. From the beginning of the master's program, however, I knew that the path would be very different from the one I had imagined. The support and mentorship that I had hoped for did not materialize. In their place were competition and fear. Students were pitted against one another and faculty did not model the behaviours that I had associated with a profession based on compassion and respect. I coped by keeping to myself and by looking forward to getting out into the "real" world of a psychologist. Once again, I encountered disappointment. The chartering process was more adversarial than supportive. I kept looking for mentors and guides, but they did not appear.

During this experience, I vowed to myself that I would make a difference once I was a psychologist. Following graduation, the Psychologists' Association of Alberta asked me to form a Women in Psychology special interest group. The journey toward forming such a group was initially a rocky one. My doubts were many. Would this kind of group work? How would it work? What would its purpose be? Part of the answer to these questions came unexpectedly from my husband's suggestion that we have the first meeting in our home. Meeting in a comfortable and personal setting fit well with having a flexible and egalitarian approach to forming our women's group. The group slipped easily into a kind of "talking circle" where each member had an equal opportunity to participate and share.

As the group met together over the next months, we developed connections with one another, sharing stories of graduate school, work environments, our profession, and our personal beliefs. We soon decided that our reasons for coming together would include both professional advocacy, specifically around issues affecting women, and personal support. The supportive part has expanded to include a focus on creativity. A few months ago, Denise suggested that we start a quilting project; she had participated in several such projects at a cancer hospital. We eagerly agreed to combine our somewhat limited experience of fabric, needles, thread, and stitch-witchery to express our visions of psychology and the group. I have been continually amazed at the level of focus and absorption, as well as the kind of "by-product" discussions, that quilting has released in our group. It has been an enriching experience and another reminder of what can happen when we trust the process and ourselves. One year ago when this small group of women first met, I would not have imagined that we would connect as we have or that we would put our energies together into the creation of a quilt and a paper.

Reflecting on the past year of our group, I feel gratified with the path we have taken. Something real has resulted from an obscure beginning. And the journey continues. I trusted that the group would form itself and that we would connect in an equal and shared way. I trusted that a group of women could come together and support one another. I have found the mentors and guides I have been looking for all along. I am proud to be where we are today.

Diane's quilt square: The circle of life (and therapy!)

The themes and images in my quilt square are strongly influenced by Aboriginal culture and teachings. The central part of my square shows a circle, a prominent symbol within Aboriginal culture. To me, the circle is important in that it represents continuity, both in life and in therapy. I believe that there is no strict beginning or end in therapy; it is an ongoing process. The life cycle of a sunflower is depicted in the centre of the circle as a way of symbolizing this continuity. The four female symbols and four red sashes represent the "four directions," another significant Aboriginal teaching, and I conceptualize these four areas as being the core of all human beings: emotional, spiritual, physical, and mental. Restoring balance is the main goal of psychological intervention.

2) *Linda's story: "Coming home"*

In many ways, the experience of attending the Women in Psychology group reflects my vision of psychology. That first evening, I experienced a feeling of coming home. Although I had never met these women before, I found myself freely listening, talking, and sharing experiences, hopes, and plans. We talked of so many things that resonated with me and that reflected and validated my experience of being a woman in the field of psychology.

How familiar was the awareness of the possible repercussions of being identified as a feminist! It was not just the communicating that was important. It was the honesty, openness, and respect of the communication that made the evening particularly meaningful to me. There was space in the room: space to listen to one another, to share experiences, to plan with excitement and anticipation. We started the quilt at the following meeting and "worked" on our squares while we talked.

After one meeting, I had an experience that highlighted a part of the struggle I felt in being a woman in the field of psychology. I left the meeting feeling very uplifted and strengthened, and as I was driving home, I found myself thinking about how to communicate this experience to the larger psychological community, my colleagues, beyond this group. I also found myself realizing that to communicate the experience in a way that would be valued and accepted by the psychology community at large would change the experience. I would be making the experience fit others' conceptualizations of psychology rather than showing what the experience was truly like for me. I would have to re-language it, change it to make it presentable, thereby losing its real essence. It would be like fitting a woman's body into a girdle. This experience has shown me the challenge we, as women, face in contributing to a vision of psychology that authentically reflects our experiences. Coming home is about being who we are. I believe that there is a freedom in breaking the old mould of psychological expression and thought and stretching into who we know ourselves to be.

Linda's quilt square: Breaking the mould

My piece shows a tree in the shape of the psychology symbol. The similarity between the psychology symbol and the symbol for women is significant in the piece. I chose the symbol of a tree because it is important both personally and professionally to me. For me, the tree is symbol of life, growth, and change. It also symbolizes the six core members of the Women in Psychology group. The six roots represent the rootedness we experience in the group and the support we give to one another. The fiery background reflects the destructiveness of the unsupportive and at times hostile climate for women in graduate school, in the profession of psychology, and in society. The image overall shows the transforming process of going through great difficulty. New shoots of green occur after a forest fire. The tree continues to grow through difficulty. Women in psychology, too, continue to grow through the, at times, destructive ways of the training they get and the professions and society in which they live.

3) Denise's story: "Sewing a new vision"

Profound experiences can arise in the most unexpected of circumstances. I held a little bias until not long ago: to my way of thinking, groups were generally for other people. I believed that professional women held the potential for collegiality born of the desire to nurture, but rarely had I actually experienced this first-hand. I wondered why, in a profession based on the desire to help, my experience had so often been tempered with competition and distance.

I admit to healthy scepticism. As I anticipated our first meeting, I wondered whether our commonality as women in psychology would provide enough foundation for connection or a common vision. I hold very strong convictions regarding the importance of mentorship and support in professional development and practice. Secretly, I hoped that this would be a place to discuss my professional hopes and frustrations, excitement and disappointments. I hoped that this would be a place to explore the challenges of putting visions of professional mentorship into practice.

From the beginning, a quiet and powerful energy was present in the group, and in time, compassion grew among us. With the decision to use creative means, through quilt-making, to articulate our experiences and dreams, the group seemed to turn a corner, and new ways of understanding our own experiences and those of others opened before us. At times, the room rang with laughter. At other times, absorbed in our creations, a respectful silence filled the space. With no direct objective, we found ways to appreciate our commonality and respect our differences through conversation. A part of me was deeply touched that I should have the opportunity to share in the dreams of my women colleagues and that I felt safe enough to share my own visions. Our risks to share as well as support and mentor one another gave birth to community.

I was getting to know my sister-group members much differently than if we had begun with an agenda, a stated goal, or some particular cause for which to lobby. I was proud of the way in which we had acknowledged our experiences and embraced our desire to try to make a difference. The group's journey itself evolved, taking form only as a shared spirit seemed to guide us. On a more personal level, I was learning. Perhaps there was a community for me and perhaps I need not always shield myself with scepticism in the face of offers of support.

Denise's quilt square: Beauty and abundance

This piece represents my view of the beauty and abundance of life. I believe in and sense a growing respect in psychology for holistic approaches to healing mind, body, and spirit, approaches that acknowledge both intellect and intuition. The image of the tree symbolizes natural relational approaches to working with others. In the background, an outdated mechanical device representing mechanistic approaches to our work is superseded by a warmer, gentler, fuller vision of the helping relationship.

4) *Jennifer's story: "Fertile soil to sow seeds of professional support and development"*

When I started university, I was under the impression that female psychology professors were readily available to foster the potential of undergraduate students such as myself. This assumption quickly withered during my undergraduate years, as I learned that such mentoring opportunities rarely presented themselves. Female academics, like exotic plants, were few and far between, and those who did exist did not appear to thrive in conditions conducive to mentoring. This lack of exposure to feminist mentors has led me to perceive the academic climate as arid and barren.

Upon graduation, I became aware of my need to experience a more enriching context, one that would ensure the sowing of seeds of professional support and development. I have found the Women in Psychology group to provide fertile soil for the "blooming" of interests and the "blossoming" of future vocational pursuits. In meetings with these five women, important relationships of mentorship, partnership, and friendship have been planted and tended with care. Our combined quilting efforts have enabled me to see how creative activity may be employed as a means of cultivating professional support and development. A strong sense of community, connection, and compassion was nurtured in our quilting sessions.

Apart from sharing experiences, I realize how together we share a vision of feminist psychology. With each meeting, we have mutually created a space to celebrate achievements, challenge and encourage one another's potential for growth, and experience collegiality. These five women have taught me that where women gather, there is a rich, relational atmosphere. Like a tree, I have flourished in my chosen field as a result of having found female mentors able to provide those nutrients essential to my growth.

Jennifer's quilt square: Journeying the landscape

My panel is a landscape of my educational journey in feminist psychology. The primary component of this journey is represented by the stream and two hills: each embodies an educational experience that I have encountered or seek to encounter as I travel toward my destination of feminist psychological practice. The brown hill is symbolic of my undergraduate experience in "patriarchal" psychology. I felt somewhat isolated in my feminist focus as an undergraduate psychology student; this is apparent in the single female symbol and its lone shadow. The green hill embodies my hope to expand this interest in my exposure to feminist psychology as a graduate student. I foresee my ability to relate to and identify with other women in psychology: hence, the multiplicity of female symbols and their connecting shadows.

The stream signifies the role the Women in Psychology group has played in channelling my energies toward my chosen field. Like a stream, the group has an "ebb and flow," which has served to influence my vision of psychology. My involvement in the group has proven to be a unique learning experience in itself and has enabled me to envision my future as a feminist practitioner in this psychological "landscape."

Our stories and squares: An analysis of our data

It has been a challenge to identify the many threads that weave through the fabric of our experiences and to construct a framework for communicating the essence of our collective experience. For the purposes of this research analysis, our methods were informed by content analysis techniques as described by Mirriam (1988) and phenomenological thematic techniques as outlined by Moustakas (1994).

In keeping with the overall experience of the Women and Psychology group, the data analysis was collaborative: one group member (J.A. Boisvert), after conducting preliminary analysis of the written narratives, shared her findings and invited feedback from all other group members. The role of other group members in providing feedback was pivotal to understanding the emergent themes and eliciting important additional data from the group.

Our collective experience: Themes and discussion

Compiling and synthesizing the stories revealed unanticipated individual benefits and a unique shared experience in the journey to create a healthy professional community. We found four main interrelated themes as we reviewed our experiences. A key commonality across all four is the power of relationships and caring within the group. With this in mind, the four central themes are the following: (1) mentorship and mutual support; (2) possibilities for change; (3) cool and warm climates; and (4) quilting and creating a vision.

1) *Mentorship and mutual support*

Together, we established a group environment where each of us could be both teacher and learner (Huang and Lynch 1995), finding opportunities to mutually mentor and enrich one another's lives across differences in education levels and professional experiences. As the trust within the group developed, stories of professional development and the messages that we had each received about our place within the profession began to emerge. The stories often contained the seeds of negative messages about ourselves within the profession, planted at times when we were developing and vulnerable. The potential and real trauma experienced as a result of such professional experiences were revealed, often for the first time, in the company of others, and we each began to learn that we were not alone.

Reflecting on our experiences, we saw that female mentors were few and far between in academic and professional settings. Indeed, at the outset of the Women in Psychology group, many of us approached the group guardedly. Previous experience had led many of us to question the likelihood that we would find a supportive atmosphere with our professional colleagues. Gratifyingly, our willingness to explore new group mentorship possibilities was rewarded with the opportunity to experience new and healthy ways of being with our women colleagues. Tikker, one of our group members, shares the value of mentorship and natural support: "Within this group of women, I feel that I have at last found the collegiality and mentorship that was so lacking in my journey to become a chartered psychologist."

This theme, a hallmark of our particular group experience, is found in feminist and other psychological literature and research (*e.g.*, Hazler and Carney 1993; Kerlin 1997). Our experience as under/graduate psychology students lacking mentorship and support leads us to hope for better opportunities for women in our field to develop a feminist identity that will enhance professional development and growth.

Several feminist writers have proposed that female identity is relational, suggesting that women experience and understand themselves in relationships and not as separate entities (Belenky *et al.* 1997). By way of example, Kmiec, Crosby, and Worrell (1996), in their chronicle of female faculty collaborating with female undergraduate students, explore the implications of feminist mentorship. As female psychologists, they cite the potential benefit of the mentoring relationship, identifying ways in which it has allowed them to behave in accordance with feminist ideology relative to their individual and collective interests. They thereby attest to the importance of relational and more collegial professional relationships.

2) *Possibilities for change*

The mentorship, support, and encouragement fostered in the group enabled each of us to develop greater trust in our potential to create professional change. The group experience heightened our sense of ourselves as capable of making professional change, of doing things differently from the way we had experienced them. The experience has allowed us to witness one another's successes, be they in graduate work or in the workplace. Jennifer shares how the group has come to shape her future vision of psychology:

> Apart from sharing the experiences, I realize how together we share a vision of feminist psychology. With each meeting, we have mutually created a space to celebrate achievements, challenge and encourage one another's potential for growth, and experience collegiality. We come together to make a significant impact in the profession, be it through teaching, research, or practice.

Feminist research on women's experiences of professional development highlights power hierarchies within academic and professional settings, drawing attention to the need to create a more relational atmosphere in psychology and the academy. Klonis *et al.* (1997), in their explorative study of the link between self-labelled feminist psychology professors, found that feminism, especially in the form of relationships with other women, served as a "life raft." The theme of feminism as a coping device in academia corresponds with our experience of the importance of relationship and its power to effect change within institutions.

3) Cool and warm climates

The Women in Psychology group provided a "warmer" and more nurturing climate when compared to our experiences of university settings, which were often found to be cool and competitive (Mintz 1994). Most of us did not feel a sense of warmth or welcoming upon entrance to a graduate program or when embarking on the chartering process. Such "cool" experiences led many of the women in our group to perceive the academic and professional climate in negative terms and to feel thwarted in our attempts to pursue education and training with a feminist focus. As a result, together we describe the group as having become a "safe place" where we can speak openly without fear of reprimand or social reprisal.

As feminists, we pride ourselves in enhancing our academic and professional environments by changing the ways we educate and relate to others with the purpose of "defrosting" these "chilly" climates (Belenky *et al.* 1997; Crawford and Macerek 1989). Amidst alternative methods of creating change, numerous elements of feminist pedagogy have been identified by women writers and investigators (*e.g.*, Forrest and Rosenberg 1997; Hoffman and Stake 1998). One element in particular, that of the validation of personal experience and development of confidence, is accomplished by encouraging students to consider connections between their subjective realities and formal course content within an atmosphere of respect and support (Forrest and Rosenberg 1997; Maher 1987; Morley 1992; Stake and Hoffman 2000; Weiler 1988). Though not a training group, our group became a space where we were able to speak more freely about our subjective experience and our professional selves.

4) *Quilting and creating a vision*

Throughout our group discussion, quilting was used by group members as a means of expressing experiences and visions of psychology and as a way of facilitating a strong sense of community, connection, and collegiality. While working to put our visions of career and profession into fabric, our conversations focussed on our individual dreams in the profession of psychology.

The fact that quilt-making was traditional women's work was not lost in our conversations. We were acutely aware that we had chosen to participate in an activity unusual for our profession. Yet, rather than diminish the status of our profession, we had the feeling that we were once again pioneers. We explored new ways of seeing ourselves and our futures. We had found a way to surmount the common mistrust and tensions among professionals in psychology, and we had begun to openly discuss our professional past, our passions, and our hopes. In a sense, our foremothers had taught us about community through quilting, and we had found in it a way to make our current work as women healthy and supportive. The themes and images that emerged in the quilt speak to making the personal political. Our pieces stand collectively in the quilt, publicly expressing our individual and professional convictions. Jocelyn tells of the importance of the connections made while quilting in the group: "With each meeting [over the quilt], my spirit feels lighter, my frustrations seem more manageable, and I feel like a happier, healthier person. I feel more capable and stronger in facing the next challenge that arises and take comfort that there are other women near."

In creating our quilt panels, we found that we were in the good company of our foremothers in putting the important aspects of our lives into fabric form (*e.g.*, Miles 1999; Gunkel 1996). We also found ourselves in good company with feminists who have remarked on the presumption that "if we do cutting edge feminist work, it is not seen as psychology" (Unger 1998, 198–99). In some sense, in bringing the possibility of quilting and other creative endeavours into the professional and academic realms, we were approaching our group from a "cutting-edge" perspective. In fact, it was not simply the message of our experience that became important. The quilt itself was important as a representation and testament to our experience together.

Conclusion

The application of a unique method and, more importantly, the conviction to create a professional haven for mentorship and support gave birth to the unique experiences of the group of psychology students and practitioners described in this paper. In developing our Women in Psychology group, our six group members began by implicitly focussing on relationship, listening, and honouring professional experiences. In the course of our meetings, a series of themes emerged that are consistent with feminist literature addressing issues of mentorship and mutual support in psychology and the academy. The four primary themes presented were mentorship and mutual support, possibilities for change, cool and warm climates, and quilting and creating a vision. Given our positive and powerful group experience, we suggest and hope that others will choose to experiment and play with possibilities for creating wholesome and necessary places for professional growth.

Chapter 10

SEXUAL HEALTH OF YOUNG WOMEN: CONTEXT AND CARE MAKE A DIFFERENCE

Mary Rucklos Hampton, Barb McWatters, Bonne Jeffery, and Pamela Smith

Introduction

Little money is spent on adolescent sexual health care due to predominant perceptions of policy-makers and health care providers that these issues lie outside the domain of medical care (Dougherty 1999). Sexual health of adolescents receives attention only when it is constructed as a problem within individuals (*e.g.*, teen pregnancy, STIs); solutions are seen as the responsibility of parents and schools. Recent research has demonstrated that the health care system does not respond to the unique sexual health care needs of young people. Only 40 per cent of primary-care physicians in the U.S. report screening for sexual activity in their adolescent patients, and only 4 per cent offer condoms to sexually active patients (Mahler 1997; Millstein, Igra, and Gans 1996). Epidemiological patterns of sexual health are different for adolescents than for adults, with *Chlamydia* currently the most prevalent STI in this age group (Shenkman *et al.* 1996; Saskatchewan Health 1996). However, routine screening for *Chlamydia*, which is often asymptomatic, is conducted by only half of physicians (Schreck 2001). There is general consensus in the literature that young women live in an environment where their sexual health care needs are not being met.

The sexual health care needs of adolescents and young adults are developmentally different from other age groups (Shenkman *et al.* 1996). For example, depending on their age, cultural context, familial connections, and other factors, adolescents and young adults are more or less dependent on parents or guardians. The implications of this dependency, combined with their emerging need for autonomy, means that health care must be accessible directly to them and must be developmentally appropriate. There are also gender differences in health care access. Young women use health services for sexual/reproductive concerns, as well as other health-related issues, more often than young men do (Bernzweig *et al.* 1997). Research conducted in Canada confirms findings in the U.S. – that young women face significant barriers when attempting to access sexual health services (Langille *et al.* 1999). These barriers include difficulties accessing appropriate physician services and lack of comfort with and lack of effective communication in health care settings.

Young women's need for sexual health services and the ways in which they interact with the health care system have received little attention from health researchers. Research conducted in "real world" settings in which adolescent girls receive care has been targeted as potentially generating the most useful findings (Dougherty 1999). Researchers are gradually recognizing that young women are capable of and interested in commenting on their own health care. Research that explores young women's perceptions of ways in which they are treated could offer insights into improving service delivery.

Feminist scholars researching young women's sexuality have listened to young women's lived experience and have discovered that the context within which they enact their sexuality is important (Tolman and Szalacha 1999). Recent theoretical contributions describe the importance of understanding the complex relational contexts within which a young woman's decision-making occurs (Tolman 1999). This relational context constitutes her immediate environment and includes sexual partners, friends, parents, and others who affect a young woman's sexual decisions. In addition, socio-cultural and socio-political environments impinge upon young women's sexual autonomy. School settings, such as public schools, reinforce patriarchal gender role socialization and tolerate a level of sexual violence against girls and young women (Fine 1988). Recent research recommends extending the relational paradigm into educational settings through sex education (Manning , Longmore, and Giordano 2000). Feminist deconstruction of the dominant conservative political agenda demonstrates that public policy is hostile to young women and does not enhance sexual health (Wilcox 1999).

Even though recent feminist theorizing has made contributions to understanding the influence of context on young women's sexuality, this framework has only minimally extended into sexual health care delivery. Given the environmental and contextual constraints, can sexual health service delivery be offered in ways that empower young women and mediate the negative effects of these environmental factors? Our research team conducted a developmental program evaluation of a sexual health centre whose mandate is to promote healthy sexuality for young people. This evaluation of Planned Parenthood Regina's Sexual Health Centre

(SHC) provided extensive data on sexual behaviour and health issues of young women and men. Our chapter presents a sample of findings from this research and discusses whether these data can shed light on three questions: (1) What are the contexts of young women's sexual activity in our city? (2) What are client views of how they have been treated at the Sexual Health Centre? (3) Can these views/perceptions offer any insights into whether environmental context of care in this setting makes a difference? A combination of quantitative (surveys) and qualitative (focus groups) methods were used to answer these questions.

Method

Data collection

1) *Youth and client satisfaction surveys.* A youth survey was developed using sexual health surveys previously used with adolescents and young adults as a template (Card 1993; King, Coles, and King 1988; Schissel and Eisler 1996). The final instrument was a seventy-three-item survey that took approximately forty minutes to complete. Topics included questions on basic demographic information, knowledge of sexual health issues, sexual and contraceptive behaviour, and the use of specific health services. A twenty-item anonymous Client Satisfaction Survey was also developed to collect demographic information, reasons for using the Sexual Health Centre, and dimensions of client satisfaction with staff and services.

2) *Focus groups.* Eight focus groups were conducted. Two groups were conducted with clients of the Sexual Health Centre (SHC): a younger client group (n=3; average age=15) and an older client group (n=23; average age=17). One community-based, teen-parent group participated in a focus group (n=3; average age=19). A community-based, at-risk-youth group participated in another focus group (n=12; average age=17). The final group was a parents focus group (n=3) consisting of members of PTAs from three different high schools. All focus group participants responded to invitations to participate and signed consent forms.

Participants

1) *Youth and client satisfaction surveys.* Gender-balanced teams of youth research assistants visited grades 10 and 12 English classes of Regina high schools to describe the study and distribute parental consent forms. They returned three days later to administer surveys to

students who returned consent forms. Client Satisfaction Surveys were distributed to all clients who used the Centre over a four-month period. They were handed to each client by the receptionist and completed; the surveys were returned anonymously by clients to a covered box at the door.

2) *Focus groups*. Client and teen mom focus groups were facilitated by trained research assistants more similar in gender, age, and ethnicity to the focus group participants (Greenbaum 1998; Rubin and Rubin 1995). All focus groups were tape-recorded and the results were transcribed for analysis. Focus group data were analyzed using grounded theory methods (Strauss and Corbin 1998).

Contexts of young women's sexual activity in Regina
Sexual activity by gender

Overall, 44 per cent of all grade 10 and 12 students reported having had sexual intercourse. This result is similar to previous research conducted in Saskatchewan (Schissel and Eisler 1996). As has been found in most sexual health research, age is significantly related to having had sex: 33 per cent of grade 10 students have had sex, and 54 per cent of grade 12 students have had sex. Data analysis indicated that more grade 10 and 12 females than males have had sex (see Table 1). This result is similar to previous research conducted in Regina (Storey and Moore 1998) but is contrary to trends found in U.S. and Canadian samples (King, Coles, and King 1988; Ku *et al.* 1998). This gender difference holds true for both grade 10 and 12 students.

Table 1: Students who have had sexual intercourse.

Grade of students	MALES		FEMALES	
	n	%	*n*	%
All grade 10/12 students	483	41	592	48.6***
Grade 10	173	31	190	34***
Grade 12	310	50	356	59***

***p<.001

Average age at first sexual intercourse in our sample was fifteen (gender differences = N.S.). Teen moms, however, were significantly younger than other students, with the average age at first sexual intercourse being fourteen.

Partners: Who are they having sex with?

Female students are more likely than males to have first had sexual intercourse with someone older by about two years. This was particularly true for grade 10 females. While the average age of first sex reported by grade 10 females was 14.5, their partners were likely to be sixteen years old. In grade 12, the average age of first sex for females was 15.5, while their partners were likely to be only one year older, or 16.5. Male students were more likely to have had sex with partners of the same age (average age at first sex = 15) or half a year older (15.5). Teen moms reported that they first had sex with partners who were significantly older (2.5 to 4 years older). These results are similar to previous research on teen pregnancy (Coley and Chase-Lansdale 1998).

Ever been physically forced to have sexual intercourse?

Findings from the youth survey analysis indicated that 15 per cent of all respondents had been physically forced to have sex. More than twice as many females as males had been forced. The younger the students were at first intercourse, the more likely they were to have reported being forced. Almost half of the teen parents (all female) indicated they had been forced to have sex (see Table 2). Further analysis indicated that teen parents who were physically forced were more likely to have had first sex with a partner who was eighteen years or older. Students who had been forced to have sex also report having had sex with more partners. Three times as many grade 10/12 students who had (39%) rather than had not (13%) been forced, have had sex with six or more people. Students who had not been forced to have sex have on average had sex with one to two people.

Participants in the focus group, however, were not specifically asked whether they had ever been forced to have sex. Only one participant disclosed forced sex: "That wasn't my first experience, though. I was raped at twelve, twelve and a half. So that was my first experience. My first, like, consensual experience was at thirteen years old. I think it was because I was with an older guy, probably. I was a lot younger, he was older ... it kinda happened" (sixteen-year-old female).

Table 2: Ever been physically forced to have sexual intercourse?

	FEMALES: YES		MALES: NES	
	n	%	n	%
Grade 10/12 students	538	21	471	9***
Teen parents	20	46***		

***p<.001

However, many of the female participants of the focus groups alluded to coercion but did not consider this a form of forced sex: "He said, if you do not give me sex, I'll get it somewhere else" (seventeen-year-old female). Our survey results underestimate the prevalence of forced sex experienced by young women since our definition is limited to physical force.

Ever had intercourse when feeling drunk?

Among all sexually active grade 10/12 participants, 63 per cent reported having had sex when feeling drunk (see Table 3). This relationship between alcohol use and sexual activity is similar to previous findings (Kowaleski-Jones and Mott 1996; King, Coles, and King 1988). While not significantly different, more males than females reported this experience (females = 60%; males = 66%). There were no differences in percentage of grade 10 (63%) and grade 12 (63%) students who reported this experience. Teen parents were significantly more likely to have had sex when feeling drunk.

Table 3: Ever had sex when feeling drunk?

	YES		NO	
	n	%	n	%
Grade 10/12 students	640	63.1	387	37.1
Teen parents	35	77.8	10	22.2

***p<.05

Focus group participants stated that alcohol and peer pressure strongly influence both young women's and men's choice to have sex the first time: "They think it is cool [to have sex] when they are drunk" (fifteen-year-old female); "I think some people have sex because someone pushed them, pressured too quick" (seventeen-year-old female).

The focus group analysis revealed that the most common reason cited by teen moms for first having sex was that they were drunk. Five participants stated: "I was drunk." Others made similar statements: "I don't know why, I was drunk;" "I just got to the point when I didn't care anymore, I was drunk." Given that these moms were also younger and were having sex with older males, their choice to voluntarily engage in their first sexual experience is questionable.

Sex education curriculum

All focus group participants (male, female, and parent) were dissatisfied with sex education as it is provided in schools. They described the school context as reinforcing gender role socialization: "It teaches them that boys, guys are studs and girls are sluts" (s h c client). Participants state that these negative messages encourage women to be ashamed of and to restrict their sexuality:

> Guys never feel ashamed of being sexual or they don't have
> to feel that they are doing something wrong. But, when I
> was growing up, it just felt like we weren't supposed to think
> about it, as girls. We weren't supposed to, you know, want to
> kiss a boy or anything like that. And it felt like your feelings
> were unnatural. I think it is more of a focus on the girls'
> responsibility to not, you know, to push the boys away. And just
> that is a damaging thing to your self-esteem. You feel that you
> are not right or something like that. Because after all, you're
> just being human. (twenty-one-year-old client)

The message young women reported receiving about having relationships and sex is fear-based: "I just remember the dating ones, like okay, I'm gonna put this duct tape on my arm. Once you have sex, it hurts the first time and then (rips tape off arm) ... you're going to get into relationships, then it's gonna hurt you bad and you're going to be sorry. That is how they explained how relationships and sex are" (twenty-year-old client).

Young women and men are generally taught about condoms as the only form of contraception in school: "Just condoms, they just talked about condoms, not anything else" (fourteen-year-old client). Teen moms stated that they learned about birth control after they became pregnant: "I learned about birth control in prenatal class" (teen mom). The type of sex education all focus group participants described receiving is "abstinence-plus," which may have included condom education for prevention of STIs (Lippmann 2000). However, all participants would prefer the comprehensive model of sex education: "Birth control, spend more time on it" (sixteen-year-old female).

Summary: Context of sexual activity in Regina

Results of the youth survey analysis indicate that by grade 12, more young women than men have had sexual intercourse. Because more than half of eighteen-year-old women in Regina are sexually active, there is a need for sexual health care that addresses the unique needs of this age group. Additional findings add to our understanding of the context by suggesting that the relational and socio-cultural contexts leave women vulnerable to sexual violence and patriarchal gender role socialization. Women who have been forced to have sexual relations also report more sexual partners, which increases their risk for unplanned pregnancies and STIs. Results from the focus group analysis validate survey results: alcohol use, peer pressure, and coercion are correlated with sexual activity in adolescence, which is consistent with social influence models of sexual behaviour (Health Canada 1999; Manning, Longmore, and Giordano 2000). These results reinforce the need for sexual health care that may mediate these harmful contextual factors.

What do young women and men want in a sexual health centre?

Our evaluation of Planned Parenthood Regina's Sexual Health Centre offered multiple data sources from which to understand the unique sexual health care needs of young women. The youth survey asked participants to specify the most important quality to them in a sexual health care setting. Both women and men stated that "caring staff" is the most important quality for them (see Table 4). This aspect is more important for young women.

Table 4: Most important qualities of a sexual health centre.

Quality	WOMEN		MEN	
	n	%	n	%
Caring staff	556	50	353	34***
That no one know I had gone there	156	14	209	20
The place is easy to get to	136	12	198	19
No or low cost for services	141	13	173	17

***p<.001

Previous research has also found "caring" to be the most highly valued sexual health care quality to adolescent girls (Hardy and Zabin 1991). Our results contribute additional data to these previous findings and further suggest that it is the most important quality for both sexes.

Who's using Planned Parenthood services?

Among all grade 10/12 sexually active respondents in the city, youth survey results indicate that significantly more women (44%) than men (16%) have used the Sexual Health Centre. The majority of the teen parents (73%) have used the Centre. The shc seems to be a resource for young people who have been physically forced to have sex or who have had intercourse while drunk: more students who have been physically forced (38%) than who have never been physically forced (29%) used the Centre; more students who have had intercourse while drunk (33%) than who have never had intercourse while drunk (25%) used the Centre. These results suggest that the shc may mediate the negative effects of sexual abuse and alcohol use among young women and men.

shc Client Satisfaction Survey

The Client Satisfaction Survey offers another source of data on what young people want in a health care setting. Of the clients who chose to complete the survey, 60 per cent were nineteen years old or younger and 98 per cent were female. Using a five-point Likert-type scale, we note that 95 per cent of clients reported being very satisfied with staff at the shc and 92 per cent were very satisfied with services provided. We conclude that clients are satisfied with the shc.

Analysis of one open-ended question gave us the opportunity to hear how young women constructed their response to "What did you like the most about your visit to Planned Parenthood Regina?" Of the 486 clients who responded to this item, two words appear most frequently: "friendly" was cited by 169 participants (35%) and "comfortable" by 83 (17%). The fact that these two qualities were mentioned consistently and spontaneously in this open-ended format suggests that they are important to the women who use the SHC. These two words were also used most frequently in focus groups when young women described their experience with the Sexual Health Centre.

The word "comfortable," particularly, is ubiquitous in health research but has not been well-defined. For example, "discomfort" with physicians or "discomfort" with procedures is routinely used in literature to describe relationships as well as physical procedures (Langille *et al.* 1999). However, "comfortable" is a perception that may differ with gender and age of respondent as well as with focus of perception (*i.e.*, relationship or procedure). Qualitative data analysis indicates that young women use the term "comfortable" to describe four different aspects of care: physician or nurse/client relationships; physical space; physician or nurse/client communication; and medical procedures (see Table 5, discussed below).

Table 5: The SHC provides a caring environment that mediates negative contextual effects of young women's lived sexuality.

"Comfortable" Response of SHC Client	Mediator- Environment of SHC	"Discomfort" Context of Sexuality
(1) *Relationship* Comfortable/safe/ respect	Caring staff/ friendly Non-judgmental	Gender role stereotypes "Sluts," "Teen moms"
(2) *Physical Space* Autonomy	Home (normalizes sexual health) TV/couches	Sterile, clinical lab coats, disease Child status
(3) *Communication* Comfortable / confidential	Choice, empowerment Quality information	Physician/ patient (power) Sex ed. info lacking
(4) *Medical Procedures* Comfortable	PAP/exam Choice/information	Sexual violence Pain, coercion

Participants in our research used the word "comfortable" most often to describe the relationship of care: "How nice everyone was, how comfortable they make you feel, much more so than my family doctor" (client). Young women described this relational context as "really comfortable, and I feel like I could talk to them and they weren't judging me. They were just there to help" (sixteen-year-old client).

This non-judgmental attitude conveyed by staff communicates caring that extends beyond the young women's physical needs to their emotional and psychological needs: "There's not a bunch of pressure, you know, they welcome you in their arms. They make you feel comfortable there. Just knowing they are there for you. Just to help you get back on your feet and build your confidence up" (seventeen-year-old female).

Friendliness conveyed to clients by staff is an important aspect of "caring," yet what the clients mean is more instrumental than the attitudinal "caring" described in the literature: "It's friendly. They're quick. You immediately feel comfortable in the atmosphere. You are not waiting with your thoughts or concerns or uncomfortableness, ever. All positive stuff. All positive" (client). This finding validates feminist theorizing that relational context is important to young women (Tolman 1999).

A hierarchy of values emerged in clients' description of good care. Being met in a friendly way in this setting surprises clients since sexually active young women are usually met with negative and disapproving attitudes: "The friendly and open atmosphere, you don't belittle people, yet you make a person feel dignified" (client).

The non-judgmental attitude is as important as high quality information: "Clients appreciate the friendliness of the staff and all the information given." Friendliness is an active relational quality that creates an atmosphere within which young women feel comfortable receiving sexual health care. The word "atmosphere" was commonly used by participants to describe the shc. Friendliness seems to be extremely important in establishing this environment of care: "Here people are friendly. It's a nice cozy atmosphere instead of a walk-in clinic" (sixteen-year-old client).

Seventy-three per cent of the teen parents surveyed use the shc as their regular sexual health care provider. Focus group analysis indicated that the environment at the shc mediates the negative effects of discrimination that teen moms face in other health care settings. "Comfortable," to teen moms, means being treated with respect: "It was comfortable, there was no one to stare at us 'cause we were young" (teen mom).

"Comfortable" also describes the physical space at the sнc: "The entire comfortable setting not set up like a doctor's office. I liked how I could feel comfortable, how the waiting room is like a home" (client). The space that greets young women when they enter the sнc normalizes sexual health: "It's less formal. Quiet and comfortable. Not so formal. You do not see people walking around in stark white jackets. And comfortable couches" (sixteen-year-old client).

The Centre is located in a house, which, to clients, feels like coming home. This sends the message to young women that sexual health is natural, rather than a clinical, medical "problem." Participants wrote comments such as "the friendly staff and the house-like environment, felt very calm." For young women, this environment reverses the messages they receive in sex education, for example, about sexuality causing pain and fear.

When young women enter the sнc, they sit in a "comfortable" space on couches. The importance of these couches as perceived by clients cannot be minimized: "The couches are comfy." The space also includes a TV that is tuned to youth-oriented programming: "They have two couches and a TV so you can watch TV" (client); "You get to watch TV while you're waiting" (client).

When asked about the TV, staff at the sнc stated that clients control the TV stations. This gives the message to clients that they are "in control." The couches, the house setting, TV, and friendly staff all contribute to a warm environment: "Makes me feel comfortable. Less like a cold clinic and more like a friend's house but with nurses and doctors" (client).

Focus group participants juxtaposed the "relaxed" atmosphere of the sнc with the "sterile" hospital environment that can have "uncomfortable" associations: "I like that it is not so sterile. 'Cause I am uncomfortable in those kind of places. When I was little I was in the hospital for a while. Going back to something like that to discuss sexual health, I don't know, I would just feel like a little kid. So here I feel like an adult" (twenty-three-year-old client).

Comfortable also means safe: "If you're looking at youth and targeting that population ... medical clinics and hospitals, like, that's the adult world. And I don't think they [youth] feel that they have a place of their own or that they can feel safe or comfortable in. But you have a place like this where, hey, I go there and ... now my friends are there and we're learning and hanging out at Planned Parenthood. Like, that's good. That's really important" (twenty-one-year-old client).

High quality information delivered in a non-judgmental way by friendly people is highly valued by young women: "I felt very comfortable with the nurse; she was very knowledgeable about the questions I had."

Participants stated that the s h c provides a safe and non-judgmental atmosphere for young women and men who are in crisis: "Me and my friends called from a pay phone at school and made an appointment. It was hard 'cause we had never been here before. And when I got in that room, I was sitting there freaking out. It was all okay, though, it was all good. 'Cause you don't walk in that room and instantly, what are you here for, go away ... like, they are friendly" (fourteen-year-old female). This acceptance of their experience is actively communicated to them by staff; their sexual health concerns are validated as serious and important.

Another message communicated to clients is one of empowerment. This philosophy counters sexist messages by treating young women as capable of informed choice, and that idea is communicated in many ways. Developmentally appropriate information is posted everywhere: "So here I felt like an adult. And I can make my own choices like this. Things are posted everywhere. And, like, all different viewpoints. You can make your own choices. Not feel like they are telling you that you have to do this or that" (twenty-year-old client).

Teen moms, for instance, choose the s h c because they receive better quality information: "I'm fairly comfortable with my doctor, but Planned Parenthood has better options than your doctor" (teen mom). One client describes how the relational context provided at the s h c supports autonomy and informed choice during crisis points when young women may be most vulnerable:

> When I came here [s h c] I was really scared because that's when I was coming to see if I was pregnant or not. I came here with my baby's father. He was actually the one who told me to come here. So I was just a freaking mess. And he was like, okay, we are gonna go to Planned Parenthood tomorrow to find out what's going on. And I was really, really, really scared. But then once I talked to someone and they had told me I was pregnant and of course I didn't know what I was gonna do or what I wanted to do or how I felt. And they stopped there and they

talked to me and they calmed me down and they told me what
I could do or like whatever they talked to me. Everything was
completely my choice. (twenty-year-old client)

The SHC provides sexual health services and education in ways that support young people's autonomy and agency.

Comfortable also means confidential. Clients provided comments such as "confidential and very comforting place to be"; "confidential, didn't feel uncomfortable." Young women want the privacy of their own sexual health centre with providers who will not disclose information to their parents:

I kinda figured that if I came here it's because ... I mean, I
wasn't as young as probably a lot of the teenage females that
do come here, but it's more comfortable a setting. 'Cause I
mean if I was say fifteen or sixteen, however old, and I needed
to talk to a doctor. Most people go to their family doctors, in
which they're with their parents. And they're panicking and,
oh my God, they're going to tell my parents. And even if the
doctor says, no, I mean, I'm sure you are going to be scared
that they're going to say something. Planned Parenthood really
helped me feel comfortable. (twenty-one-year-old client)

Comfortable with medical procedures

Focus group participants stated that the comfortable relationships contributed to their ability to tolerate uncomfortable physical procedures such as PAPs.

When I first came here, my friends told me that if you are
over eighteen you have to come in for a PAP. Even though you
haven't had sex you have to do it. So I came in here like going,
"Oh my God, I've never had this, don't know what" ... And then
the doctor says, "No, you do not have to have one." And then
we just talked about birth control and stuff like that. And it
was like AHHH ... Right on! And she was like, oh come back
after you've had sex; when I did come back she made me feel so
comfortable and everything. It wasn't a bad experience at all.
(twenty-year-old client)

The comfortable environment of care makes it easier for young women to tolerate uncomfortable medical procedures.

Conclusions

Results from our research validate recent feminist theorizing about young women's sexuality (Johnson, Roberts, and Worrell 1999). They are empowered and are sexually active in greater percentages than young men. The majority of young women in our city are sexually active before they leave high school. However, their lived environment exposes them to sexual violence and patriarchal gender role socialization (Johnson, Roberts, and Worrell 1999). A large percentage of women in our research have been physically forced to have sex. Participants who are physically forced are younger at first intercourse and report having had sex with more partners, which puts them at greater risk for STIs and unplanned pregnancies. Alcohol use and sexual activity are correlated, and young women are having sex with older partners, further suggesting that young women are vulnerable in their socio-cultural context. Because young women are sexually active, yet confronting a dangerous environment, we conclude, as previous researchers have suggested, that young women have unique sexual health care needs (Dougherty 1999). Responsibility for this care cannot be left to schools, since, as Michelle Fine states (1988, 42), "public schools may actually disable young women in their negotiation as sexual subjects. They travel through and into positions of passivity and victimization; young women are currently educated away from positions of sexual self interest."

Our findings agree with other researchers who state that young women need their own place for sexual health care (Langille *et al.* 1999). However, through listening to the participants in our research, we conclude that this "place" must provide an environment that mediates the negative effects of the socio-cultural context within which they enact their sexuality. Girls and young women have clearly articulated in previous research what does not work for them. Results from analysis of multiple data sources in our study provide a picture of what does work. The voices of young women in our study lead us to conclude that the environment of care provided by settings such as the s н c works. In the real world of girls' lived environments, the context of sexual health care makes a difference. Listening to young women's voices, we have heard that their setting must include certain qualities, especially caring, friendly staff who create a comfortable environment for care. In fact, both young women and men stated that caring staff is the most important quality in a sexual health centre. The results of our research extend the importance of the feminist relational paradigm into sexual health care delivery (Manning, Longmore, and Giordano 1999).

For girls and young women, a comfortable environment where sexual health care is provided is important. According to our research, "comfortable" for girls and young women includes four dimensions: (1) the relationship of care; (2) the physical space; (3) communication; and (4) medical procedures. The relational domain between physician/nurse and client is fundamental. Friendliness is an instrumental aspect of caring that is communicated to clients. Being met by friendly staff in a homey and relaxed environment helps young women feel safe and reverses negative gender stereotypes that sexually active women may receive elsewhere. A comfortable physical space deconstructs the message that young women's sexuality is a "problem." A house setting and comfortable couches condone sexual health. Young women immediately feel as if they belong in a setting where other young women gather. Control of TV programming and information posted everywhere sends the message that they are being treated like adults. Empowerment and autonomy is encouraged when staff communicate full acceptance of young women's experiences and give them unbiased information. Even uncomfortable medical procedures such as PAPs are tolerated as a result of the comfortable relationships of care given to young women in such a setting. These results enhance our understanding of the word "comfortable" when young women describe sexual health care.

Sexual health care of young women does belong within the domain of medical care, contrary to the dominant views of policy-makers and health care providers (Dougherty 1999). However, service delivery must be implemented in ways that meet the unique needs of girls and young women. Our findings suggest, as feminist theorists recommend, that health care providers can be empowering agents (Tolman 1999). Sexual health centres such as the one we evaluated mediate the oppression that young women encounter in our society. The empowerment philosophy of Planned Parenthood supports the autonomy and agency that young women are exercising today. Our findings give suggestions for ways to construct a comfortable environment of care. Results of our research remind us of the importance of supporting these kinds of services for the future health of young women and men.

Acknowledgment

This project (HTF SK334) was supported by funding from the Health Transition Fund, Health Canada. Views expressed do not necessarily reflect official policy of Health Canada.

Chapter 11

VOICES OF DANCERS WITH MOBILITY IMPAIRMENTS

Donna L. Goodwin, Joan Krohn, and Arvid Kuhnle

Introduction

Every Wednesday afternoon, a group of young dancers comes together to go over routines and share the joy of expressive movement. The parents, who have rushed to arrive on time, quietly retreat to the sidelines to watch the day's lesson unfold. As the music begins, the young dancers glide and twirl as they rehearse their dance compositions. This scene is repeated over and over in innumerable communities across the country. What is unique to this particular Wednesday program, however, is that the dancers are children with mobility impairments and they dance from their wheelchairs.

At first glance there appears to be a strong contradiction between the notion of ballet, ballroom, or modern dance and dancers with mobility impairments. Upon further reflection, however, the notion of people dancing from wheelchairs conveys a sense of adventure, risk, challenge, and new possibilities. The Kids in Motion Dance Program in Saskatoon, Saskatchewan, under the direction of Joan Krohn, has looked beyond the contradictions. The artistic success of the program is a reflection of the experimental and collaborative approach shared by the dancers, parents, and instructors.

Dance and movement exploration programs have been conducted for children with disabilities for more than thirty years (Riordan 1989; Zimmer and Krombholz 1994). Dance has been used in clinical and educational settings as a form of therapy, as a means of achieving physical and psychological well-being, for recreational purposes, and as a form of personal expression (Boswell 1989; Elliot 1998; Schwartz 1989).

Dancing from wheelchairs has four overlapping aims. The first is the physical development that occurs through muscle strengthening, flexibility development, and balance training. The second involves the development of new movement patterns and the improvement of existing ones.

This can translate into improved posture, enhanced manoeuvrability of the wheelchair, and improved coordination of movements. Psychological benefits, aim three, are reflected in such constructs as improved self-esteem and self-confidence, and an expanded form of self-expression. And lastly, the social aspects of wheelchair dance are obvious, as teamwork and co-operation are required for success in pair or group formations (Zimmer and Krombholz 1994).

Peters' (1996) model of disablement helps explain how parents, dancers, and instructors have explored and expanded our traditional perceptions of the body, definitions of personal success and feelings of self, and able-bodied norms to make the experience of these dancers a reality. Disablement refers to the "process" of becoming disabled. Disablement models conceptually link functional change occurring within the individual to social activities in response to that individual (Peters 1996). Recently, these models have begun to emphasize strength rather than weakness, environmental and social context rather than the isolated individual, and the role of mediators in the disablement process (Depauw 2000).

Peters' model of disablement also reflects three perspectives, that of the outsider, the interventionist, and the insider. The outsider's perspective is characterized by objective descriptions of disablement such as those found in textbooks, professional journals, and classification systems (including sport). As outsiders, we emphasize, measure, or classify. The interventionist's perspective is characterized by concrete application of the outsider's knowledge to maximize the individual's abilities. Interventionists work with physical structure and abilities toward maximizing function through rehabilitation regimes. Normalization within the contexts of home, school, or work is the primary goal.

The unique contribution that Peters makes is the inclusion of the insider perspective in his model, or disablement as it is experienced. The insider perspective can be contextualized on three levels: the body as it is experienced, the individual's unique sense of self, and experiences within the larger social context. The body experienced refers to the structural or functional changes that have resulted from impairment: how the body moves is the focus. From an insider's perspective, a person may recount that she moves more slowly than other people do, while an outsider may indicate that the person has *hemiparesis* (muscular weakness on one side of the body brought about by hemorrhagic stroke).

The "person" in Peters' model makes reference to the aggregate of attitudes and abilities that contribute to an individual's unique sense of self. It is what gives a person a sense of personal integrity and is that which may be threatened by impairment. A person's sense of self can result in restriction in activities that may be accompanied by feelings of frustration, anger, and/or grief, or conversely, it may result in the pursuit of new activities due to an acceptance of self.

"Society" within Peters' model refers to the insider's experience of societal context. The social context can lead to disadvantages or advantages, depending upon the circumstantial interaction of outsider attitudes and norms of behaviour with the insider's vulnerability, ambivalence, or self-reliance. The insider's perspective can be understood through a phenomenological lens that provides a changing context against which personal meaning is experienced across time, through aging, personal history, and social influences. Only the insider fully embodies the events that take place within the context of his/her body, person, and society.

Purpose of the study

The psychosocial experience of children with disabilities has been largely ignored in the literature (Blinde and McCallister 1998). The lack of research interest in the experience of dancers with disabilities is even more pronounced (Fraleigh 1991; Kleinman 1992). The purpose of this study is to describe how children and youth with mobility impairment experience movement and dance. More specifically, the objectives of the study are to let children speak for themselves on the subjects of (a) their bodies (how they describe themselves); (b) their experiences as dancers (the role that this form of physical activity and personal expression plays in their perceptions of their disability); and (c) their wheelchairs as implements of dance (the semiotic importance of this mobility device).

Method

A hermeneutic, phenomenological approach was used in the study. Hermeneutic phenomenology, or the study of the interpretation of texts for the purpose of obtaining a common understanding of the meaning assigned to everyday experiences, enables researchers to ascertain underlying structures (themes) that emerge from the descriptions of participants and the commonalties in meanings understood (Moustakas 1994; Packer 1985; Van Manen 2000).

Participants

This study is part of a larger investigation that examined the experiences of the dancers in the Kids in Motion Dance Program. The one male and five female dancers varied in age from six years to fourteen years (M= 8 years). Due to mobility impairment caused by *spina bifida*, all of the dancers participated in the program from their wheelchairs. The exception in the group was a six-year-old dancer who did not have a disability but who preferred to dance from a wheelchair rather than participate in what she referred to as "regular dancing."

The experiences presented here are those of the two senior female dancers, aged ten and fourteen years, and their mothers. The senior dancers' ages, their love of dance, and the length of time they had been involved in dance suggested that their experiences were worthy of in-depth examination.

The mothers of these two older dancers have also worked through developmental changes and experienced the challenges of fostering an active lifestyle for their daughters over a longer period of time than have the parents of the younger dancers.

Data collection

A combination of several data sources was used to triangulate the data (Janesick 1994). To gain a broad view, information was collected in the form of interviews, visual documentations, journals, and field notes over a five-month period.

The dancers participated in two one-hour, semi-structured, audio-recorded, one-on-one interviews (Graue and Walsh 1998; Maybin 1996). (See Appendix A for sample questions.) To augment the spoken descriptions, the dancers were also invited to keep journals or draw pictures of their dance experiences (Emmison and Smith 2000; Harper 2000). The journals and drawings facilitated rapport development, provided a stimulus for discussion, and offered another way for the participants to symbolically express their thoughts and feelings about their dance experiences. One dancer preferred to keep a journal but did not complete any drawings, while the other dancer completed drawings but did not keep a journal.

The mothers, like their daughters, participated in two one-hour, semi-structured, one-on-one interviews. They were also given one-time use of cameras (with twenty-four images) and encouraged to capture images that they felt represented their daughters' experiences in the dance program (Van Leeuwen and Jewitt 2001). The participants were encouraged to be creative in their use of the camera. Images of things, places, classmates, groups, individuals, and staged or spontaneous action shots were all encouraged. The significance of each image was explained to the researcher during the parents' second interviews and became part of the textual record, thereby clarifying the significance of the images and removing researcher bias (Pink 2001; Walker 1993). Both mothers voluntarily augmented the images with photographs from their family photo albums. One parent also shared her thoughts in journal format.

At the end of each interview session, the researchers recorded reflections in the form of field notes on what was said that day, ideas for further probing on subsequent days, and preliminary thoughts about themes emerging from the data. These notes permitted the researchers to return conceptually to the interview during the analysis of the data (Bogdan and Biklen 1992).

Method of analysis

The structures of the experience, or phenomenological themes embodied in the participants' words, were generated through a line-by-line semiotic clustering analysis of the verbatim transcripts. Semiotic clustering analysis is the research for and interpretation of categories and linguistic structures found in the text (Feldman 1995). Following the semiotic linguistic tradition, not only were the words and their linguistic structures considered and interpreted, but the context that triggered the response also received attention (Manning and Cullum-Swan 1994). The transcripts, journal entries, and field notes were read over in entirety. Essential or particularly revealing phrases were highlighted and coded with meaningful labels. Those that were conceptually similar were gathered together into thematic statements. Descriptions of the symbolic meaning of the visual representations were derived from the descriptions provided by the participants during the interviews (Walker 1993).

Results

The daughters and mothers brought their own unique perspectives to the dance phenomenon and yet their descriptions were experientially similar (Table 1).

Table 1: Thematic analysis summary.

THEME	DANCERS	MOTHERS
Breaking the mould	"A dream come true"	"I am so proud"
Beyond the wheelchair	"They see me, not the chair"	"They can be themselves"
More than an extracurricular activity	"Younger children look up to me"	"Parents learn from each other"
Share the canoe	"We get a roar of applause"	"Promotes disability awareness"

Four themes encapsulated the experiences described by the dancers and their mothers: breaking the mould, beyond the wheelchair, more than an extracurricular activity, and sharing the dance.

Breaking the mould

There is a tension between the bodies we often associate with dancers and those of persons with disabilities. As one parent very astutely said, "I don't think a lot of people use dance and wheelchair in the same sentence that much." And yet, these young people identified themselves as dancers. They confronted the traditional image of the slender, symmetrical, and agile body of the dancer and broke the mould as they identified themselves not only as dancers, but also as graceful, strong, and soft in their movements. One mother commented, "When I watch her do a pirouette, she uses her arms and her body and she pulls it into the chair and the chair is moving with her, she is the one in control." The dancers were also keenly interested in providing input into the music selections, the choreography, and the costumes. It was a dream-come-true for these young dancers.

When she reflected upon being told that her baby had *spina bifida*, one mother commented on the uncertainty she felt at that moment about the future. Uncertain as this time was, however, she also had a sense of optimism for her daughter. In her journal, one mother recalled her baby's first day: "[S]he may not be a ballerina, but there are a lot of things she will be able to be and to do." Little did this mother know that her daughter would prove her wrong.

From the parents' perspectives, the dance program provides them with a deep sense of pride in the accomplishments of their children. "There wasn't one parent there who watched them that didn't cry" (Telemiracle 2000). Parents are also grateful "to have this opportunity to have [their children] be able to be all that they are. They can be whatever they want to be here."

Beyond the wheelchair

For these dancers, the wheelchair has become more than a means by which to get from point A to point B. It has facilitated their expression of emotion and creativity through movement. One of the dancers indicated that she had been disappointed in the past by others' views of her disability: "Being in a wheelchair kind of discouraged me [because] people think you can't do anything." Then "we found Joan [the dance instructor]!" And now "I am learning how to move my chair." Before, her wheelchair was "just a thing to get around in"; her dance experiences have shown her that "you can actually do something with your wheelchair."

The wheelchair was not a limiting factor for the dancers, but rather provided emotional, creative, and physical freedom. One mother said, "The wheelchair has become a very instrumental tool in her just being free." Whereas the mothers were pleased that the dancers could be themselves in a learning environment that maximized their abilities, dance provided the daughters with an opportunity to demonstrate the outermost limits of their abilities. The daughters strove to move beyond the wheelchair and the constraints often imposed by others' perceptions of ability.

The wheelchair was always secondary to the dance itself. Whereas some viewers will always see the wheelchair first and foremost, one dancer remarked, "I've seen them watching [me], not the wheelchair."

More than extracurricular activity

Although the outcomes of this dance program are predictably similar to those of other dance programs, there are some aspects that appear to be unique to these dancers. The younger dancers looked up to the older dancers as they shared their vision, their dance, and their personal life stories. The opportunity to learn from each other was not overlooked. The older dancers model movement possibilities, how the wheelchair can be used as a form of personal expression, and independence in physical management. One mother of an older dancer commented, "The parents have told me how much they appreciate her being in the class because for their children she is a very positive role model."

The parents talked about the growth they have witnessed in their daughters. Their daughters are learning to dance (and also learning rhythm and patterns of moving, and using their muscles), but they are also connecting with others with mobility impairments, learning to work co-operatively, developing patience, supporting each other's efforts and accomplishments, and building confidence. One parent reflected on a comment from the dance instructor directed to her daughter: "She choreographs, she designs the costumes, she picks the music, and she has the dance in her head."

The mothers also identified with and learned from each other's experiences. It's "the people that you meet. It's the people around you that just make so many special memories for other people." The dance program was more than an extracurricular activity; it promoted growth in both the dancers and the parents.

"Gotta share the dance"

The dancers expressed a strong desire to share their hard work and accomplishments through public dance performances. It was their time to show off and receive acknowledgment for their efforts. Although the preparation was tiring, and the actual performance days could place extra stress on the dancers and their families, these were sacrifices that were made freely. A drawing completed by one of the dancers depicts her image of a piece of abstract art that evoked images of dance for her: "It reminded me of dance because it was so colourful and ... because of the words on it, 'Dance Man, Dance!' I love performing dance. It just makes me feel really, really happy ... I have actually accomplished something."

The parents were also supportive of the public dance performances, which brought closure to a term of dance classes and provided them with an opportunity to enjoy the aesthetics of the performance. But in addition, there was also a sense that it was important for other people to witness the accomplishments of the dancers. Public education was a prominent theme in the parents' support of the dance recitals: "Showing off their ability was important ... all the parents felt that the rest of the province needed to be educated about what kids in wheelchairs can do." Another parent added, "Just because you're in a wheelchair doesn't mean that you can't dance, that you can't be beautiful and graceful."

Discussion

In reflecting upon Peters' model of disablement and the demarcations of body, person, and society, we see that the bodily experience of disability in dance manifests itself in a number of significant ways.

The body

The dancers, with the support of their mothers, challenged able-body-ism and the traditional dance aesthetic as the standard against which dance can be expressed and experienced. These dancers chose not to acquiesce to the traditional image of a dancer's body, but rather to live their dream of dancing. Whereas the stares of others can separate the body from the mind and create a sense of dualism both in the observer and the person being observed, these dancers maintained their identity as dancers irrespective of the stereotypical image a wheelchair can evoke (Phillips 1992).

The dancers experienced movement on their own terms, exploring the capabilities of their bodies to the fullest. They demonstrated optimism about what the future holds in light of a society that is quick to reinforce the norm but slow to acknowledge potential.

The Kids in Motion Dance Program gave the dancers an opportunity to explore their wheelchairs as implements of dance. Although perceived as a way to get from point A to B, the wheelchair also created a means by which to express emotion, portray creative expression, and share the love of dance with others. Whereas a wheelchair can be viewed from an outsider's perspective as a symbol of weakness and dependence, from the dancers' perspective it provided personal freedom and an opportunity to experience their bodies in new ways. The wheelchair, although essential to the dance experience, was secondary to their identities as dancers, however. The wheelchair is an inanimate object; it is the dancer in the chair who makes the dance (Flanderson 2000).

The person

The mothers indicated that the dance program provided an opportunity for their daughters to be their own persons and experience the world on their own terms. They also learned from each other, developed leadership skills, and experienced personal growth. This personal growth experienced by the dancers is clearly demarcated in Peters' model. Participation in the dance program also provided the older girls with an opportunity to be role models for others. They were looked up to by younger dancers and took pride in their roles.

Society

The dancers and their mothers also saw the dance program as a means by which to overcome the myths of weakness, passivity, dependency, and helplessness imposed on persons with disabilities by society. The public performances provided an opportunity to showcase the accomplishments of the dancers and educate the general public as to the abilities of persons with disabilities. The concomitant benefit to society is an expanded and enriched understanding of how success must be personally determined. Observing dancers who use wheelchairs causes us to come to terms with our own assumptions of the "appropriate place" for persons with disabilities (Marley 1997). We are asked to reassess our pursuit of normalization, a pursuit that labels people according to ability (or disability). The experiences of the daughters and mothers calls into question the "try harder" dilemma, or the cultural notion of perseverance in efforts to overcome disability that is unwittingly imposed by rehabilitation practitioners, employers, family members, and potentially the person him or herself (Phillips 1992). As is so aptly stated by Mary Verdi-Fletcher, co-artistic director and founding director of the Cleveland Ballet Dancing Wheels, "[T]he vision of the dance eliminates stereotypes. When we perform, we talk about the fact that disability comes from perceptions and a lack of understanding about ability" ("Innovative dance" 1998).

Conclusion

The Kids in Motion Dance Program is enriching the arts community of Saskatoon and the province of Saskatchewan. The dancers have changed the way we think about the aesthetics of dance and the richness of the dance experience. Plans are underway to expand the present program to bring together dancers, instructors, and choreographers, with and without disabilities, and to bring the gift of dance to a larger audience. Outreach programs, appearances by guest artists, school performances, the involvement of College of Music students, video production, and syllabus development are envisioned for the future. Protecting the dancers and their efforts from being trivialized has been one of the principles guiding the Kids in Motion Dance Program. The troupe will continue to perform only when ready and only at venues that will further the goals and objectives of the program.

The focus of the program will always be the dancers with mobility impairments. The incorporation of stand up dancers, or dancers without mobility impairments, will bring a new dimension to the program. Moving beyond floor patterns created by the wheelchairs, stand up dancers will bring expanded and seamless movements to the troupe's repertoire as fluidity from the wheelchair to the floor can occur through shared weight sustainment, complex balance moves, and flight (Siciliano 2000). Opportunities and choice are expanded for dancers both with and without disabilities.

The dancers' dreams are clear and the future is bright, whether the benefits are the education of patrons of the arts, personal expression, a sense of physical well-being, enhanced career opportunities, or the sheer joy of movement.

Authors' Note

The President's SSHRC Fund, University of Saskatchewan supported this study. We thank Laura Harris for her support in the completion of this study. A very warm thank you is also extended to the mothers and daughters who so willingly shared their stories.

Appendix A

Sample Interview Questions

DANCERS
1. Tell me about the children who attend this program.
2. What are you and your dance friends learning in the dance program?
3. What words would you use to describe your body when you are in dance class? Do you have any stories that would help you describe your body?
4. In what ways do you think differently about your wheelchair when you are at the dance program than other times during your day?
5. Tell me about your public performances. How important are they to you?
6. If you had a friend who you wanted to join the program, what would you say to him or her?

PARENTS
1. How did you come to be involved in the Kids in Motion Dance Program?
2. How do you think your son or daughter would describe their physical self?
3. What have you taken away (learned) from the program? What part do parents play in the program?
4. Does your child think of him or herself as a dancer? How and why has this identification developed?
5. Tell me about the role of the wheelchair in your child's dance experiences.
6. Tell me about the public performances. What is their significance, for you, for your child, for the audience?

References

Abel, S., and R. Kearns. 1991. Birth places: A geographical perspective on planned home birth in New Zealand. *Social Science and Medicine* 33 (7): 825–34.

Aboriginal Justice Council. 1999. *Our mob, our justice: Keeping the vision alive.* Perth: Aboriginal Justice Council Secretariat.

Ahrentzen, S. 1992. Home as a workplace in the lives of women. In *Human behavior and environment: Advances in theory and research*, vol. 12, ed. I. Altman and S. Low, 113–38. New York: Plenum Press.

Ajemian, I., and B. Mount. 1980. *Royal Victoria Hospital manual on palliative/hospice care.* New York: ARNO.

Allen, P.G. 1986. *The sacred hoop: Recovering the feminine in America Indian traditions.* Boston: Beacon.

Aptheker, B. 1989. *Tapestries of life: Women's work, women's consciousness, and the meaning of everyday experience.* Amherst: University of Massachusetts Press.

Aranda, M.P., and B.G. Knight. 1997. The influence of ethnicity and culture on the caregiver stress and coping process: A sociocultural review and analysis. *The Gerontologist* 37 (3): 342–54.

Austen, T. 1998. *A cry in the wind: Conflict in Western Australia, 1829–1929.* Darlington: Darlington Publishing Group.

Backhouse, C. 1999. *Colour-coded: A legal history of racism in Canada, 1900–1950.* Toronto: University of Toronto Press.

Bain, M.A. 1982. *Full fathoms five.* Perth, Western Australia: Artlook Books.

Belenky, M., B. Clinchy, N. Goldberger, and J. Tarule. 1997. *Women's ways of knowing: The development of self, voice, and mind.* 10th ed. New York: Basic Books.

Bell, H.R. 1998. *Men's business: Women's business.* Rochester, VT: Inner Traditions International.

Bennett, S. 1999. *White politics and black Australians.* Sydney: Allen and Unwin.

Berger, John. 1973. *Ways of seeing.* London: British Broadcasting Corporation.

Berman, T., G. Ingram, M. Gibbons, R. Hatch, L. Maignon, and C. Hatch. 1994. *Clayoquot and dissent.* Vancouver, BC: Ronsdale Press.

Berndt, R.M., and C.H. Berndt. 1988. *The world of the first Australians.* 5th ed. Canberra: Aboriginal Studies Press.

Bernzweig, J., J.I. Takayama, C. Phibbs, C. Lewis, and R.H. Pantell. 1997. Gender differences in physician-patient communication: Evidence from pediatric visits. *Archives of pediatric and adolescent medicine* 151: 586–91.

Blagg, H. 2000. *Crisis intervention in Aboriginal family violence.* Perth: Crime Research Centre, University of Western Australia.

Blinde, M.E., and S.G. McCallister. 1998. Listening to the voices of students with disabilities. *Journal of Physical Education, Recreation, and Dance* 69 (6): 64–68.

Bogdan, R.C., and S.K. Biklen. 1992. *Qualitative research for education: An introduction to theory and methods.* Needham Heights, MA: Allyn and Bacon.

Boisevert, J.A., R.F. Jevne, and C.L. Nekolaichuk. 1997. *The experience of hope in a self-help group for women with eating disorders*. Unpublished manuscript.

Bornstein, K. 1994. *Gender outlaw: On men, women, and the rest of us*. New York: Vintage Books.

Boswell, B. 1989. Dance as creative expression for the disabled. *Palaestra* 6 (5): 28–34.

Boucher, P. 1994. Women in the shadows of the industrial forest: Silences, tensions, and contradictions. Paper presented at the *Women and Canadian Environment Conference*, Vancouver, BC.

———. 1998. Ecology, feminism and planning: Lessons from women's environmental activism in Clayoquot Sound. PhD diss., University of British Columbia, Vancouver, BC.

Braidotti, R., E. Charkiewicz, S. Häusler, and S. Andwierginga. 1995. *Women, the environment and sustainable development: Towards a theoretical synthesis*. London: Zed Books.

British Paediatric Association/Association for Children with Life-Threatening Conditions and their Families. 1966. *A guide to the development of paediatric palliative care services*. London: British Paediatric Association.

Brown, P., B. Davies, and N. Martens. 1990. Families in supportive care – part 2. Palliative care at home: A viable care setting. *Journal of Palliative Care* 6 (3): 21–27.

Browne, C.V. 1998. *Women, feminism and aging*. New York: Springer.

Buckelew, Alvin. 1984. *Terrorism and the American response*. San Rafael, CA: Mira Academic Press.

Butler, J. 1990. *Gender trouble: Feminism and the subversion of identity*. New York: Routledge.

———. 1993. *Bodies that matter: On the discursive limits of "sex."* New York: Routledge.

Buttimer, A. 1980. Home, reach, and the sense of place. In *The human experience of space and place*, ed. A. Buttimer and D. Seamon, 166–87. New York: St. Martin's Press.

Canada. Health Canada. 1999. A report from consultations on a framework for sexual and reproductive health. Ottawa, ON.

———. Indian and Native Affairs Canada. 1995. Population projections of registered Indians 1991–2015. *www.inac.gc.ca/stats/facts/1995/poppro.html*

———. Indian and Native Affairs Canada. N.d. Demographics. *www.inac.gc.ca/strength/demodr.html*

Canadian Palliative Care Association. 1996. *Palliative care: Towards a consensus in standardized principles of practice*. Ottawa: Standards Committee.

Card, J.L. 1993. *Handbook of adolescent sexuality and pregnancy*. Thousand Oaks, CA: Sage.

Carlini, Heather. 1992. *Birth mother trauma: A counseling guide for birth mothers*. Saanichton, B.C.: Morningside Publishing.

Carroll, M. 1995. *Community and the northwestern logger: Continuities and changes in the era of the spotted owl*. Boulder, CO: Westview.

Casey, E. 1993. *Getting back into place: Toward a renewed understanding of the place/world*. Bloomington: Indiana University Press.

Chesterman, J., and B. Galligan. 1997. *Citizens without rights: Aborigines and Australian citizenship*. Melbourne: Cambridge University Press.

Choose Life Report. 1999. Broome, Australia: Kimberley Aboriginal Medical Services Council.

Chowdhry, G. 1995. Engendering development? Women in development (WID) in international development regimes. In Marchand and Parpart 1995, 26–41.

Coley, R., and P.L. Chase-Lansdale. 1998. Adolescent pregnancy and parenthood: Recent Evidence and Future Directions. *American Psychologist* 53: 152–66.

Collins, P. 1990. *Black feminist thought: Knowledge, consciousness, and the politics of empowerment*. Boston, MA: Unwin Hyman.

Cosgrove, D. 1978. Place, landscape and the dialectics of cultural geography. *Canadian Geographer* 22 (1): 66–71.

Council for Aboriginal Reconciliation. 1997. *The path to reconciliation: Issues for a people's movement*. Canberra: Australian Government Publishing Services.

Coutts, J. 1997. "Health-care initiatives tentative," Rock says. *Globe and Mail*, Sept. 13, 1997.

Crawford, M., and J. Macerek. 1989. Feminist theory, feminist psychology: A bibliography of feminist epistemology, critical analysis, and applications. *Psychology of Women Quarterly* 13: 477–91.

Currie, Dawn. 1999. *Girl talk: Adolescent magazines and their readers*. Toronto: University of Toronto Press.

Dalton, J.H., M.J. Elias, and A. Wandersman. 2001. *Community psychology: Linking individuals and communities*. Toronto: Wadsworth.

Davies, Martin. 1997. *Blackwell companion to social work*. Oxford: Blackwell.

Deiter, C. 1999. *From our mothers' arms: The intergenerational impact of residential schools in Saskatchewan*. Toronto: United Church Publishing House.

Depauw, K. 2000. Socio-cultural context of disability: Implications for scientific inquiry and professional preparation. *Quest* 52: 358–68.

Depress, C. 1991. The meaning of home: Literature review and directions for future research and theoretical development. *Journal of Architectural and Planning Research* 8 (2): 96–115.

Diamond, I., and G. Orenstein, eds. 1990. *Reweaving the world: The emergence of ecofeminism*. San Francisco: Sierra Club Books.

Dougherty, D.M. 1999. Health care for adolescent girls. In Johnson, Roberts, and Worrell 1999, 301–25.

Doyle, K. 1992. The symbolic meaning of house and home: An exploration in the psychology of goods. *American Behavioral Scientist* 35 (6): 790–802.

Drill, Esther, Heather McDonald, and Rebecca Odes. 1995–2005. *www.gurl.com*

Dundgeon, D.J., and L. Kristjanson. 1995. Home versus hospital death: Assessment of preferences and clinical challenges. *Canadian Medical Association Journal* 152 (3): 337–40.

Dunk, T. 1991. *It's a working man's town: Male working-class culture in northwestern Ontario*. Montreal: McGill-Queen's University Press.

Eddy, J.J. 1992. Recognition, reconciliation and history. In *Reconciling our differences*, ed. Frank Brennan, 5–18. Richmond, Victoria: Aurora Books.

Egan, B., and S. Klausen. 1998. Female in a forest town: The marginalization of women in Port Alberni's economy. *B.C. Studies* 118: 5–40.

Elder, B. 1998. *Blood on the wattle: Massacres and maltreatment of Aboriginal Australians since 1788*. Sydney: New Holland Publishers.

Elliot, R. 1998. The use of dance in child psychiatry. *Clinical Child Psychology and Psychiatry* 3 (2): 251–65.

Emmison, M., and P. Smith. 2000. *Researching the visual*. Thousand Oaks, CA: Sage.

England, K. 1994. Getting personal: Reflexivity, positionality, and feminist research. *Professional Geographer* 46: 80–89.

Estés, Clarissa Pinkola. 1992. *Women who run with the wolves: Myths and stories of the wild woman archetype*. Toronto: Random House.

Evan, Sarah. 1958. *Services to unmarried mothers: The unwed mother's indecision about her baby as a defense mechanism*. New York: Child Welfare League of America.

Eyles, J., and A. Litva. 1996. Theory calming: You can only get there from here. *Health and Place* 2 (1): 41–44.

Farrell, William Regis. 1982. *The U.S. government response to terrorism: In search of an effective strategy*. Boulder, CO: Westview.

Federation of Saskatchewan Indian Nations (FSIN). *Treaty issues*. N.d. *www.fsin.com/Requests/ohrcweb/pages/treaty_issues_7.htm*

Feinberg, L. 1998. *Transliberation: Beyond pink or blue*. Boston: Beacon Press.

Feldman, M.S. 1995. *Strategies for interpreting qualitative data*. Thousand Oaks, CA: Sage.

Ferguson, Evelyn B. 1984. The real cabbage patch kids: An examination of the Canadian private adoption system. *Occasional Papers in Social Policy Analysis*. Toronto: Ontario Institute for Studies in Education.

Fine, M. 1988. Sexuality, schooling, and adolescent females: The missing discourse of desire. *Harvard Educational Review* 58: 29–53.

Fiske, J. 1993. Child of the state, mother of the nation: Aboriginal women and the ideology of motherhood. *Culture* 13 (1): 17–36.

Flanderson, N. 2000. To infinity and beyond. *Dance Spirit* (March): 33–34.

Fogel, B. 1992. Psychological aspects of staying at home. *Generations* 16 (2): 15–19.

Forrest, L., and F. Rosenberg. 1997. A review of the feminist pedagogy literature: The neglected child of feminist psychology. *Applied and Preventative Psychology* 6: 179–92.

Foucault, M. 1980. *Power/knowledge*. Trans. and ed. C. Gordon, L. Marshall, J. Mepham, and K. Soper. Brighton, UK: Harvester Press.

———. 1985. *The history of sexuality*, vol. 2. Trans. R. Hurley. New York: Pantheon.

Fraleigh, S. 1991. A vulnerable glance: Seeing dance through phenomenology. *Dance Research Journal* 23 (1): 11–16.

Fraser, N. 1997. *Justice interruptus: Critical reflections on the "postsocialist" condition*. London: Routledge.

Freire, P. 1972. *Pedagogy of the oppressed*. Ringwood, Australia: Penguin.

Garcia-Guadila M.P. 1995. Gender, environment, and empowerment in Venezuela. In *Engendering wealth and well-being: Empowerment for global change*, ed. R.L. Blumberg, C.A. Rakowski, I. Tinker, and M. Monteón, 213–37. Boulder, CO: Westview.

Gesler, W. 1992. Therapeutic landscapes: Medical issues in light of the new cultural geography. *Social Science and Medicine* 34 (7): 735–46.

————. 1993. Therapeutic landscapes: Theory and a case study of Epidauros, Greece. *Environment and Planning D: Society and Space* 11: 171-89.

Gibson, K. 1992. Hewers of cake and drawers of tea: Women, industrial restructuring and class processes on the coalfields of central Queensland. *Rethinking Marxism* 5: 29-56.

Gibson-Graham, J.K. 1994. Stuffed if I know: Reflections on post-modern feminist social research. *Gender, Place and Culture* 1: 205-24.

Glasser, G., and A.L. Strauss. 1967. *The discovery of grounded theory: Strategies for qualitative research*. Chicago: Aldine.

Glenn, E.N. 1994. Social constructions of mothering: A thematic overview. In *Mothering: Ideology, experience, and agency*, ed. E.N. Glenn, G. Chang, and L.R. Forcey, 1-29. New York: Routledge.

Goffman, Erving. 1963. *Stigma: Notes on the management of spoiled identity*. New York: Simon and Schuster.

Gradine, J. 1995. Embracing the family. *Canadian Nurse* 91 (9): 31-36.

Grant, J. 1993. *Fundamental feminism: Contesting the core concepts of feminist theory*. New York: Routledge.

Graue, M.E., and D.J. Walsh. 1998. *Studying children in context: Theories, methods, and ethics*. Thousand Oaks, CA: Sage.

Gray, J. 1998. Mentoring the young clinician-scientist. *Clinical and Investigative Medicine* 21: 279-83.

Greenbaum, T.L. 1998. *The handbook for focus group research*. 2nd ed. Newbury Park, CA: Sage.

Griffith, Keith. 1991. *The right to know who you are: Reform of adoption law with honesty, openness and integrity*. Ottawa: Katherine Kimbell.

Gunkel, C.S. 1996. Nancy Reddick's quilts: Autobiographical statements. In *Uncoverings*, ed. L. Horton, 1-28. San Francisco: American Quilt Study Group.

Haebich, A. 1992. *For their own good: Aborigines and government in the southwest of Western Australia 1900-1940*. 2nd ed. Perth: University of Western Australia Press.

Hall, J. 1986. Disorderly women: Gender and labor militancy in Appalachian south. *Journal of American History* 73: 354-82.

Hall, Stuart. 1991. Ethnicity, identity and difference. *Radical America* 3: 9-22.
————. 1992. New ethnicities. In *Race, Culture and Difference*, ed. J. Donald and A. Rattansi, 21-33. Newbury Park, CA: Sage, in association with Open University.
————. 1997. Cultural identity and diaspora. In *Identity and difference*, ed. Kathryn Woodward, 51-59. London: Sage.

Hanson, S., and G. Pratt. 1995. *Gender, work and space*. New York: Routledge.

Hardy, J.B., and L.S. Zabin. 1991. *Adolescent pregnancy in an urban environment: Issues, program and evaluation*. Washington DC: Urban Institute Press.

Harper, D. 2000. Reimagining visual methods. In *Handbook of qualitative research*, 2nd ed., ed. N.K. Denzin and Y.S. Lincoln, 717-32. Thousand Oaks, CA: Sage.

Harris, W. Herbert. 1995. Introduction: A conceptual overview of race, ethnicity, and identity. In *Racial and ethnic identity: Psychological development and creative expression*, ed. Herbert Harris, Howard Blue, and Ezra Griffith, 1-14. New York: Routledge.

Hartley, Shirley Foster. 1975. *Illegitimacy*. Berkeley: University of California Press.

Hayes M., S. Taylor, L. Bayne, and B. Poland. 1990. Reported versus recorded health service utilization in Grenada, West Indies. *Social Science and Medicine* 31: 455–60.

Hazler, R., and J. Carney. 1993. Student-faculty interactions: An underemphasized dimension of counselor education. *Counselor Education and Supervision* 33 (2): 80–89.

Healy, M., and L. Acacio. 1998. *Regional social indicators for Aboriginal people in Western Australia*. Perth, Western Australia: Aboriginal Affairs Department.

Henry, Frances. 1997. Racist discourse and the media. *Ontario Council of Agencies Serving Immigrants (OCASI) Newsletter* 4.

Herman, Judith. 1992. *Trauma and recovery: The aftermath of violence from domestic abuse to political terror*. New York: Basic Books.

Hewitt, R. 1986. *White talk, black talk: Inter-racial friendship and communication among adolescents*. Cambridge: Cambridge University Press.

Hilty, L. 1980. A passion for quilting. In *Uncoverings*, ed. L. Horton, 13–17. Mill Valley, CA: American Quilt Study Group.

Hobsbawm, Eric. 1991. Introduction. *Social Research* 58 (1): 65–68.

Hoffman, L., and J.E. Stake. 1998. Feminist pedagogy in theory and practice: An empirical investigation. *National Women's Studies Association Journal* 10: 71–97.

Hogan, R.A. 1964. Issues and approaches and supervision. *Therapy: Theory, Research and Practice* 1: 139–41.

Horton, L. 1985. South Carolina quilts and the Civil War. In *Undercoverings*, ed. L. Horton, 53–69. San Francisco: American Quilt Study Group.

———. 2000. An "old-fashioned quilting" in 1910. In *Undercoverings*, ed. V. Gunn, 1–26. San Francisco: American Quilt Study Group.

Hovane, V.E. 2000. *An investigation of the multiple responses to oppression and implications for identity among Aboriginal adolescents*. Unpublished manuscript.

Huang, A., and J. Lynch. 1995. *Mentoring: The tao of giving and receiving wisdom*. San Francisco: HarperCollins.

Huggins, J. 1998. *Sister girl*. St. Lucia: University of Queensland Press.

Hunt, Mary. 1991. *Fierce tenderness: A feminist theology of friendship*. New York: Crossroad.

Hunter, B. 1999. *Three nations, not one: Indigenous and other Australia poverty*. Canberra: Centre for Aboriginal Economic Policy Research, Australian National University.

Hunter, E.M. 1991. The intercultural and socio-historical context of Aboriginal personal violence in remote Australia. *Australian Psychologist* 14 (2): 89–98.

Ingraham, Chrys. 1994. The heterosexual imaginary: Feminist sociology and theories of gender. In *Materialist feminism: A reader in class, difference, and women's lives*, ed. Rosemary Hennessy and Chrys Ingraham, 275–90. New York: Routledge.

Innovative dance group inspires as it performs. 1998. *People Weekly* 50(1).

Jackson P. 1989. *Maps of meaning*. London: Unwin Hyman.

Jain, Ajit. 2001. Complaints of harassment of Muslims riding in Montreal. *www.rediff.com/us/2001/oct/12ny31.htm*

James, Allison. 1998. Imagining children "at home," "in the family" and "at school": Movement between the spatial and temporal markers of childhood identity in Britain. In *Migrants of identity: Perceptions of home in a world of movement*, ed. Nigel Rapport and Andrew Dawson, 139-60. New York: Berg.

Janesick, V.J. 1994. The dance of qualitative research design: Metaphor, methodolatry, and meaning. In *Handbook of research*, ed. N.K. Denzin and Y.S. Lincoln, 209-19. Thousand Oaks, CA: Sage.

Johnson, N.G., M.C. Roberts, and J. Worrell, eds. 1999. *Beyond appearance: A new look at adolescent girls*. Washington DC: American Psychological Association.

Jones, K., and G. Moon. 1993. Medical geography: Taking space seriously. *Progress in Human Geography* 17: 515-24.

Jordan, V.J., J.L. Surrey, and A.G. Kaplan. 1991. Women and empathy: Implications for psychological development and psychotherapy. In *Women's growth in connection: Writings from the Stone Centre*, ed. J.V. Jordan, A.G. Kaplan, J. Baker Miller, I.P. Stiver, and J.L. Surrey, 27-50. New York: Guilford Press.

Kearns, R. 1993. Place and health: Towards a reformed medical geography. *Professional Geographer* 45 (2): 139-47.

———. 1995. Medical geography: Making space for difference. *Progress in Human Geography* 19 (2): 251-59.

———. 1997. Narrative and metaphor in health geographies. *Progress in Human Geography* 21 (2): 269-77.

Kearns, R., and W.M. Gesler, eds. 1998. *Putting health into place: Landscape, identity and well-being*. Syracuse: Syracuse University Press.

Kearns, R., and A. Joseph. 1993. Space and its place: Developing the link in medical geography. *Social Science and Medicine* 37: 711-31.

Kearns, R., S. Taylor, and M. Dear. 1987. Coping and satisfaction among the chronically mentally disabled. *Canadian Journal of Community Mental Health* 6: 13-22.

Keating, N.C., J.E. Fast, I.A. Connidis, M. Penning, and J. Keefe. 1997. Bridging policy and research in eldercare. *Canadian Journal on Aging/Canadian Public Policy* Supplement: 2-41.

Keating, N.C., J.E. Fast, J.A. Frederick, K. Cranswick, and C. Perrier. 1999. *Eldercare in Canada: Context, content and consequences*. Ottawa: Statistics Canada.

Kelly, Judy. 1999. *Birthmother research project. The trauma of relinquishment: The long-term impact of relinquishment on birthmothers who lost their infants to adoption during the years 1965-1972*. Plainfield, VT: Goddard.

Kerlin, R.A. 1997. *Breaking the silence: Toward a theory of women's doctoral persistence*. PhD diss., University of Victoria, Victoria, British Columbia.

Kilbourne, Jean. 1999. *Can't buy my love: How advertising changes the way we think and feel*. New York: Touchstone.

Kimberley Aboriginal Medical Services Council. 2000. *Issues for Aboriginal controlled health services in the Kimberley*. www.hcn.net.au/kamsc/hlthstat.htm

Kimberley Development Commission. 1997. *Kimberley Region, Western Australia: Economic development strategies – 1997 to 2010*. Broome: Kimberley Development Commission.

King, M.A., B.J. Coles, and A.J. King. 1988. *Canada youth and AIDS survey*. Kingston, ON: Social Program Evaluation Group, Queen's University.

Klein, Naomi. 2000. *No logo: Taking aim at the brand bullies*. Toronto: Knopf Canada.

Kleinman, S. 1992. Researching lived experience in movement and dance. *Kinesiology and Medicine for Dance* 14 (10): 33-43.

Klonis, S., J. Endo, F. Crosby, and J. Worell. 1997. Feminism as life raft. *Psychology of Women Quarterly* 21 (3): 333-45.

Kmiec, J., F. Crosby, and J. Worrell. 1996. Walking the talk: On stage and behind the scenes. In *Women's ethnicities: Journeys through psychology*, ed. K.F. Wyche and F. Crosby, 49-61. Boulder, CO: Westview.

Kobayashi, A., and B. Ray. 2000. Civil risk and landscapes of marginality in Canada: A pluralist approach to social justice. *Canadian Geographer* 40: 401-17.

Kottler, J.A. 1995. *Growing a therapist*. San Francisco: Jossey-Bass.

Kowaleski-Jones, Lori, and F.L. Mott. 1998. Sex, contraception and child bearing among high-risk youth: Do different factors influence males and females? *Family Planning Perspectives* 30 (4): 163-70.

Ku, L., F.L. Sonestein, L.D. Lindbergh, C.H. Bradner, S. Boggess, and J.H. Pleck. 1998. Understanding changes in sexual activity among metropolitan men, 1979-1995. *Family Planning Perspectives* 31 (6): 280-91.

Kunzel, Regina G. 1993. *Fallen women, problem girls: Unmarried mothers and the professionalization of social work, 1890-1945*. New Haven: Yale University Press.

Kushner, Harvey. 1998. *Terrorism in America: A structured approach to understanding the terrorist threat*. Springfield, IL: Charles C. Thomas.

Lambert, J., ed. 1993. *Wise women of the dreamtime*. Rochester, VT: Inner Traditions International.

Langille, P., J. Graham, E. Marshall, M. Blake, C. Chitty, and H. Doncaster-Scot. 1999. *Developing understanding from young women's experiences in obtaining sexual health services and education in a Nova Scotia community*. Nova Scotia: Maritime Centre of Excellence in Women's Health.

Larsen, D. 1999. *Biographies of six Canadian counselor educators: Stories of personal and professional life*. PhD diss., University of Alberta, Edmonton, Alberta.

Lawton, M.P. 1984. Introduction. In *Elderly people and the environment*, vol. 7 of *Human behavior and environment: Advances in theory and research*, ed. I. Altman, M.P. Lawton, and J.F. Wohlwill, 1-16. New York: Plenum Press.

Lee, P. 1982. Determinants of health. In *Proceedings of the Conference on Health in the '80s and '90s and Its Impact on Health Sciences Education*, 23-44. Ottawa: Council of Ontario Universities.

Leyendecker, Gertrude T. 1958. *Services to unmarried mothers: Generic and specific factors in casework with the unmarried mother*. New York: Child Welfare League of America.

Liepins, R. 1998. "Women of broad vision": Nature and gender in the environmental activism of Australia's "Women in Agriculture" movement. *Environment and Planning A* 30: 1179-96.

Lippman, H. 2000. What are they teaching in sex ed these days? *Medical Economics* 77 (8): 79-82.

Lithgow, M. 1974. *Quiltmaking and quiltmakers*. New York: Funk and Wagnalls.

Little, Margaret J.H. 1998. *No car, no radio, no liquor permit: The moral regulation of single mothers in Ontario, 1920-1997*. Toronto: Oxford University Press.

Litva, A., and J. Eyles. 1995. Coming out: Exposing social theory in medical geography. *Health and Place* 1: 5-14.

Loganbill, C., E. Hardy, and U. Delworth. 1982. Supervision: A conceptual model. *The Counseling Psychologists* 10 (1): 3-42.

Lubin, S. 1992. Palliative care: Could your patient have been managed at home? *Journal of Palliative Care* 8 (2): 18-22.

Luxton, Meg. 2001. *Family responsibilities: The politics of love and care.* 32nd Annual Sorokin Lecture. Saskatoon: University of Saskatchewan.

Maggard, S.W. 1990. Gender contested: Women's participation in the Brookside coal strike. In *Women and social protest*, ed. G. West and R.L. Blumberg, 75-98. New York: Oxford University Press.

Maher, F.A. 1987. Toward a richer theory of feminist pedagogy: A comparison of "liberation" and "gender" models for teaching and learning. *Journal of Education* 169: 91-100.

Mahler, K. 1997. Physicians often omit sexual health services for adolescents' care. *Family Planning Perspectives* 29 (2): 91-92.

Manning W.D., M.A. Longmore, and P.C. Giordano. 2000. The relationship context of contraceptive use at first intercourse. *Family Planning Perspectives* 32 (3): 104-25.

Manning, P.K., and B. Cullum-Swan. 1994. Narrative, content, and semiotic analysis. In *Handbook of qualitative research*, ed. N.K. Denzin and Y. S Lincoln, 463-77. Thousand Oaks, CA: Sage.

Marchak, M.P. 1983. *Green gold: The forest industry in British Columbia.* Vancouver: UBC Press.

Marchand, M.H., and J.L. Parpart. 1995. *Feminism/postmodernism/development.* New York: Routledge.

Marley, W.P. 1997. The disability syndrome and the instinctive wisdom of the body. *Palaestra* 13 (2): 26-29.

Maybin, J. 1996. Story voices: The use of reported speech in 10-12-year-olds' spontaneous narratives. *Current Issues in Language and Society* 3 (1): 36-38.

Mayer J., and M. Mead. 1994. A reformed medical geography reconsidered. *Professional Geographer* 46 (1): 103-106.

McColm, Michelle. 1993. *Adoption reunions: A book for adoptees, birth parents and adoptive families.* Toronto: Second Story Press.

McCorkle, R. 1988. The four essentials. *Journal of Palliative Care* 4 (1, 2): 59-61.

McWhinney, I.R., M.J. Bass, and V. Orr. 1995. Factors associated with location of death (home or hospital) of patients referred to a palliative care team. *Canadian Medical Association Journal* 152 (3): 361-68.

Mercadante, S., G. Genose, J.A. Kargar, S. Maddalone, S. Roccella, L. Salvaggio, and M. Simonetti. 1992. Home palliative care results in 1991 versus 1988. *Journal of Pain and Symptom Management* 7 (7): 414-18.

Mies, M. 1986. *Patriarchy and accumulation on a world scale: Women in the international division of labor.* London: Zed Press.

Miles, M. 1999. The Kezia D. Benton quilt: A life uncovered. In *Undercoverings*, ed. V. Gunn, 3-30. San Francisco: American Quilt Study Group.

Miller, Abraham. 1982. *Terrorism, the media, and the law.* Dobbs Ferry, NY: Transnational Publishers.

Miller, J.R. 1989. *Skyscrapers hide the heavens: A history of Indian-White Relations in Canada.* Toronto: University of Toronto Press.

Millstein, S.G., V. Igra, and J. Gans. 1996. Delivery of STD/HIV preventive services to adolescents by primary care physicians. *Journal of Adolescent Health* 19: 249-57.

Mintz, J. 1994. Challenging values: Conflicts, contradiction, and pedagogy. In *To improve the academy*, vol. 13, ed. E.C. Wadsworth. Stillwater, OK: Professional and Organizational Network in High Education, New Forums Press.

Mirriam, S. 1988. *Case study research in education*. San Francisco: Jossey-Bass.

Mojab, Shahrzad. 1998. Muslim women and Western feminists: The debate on particulars and universals. *Monthly Review* 50 (7): 19-30.

Money, J. 1986. *Venuses penuses: Sexology, sexosophy and exigency theory*. Buffalo: Prometheus Books.

Morley, L. 1992. Women's studies, difference, and internalized oppression. *Women's Studies International Forum* 15: 517-25.

Morse, J. 1994. Designing qualitative research. In *Handbook of qualitative research*, ed. N. Denzinand and Y. Lincoln, 220-35. Newbury, CA: Sage.

Moseley, H.D. 1935. *Report of the royal commissioner appointed to investigate, report, advise upon matters in relation to the condition and treatment of Aborigines*. Perth: Government Printer.

Moss, P., J. Eyles, I. Dyck, and D. Rose. 1993. Focus: Feminism as method. *Canadian Geographer* 37: 48-61.

Moustakas, C. 1994. *Phenomenological research methods*. Thousand Oaks, CA: Sage.

Naples, Nancy, ed. 1998. *Community activism and feminist politics: Organizing across race, class and gender*. New York: Routledge.

Napster. *www.napster.com*

National Film Board. 1979. *No life for a woman*. Ottawa: National Film Board.

Nelson, M.D., P. Johnson, and J.M. Thorngren. 2000. An integrated approach for supervising mental health counseling interns. *Journal of Mental Health Counseling* 22 (1): 45-59.

Neopets, Inc. 1999-2005. *www.neopets.com*

Ng, Roxana. 1981. Constituting ethnic phenomenon: An account from the perspective of immigrant women. *Canadian Ethnic Studies* 13: 97-108.

———. 1987. The social construction of "immigrant women" in Canada. In *The politics of diversity: Feminism, marxism and nationalism*, ed. Roberta Hamilton and Michele Barrett, 269-86. Montreal: Book Centre.

———. 1993. Racism, sexism, and immigrant women. In *Changing patterns: Women in Canada*, ed. Sandra Burt and Lorraine Code, 279-308. Toronto: McClelland & Stewart.

Niagara District Health Council. 1997. *Niagara's annual district service plan for long term care community services 1997-1998*. Fonthill, ON: Niagara District Health Council.

Olwig, F. Karen. 1998. Epilogue. Contested homes: Home-making and the making of anthropology. In *Migrants of identity: Perceptions of home in a world of movement*, ed. Nigel Rapport and Andrew Dawson, 225-36. New York: Berg.

Ontario Gerontology Association. 1997. *Bulletin/Newsletter*, May 7, 1997.

Origins, Inc. n.d. *Affects* [sic] *of adoption on mental health of the mother: What they knew and didn't tell us*. *www.angelfire.com/or/originsnsw/mthr.html*

Oxenham, D. 1999. *Aboriginal terms of reference: The concept at the Centre for Aboriginal Studies*. Perth: Curtin Indigenous Research Centre.

Packer, M.J. 1985. Hermeneutic inquiry in the study of human conduct. *American Psychologist* 40 (10): 1081–93.

Papanek, Hanna. 1994. The ideal women and the ideal society: Control and autonomy in the construction of identity. In *Identity politics and women: Cultural reassertions and feminism in international perspective*, ed. Valentine Moghadam, 3–26. Boulder: Westview.

Paquet, M. 1995. Prevention for caregivers of dependent elderly persons: What prevention? *Canadian Social Work Review* 12 (1): 45–71.

Pardo, M. 1990. Mexican-American women grassroots community activists: Mothers of East Los Angeles. *Frontiers* 11 (1): 1–7.

Parpart, J.L. 1995. Deconstructing the development "expert": Gender, development and the "vulnerable groups." In Marchand and Parpart 1995, 221–43.

Pattison, E.M. 1978. The living-dying process. In *Psychological care of the dying patient*, ed. C.A. Garfield, 133–68. New York: McGraw-Hill.

Pearson, N. 1999. *Our right to take responsibility*. A discussion paper for the Aboriginal leaders and community members of Cape York, Trinity Beach. Queensland: Pearson.

Pedersen, H., and B. Woorunmurra. 1995. *Jandamarra: and the Bunuba Resistance*. Broome: Magabala Books Aboriginal Corporation.

Peters, D.J. 1996. Disablement observed, addressed, and experienced: Integrating subjective experience into disablement models. *Disability and Rehabilitation* 18 (2): 593–603.

Petrie, Anne. 1998. *Gone to an aunt's: Remembering Canada's homes for unwed mothers*. Toronto: McClelland & Stewart.

Phillips, M.J. 1992. "Try harder": The experience of disability and the dilemma of normalization. In *Interpreting disability: A qualitative reader*, ed. P.M. Ferguson, D.J. Ferguson, and S.J. Taylor, 213–27. New York: Teachers College Press.

Pink, S. 2001. *Doing visual ethnography*. Thousand Oaks, CA: Sage.

Polkinghorne, D.E. 1995. Narrative configuration in qualitative analysis. *Qualitative Studies in Education* 8 (1): 2–23.

Pred, A. 1983. Structuration and place: On the becoming of sense of place and structure of feeling. *Journal for the Theory of Social Behavior* 13: 45–68.

Prior, D., J. Stewart, and K. Walsh. 1995 *Citizenship: Rights, community and participation*. Harlow: Longman.

Proctor, J. 1995. Whose nature? The contested moral terrain of ancient forests. In *Uncommon ground: Toward reinventing nature*, ed. W. Cronon, 269–97. New York: W.W. Norton.

———. 1999. A moral earth: Facts and values in global environmental change. In *Geography and ethics: Journeys in a moral terrain*, ed. J.D. Proctor and D.M. Smith, 149–62. London: Routledge.

Proshansky, H. M., A. K. Fabian, and R. Kaminoff. 1983. Place-identity: Physical world socialization of the self. *Journal of Environmental Psychology* 3: 57–83.

Prudham, W.S., and M.G. Reed. 2001. "Looking to Oregon" and other models for the sustainability of forestry and land use in coastal British Columbia. *B.C. Studies* 130: 5-40.

Pulido, L. 1996 *Environmentalism and economic justice: Two Chicago struggles in the southwest*. Tucson: University of Arizona Press.

Quadagno, J.S., R.G. Kuhar, and W.A. Peterson. 1980. Maintaining social distance in a racially integrated retirement community. In *Aging, the individual and society: Readings in social gerontology*, ed. J. Quadagno, 224-39. New York: St. Martin's.

Rando, T.A. 1995. Grief and mourning: Accounting for loss. In DYING: *Facing the facts*, 3rd ed., ed. H. Wass and R.A. Neimeyer, 211-42. Washington, DC: Taylor and Francis.

Rapport, Nigel, and Andrew Dawson. 1998. The topic and the book. In *Migrants of identity: Perceptions of home in a world of movement*, ed. Nigel Rapport and Andrew Dawson, 3-17. New York: Berg.

Ravetz, Joe. 1998. The Internet, virtual reality and real reality. In *Cyberspace divided: Equality, agency and polity in the information society*, ed. Brian Loader, 113-22. New York: Routledge.

Raymond, J. 1986. *A passion for friends: Toward a philosophy of female affection*. Boston: Beacon Press.

Razack, S.H. 1998. *Looking white people in the eye: Gender, race, and culture in the courtrooms and classrooms*. Toronto: University of Toronto Press.

Reed, M.G. 1997. Seeing trees: Engendering environmental and land use planning. *Canadian Geographer* 14 (4): 398-414.

––––––. 2000. Taking stands: A feminist perspective on "other" women's activism in forestry communities of northern Vancouver Island. *Gender, Place and Culture* 7: 363-83.

––––––. 2001. Endangered forests and endangered communities. In *Proceedings of The Nature and Culture of Forests: Implications of Diversity for Sustainability, Trade and Certification*, 113-25. Vancouver, BC: Institute for European Studies, University of British Columbia.

Reinharz, S. 1992. *Feminist methods in social research*. New York: Oxford University Press.

Relph, E.C. 1976. *Place and placelessness*. London: Routledge, Keagan and Paul.

Report of the Committee on Adoption in Alberta. 1965. *In the matter of the Child Welfare Act and in the matter of Order-In-Council No. 1871-64*. Edmonton: Government of Alberta.

Richardson, L. 1997. *Fields of play: Constructing an academic life*. New Brunswick, NJ: Rutgers University Press.

Rickarby, Dr. Geoff. 1998. NSW *parliamentary inquiry into adoption practices: Excerpts from Dr. Geoff Rickarby's submission*. New South Wales, Australia.

Riordan, A. 1989. Sunrise wheels. *Journal of Physical Education, Recreation, and Dance* 60 (9): 62-64.

Roberts, Donald. 1993. Adolescence and the mass media: From "Leave it to Beaver" to "Berverly Hills 90210." *Teachers College Record* 94: 630-44.

Rootman, I., and R. Munson. 1990. Strategies to achieve health for all Canadians. *Canadian Geographer* 34: 332-34.

Rowles, G. 1978. Reflections on experimental fieldwork. In *Humanistic geography: Prospects and problems*, ed. D. Ley and M. Samuels, 173-93. New York: John Wiley.

————. 1983. Place and personal identity in old age: Observations from Appalacia. *Journal of Environmental Psychology* 3: 299-313.

Rubenstein, R. 1990. Culture and disorder in the home care experience: The home as sickroom. In *The home care experience: Ethnography and policy*, ed. J. Gubrium and A. Sankar, 37-57. Newbury Park, CA: Sage.

Rubin, H.J., and I.S. Rubin. 1995. *Qualitative interviewing: The art of hearing data*. Thousand Oaks, CA: Sage.

Ryan, William. 1971. *Blaming the victim*. New York: Vintage.

Sachs, C. 1994. Rural women's environmental activism in the USA. In *Gender and rurality*, ed. S. Whatmore, T. Marsden, and P. Lowe, 117-35. London: David Fulton.

Sahlberg-Blom, E., B.M. Ternestedt, and J.E. Johansson. 2001. Is good quality of life possible at the end of life? An explorative study of the experiences of a group of cancer patients in two different care cultures. *Journal of Clinical Nursing* 10 (4): 550-62.

Said, Edward. 1981. *Covering Islam: How the media and the experts determine how we see the rest of the world*. New York: Pantheon Books.

Santrock, John W. 2001. *Adolescence*. New York: McGraw-Hill.

Saskatchewan Health. 1996. *Saskatchewan Epidemiology Report* 3 (2). Regina: Saskatchewan Health.

Sawicki, Jana. 1991. *Disciplining Foucault: Feminism, power and the body*. New York: Routledge.

Schachter, S. 1992. Quality of life for families in the management of home care patients with advanced cancer. *Journal of Palliative Care* 8 (3): 61-66.

Schissel, B., and L. Eisler. 1996. *Saskatchewan youth attitudes survey*. Saskatoon: Department of Sociology, University of Saskatchewan.

Schreck, L. 2001. Providers who see sexually active teenagers often fail to test them for Chlamydia. *Family Planning Perspectives* 33 (2): 93-94.

Schwartz, V. 1989. A dance for all people. *Journal of Physical Education, Recreation and Dance* 60 (9): 49-53.

Seager, J. 1993. *Earth follies: Coming to terms with the global environmental crisis*. New York: Routledge.

Seamark, S.A., C.P. Thorne, C. Lawrence, and D. Pereira Gray. 1995. Appropriate place of death for cancer patients: Views of general practitioners and hospital doctors. *British Journal of General Practice* 45: 359-63.

Seamon, D. 1979. Phenomenologies of environment and place. *Phenomenology and Pedagogy* 2 (2): 130-35.

Seitz, V. 1995. *Women, development, and communities for empowerment in Appalachia*. Albany: SUNY Press.

Seventeen. 2005. *www.seventeen.com*

Shawyer Joss. 1979. *Death by adoption*. New Zealand: Cicada Press.

Shenkman, E., J. Pendergast, J. Reiss, E. Waltern, R. Bucciarelli, and S. Freedman. 1996. The school enrollment-based health insurance program: Socioeconomic factors in enrollees' use of health services. *American Journal of Public Health* 86: 1791-93.

Shiva, V. 1989. *Staying alive: Women, ecology and development*. Delhi: Kali for Women.

Shumaker, S.A., and G.J. Conti. 1985. Understanding mobility in America. In *Human behavior and environments: Advances in theory and research*, vol. 8 of *Home Environments*, ed. I. Altman and C. Werner, 237-83. New York: Plenum Press.

Sibley, D. 1998. The problematic nature of exclusion. *Geoforum* 29 (2): 119-21.

Siciliano, L. 2000. Dancing wheels welcomes teenagers with disabilities. *The Plain Dealer* 5.

Sidanius, J., and F. Pratto. 1999. *Social dominance: An intergroup theory of social hierarchy and oppression*. Cambridge: Cambridge University Press.

Sixsmith, J. 1986. The meaning of home: An exploratory study of environmental experience. *Journal of Environmental Psychology* 6: 281-98.

Skovholt, T.M., and M. Ronnestad. 1992. Themes in therapist and counselor development. *Journal of Counseling and Development* 70: 505-15.

Smith, Brent. 1994. *Terrorism in America: Pipe bombs and pipe dreams*. Albany: State University of New York Press.

Social services for unwed parents. 1957. Ottawa: Publications Section, Canadian Welfare Council.

Solinger, Rickie. 1992. *Wake up little Susie*. New York: Routledge.

Soll, Joe. 2000. *Adoption healing: A path to recovery*. Baltimore: Gateway Press.

Somerville, P. 1997. The social construction of home. *Journal of Architectural and Planning Research* 14 (3): 226-45.

Stake, J.E., and E.L. Hoffman. 2000. Putting feminist pedagogy to the test: The experience of women's studies from student and teacher perspectives. *Psychology of Women Quarterly* 24 (1): 30-38.

Statistics Canada. 1997. Who cares? Caregiving in the 1990s. *The Daily*, August 19, 1997.

Stern-Gillet, S. 1995. *Aristotle's philosophy of friendship*. New York: SUNY Press.

Stoltenberg, C., and U. Delworth. 1987. *Supervising counselors and therapists: A developmental approach*. San Francisco: Jossey-Bass.

Stone, P. Gregory. 1962. Appearance and the self. In *Human behavior and social perspectives*, ed. Arnold Rose, 86-118. Boston: Houghton Mifflin.

Storey, K., and R. Moore. 1998. *Knowledge, attitudes and risk-taking behavior of adolescents with regard to Acquired Immunodeficiency Syndrome (AIDS)*. University of Regina: A report submitted to the Board of Education of Regina Public School Division.

Strauss, A., and J. Corbin. 1998. *Basics of qualitative research: Procedures and techniques for developing grounded theory*. 2nd ed. Newbury Park, CA: Sage.

Sturgeon, N. 1997. *Ecofeminist natures: Race, gender, feminist theory and political action*. New York: Routledge.

Sullivan, P. 1996. *All free man now: Culture, community and politics in the Kimberley Region, North-Western Australia*. Canberra: Australian Institute of Aboriginal and Torres Strait Islander Studies.

Switzer, J. 1996. Women and wise use: The other side of environmental activism. Paper presented at the Western Political Science Association Annual Meeting. San Francisco, March 14-16, 1996.

Tolman, D.L. 1999. Female adolescent sexuality in relational context: Beyond sexual decision-making. In Johnson, Roberts, and Worrell 1999, 227-46.

Tolman, D.L., and L.A. Szalacha. 1999. Dimension of desire: Bridging qualitative and quantitative methods in a study of female adolescent sexuality. *Psychology of Women Quarterly* 23: 7-39.

Tuan Y. 1974. *Topophilia: A study of environmental perception, attitudes and values*. New Jersey: Prentice-Hall.

Tuan Y. 1976. Literature, experience and environmental knowing. In *Environmental knowing: Theories, research and methods*, ed. G. Moore and R. Golledge, 260-72. Pennsylvania: Dowden, Hutchinson and Ross.

Unger, R.K. 1998. *Resisting gender: Twenty-five years of feminist psychology*. Thousand Oaks, CA: Sage.

Van Leeuwen, T., and C. Jewitt. 2001. *Handbook of visual analysis*. Thousand Oaks, CA: Sage.

Van Manen, M. 2000. *Researching lived experience: Human science for an action sensitive pedagogy*. London, ON: Althouse Press.

Vincent, Clark E. 1961. *Unmarried mothers*. New York: Free Press of Glencoe.

Walker, R. 1993. Finding a silent voice for the researcher: Using photographs in evaluation and research. In *Qualitative voices in educational research*, ed. M. Schratz, 72-92. Washington DC: Falmer Press.

Walmsley, D.J., and G.J. Lewis. 1993. *People and environment: Behavioral approaches in human geography*. 2nd ed. London: Longman Scientific and Technical.

Weiler, K. 1988. *Women teaching for change*. New York: Bergen and Garvey.

Wells, Y.D., and H.L. Dendig. 1996. Changes in carer's capacity and motivation to provide care. *Journal of Family Studies* 2 (1): 15-28.

Werner, C., I. Altman, and D. Oxley. 1985. Temporal aspects of homes: A transactional approach. In *Human behavior and environment: Advances in theory and research*, vol. 8 of *Home environments*, ed. I. Altman and C. Werner, 1-32. New York: Plenum Press.

West, G., and R. Blumberg, eds. 1990. *Women and social protest*. Oxford: Oxford University Press.

Western Australian Department of Training. 1997. *Just enough to tease us*. Perth: Australian National Training Authority.

Wheeler, Everett. 1991. Terrorism and military theory: An historical perspective. In *Terrorism research and public policy*, ed. Clark McCauley, 6-33. London: F. Cass.

White, Jonathan Randall. 2002. *Terrorism: An introduction*. Belmont, CA: Wadsworth Thomson Learning.

White, N. 1981. Modern health concepts. In *The health conundrum*, ed. N. White, 5-18. Toronto: TV Ontario.

Wilcox, B.L. 1999. Sexual obsessions: Public policy and adolescent girls. In Johnson, Roberts, Worrell 1999, 333-54.

Williams, A. 1998. Therapeutic landscapes in holistic medicine. *Social Science and Medicine* 46 (9): 1193-1203.

Williams, A., and D. Forbes. 2003. The influence of income on the experience of informal care-giving: Policy implications. *Health Care for Women International* 24 (4): 280-91.

Williams, A., M.V. Caron, M. McMillian, A. Litkowich, N. Rutter, A. Hartman, and J. Yardley. 2001. An evaluation of contracted palliative care nursing services in Ontario, Canada. *Evaluation and Program Planning* 18: 327–39.

Williams, R., P. Swan, J. Reser, and B. Miller. 1992. Australian Aborigine communities: Changing oppressive social environments. In *Psychology and social change*, ed. D. Thomas and A. Vino. Palmerston North, NZ: Dunmore Press.

Wolf, Naomi. 1991. *The beauty myth: How images of beauty are used against women*. New York: William Morrow and Company.

Young, Iris Marion. 1990. *Justice and the politics of difference*. Princeton: Princeton University Press.

Young, Leontine. 1954. *Out of wedlock*. New York: McGraw Hill.

Zimmer, M., and Krombholz, G. 1994. Wheelchair dancing. *Paleastra* 11 (1): 25–28, 65.

Zulaika, Joseba, and William Douglass. 1996. *Terror and taboo: The follies, fables, and faces of terrorism*. New York: Routledge.

www.ingramcontent.com/pod-product-compliance
Lightning Source LLC
Chambersburg PA
CBHW062025270326
41929CB00014B/2321